WITHOUT A COMPASS

WITHOUT A COMPASS

MARTIN TERRELL

CHAPEL HILL
PRESS

To my mother,

Carrie Mae Cooper,

a migrant from East Point, Georgia

CONTENTS

BOOK ONE

THIRTEENTH STREET, SETTING MY BEARINGS

should have been a burglar. I've had lots of practice. Feels like I've been crawling through transom door windows before I could walk. Daddy started it.

Most people think the transom is a small rectangular window above the regular door to let in light. If you ask me, it exists solely for fathers to boost kids through to open the doors from the inside when they've forgotten their keys.

Our building was like most other buildings on Thirteenth Street—a three-story building hunched shoulder-to-shoulder with others like it all the way up the hill to Mr. Herrmann's Bakery. Every apartment's front door opened onto the hallway from the kitchen. We lived on the first floor. And every door had a transom.

Coming home from the drive-in one night after seeing *Rear Window*, Mama, my sister Wanda, and I stopped at our door. "I'm tired out," Mama said. "Let's get inside." Daddy turned the key in the lock, and the door didn't open. He buried the doorknob in his hand and twisted hard. The door still didn't move. "Damn it!" he said, patting his pockets. "I brought the wrong key."

He looked at Mama with a smilelike grimace that said, "I lost the damn key and you better not say anything." Then he quickly fished around and hooked me with his eyes. "Junior, come over here and crawl through this transom."

Just like that: "Come over here and crawl through this transom." Before I could move he pulled me between himself and the door. I flattened my body against the door, stretched my arms above my head, placed my right foot into Daddy's cupped hands, and let him lift me high enough to reach the transom. Once there, I pushed the transom window open from the bottom to where it stayed up like an awning, with Daddy still holding my foot in his hands. Next, he boosted me up and over the transom's sill, and I slid head first until I caught the doorknob with my left hand. Still falling, I pushed myself away from the door with my right and rolled to break my fall.

Years later, Daddy's training paid off when I crawled through the transom to raid his refrigerator in his apartment on Gest Street. I hadn't slept in two days and eaten very little. His cold chicken, mayonnaise, and bread hit the spot.

The kitchen is the worst place to enter late at night in the dark. All the floors in our building tilted, and none of the doors fit snugly in their frames—an open sesame for rats. Uneven patches of color dressed the walls. Year after year Mama uselessly stuffed rags against the sills in winter. The cold never surrendered. Our apartment leaned heavily against the spongy wall of our shared first-floor toilet, a gray porcelain throne just a rat's dash from the garbage cans in the rear. Mama and Daddy both knew we had rats. Symphonies of them lived in and made nightly trips through the kitchen where I slept.

Kept covered in the front room till bedtime, I rode the roll-away bed brought into the kitchen at night like a warship in enemy seas. Familiar with the nightly kitchen attack, I unfolded the bed, set it up, and positioned it between the sink and the table as far away from the rat runs as I could. (The rats loved to explore the sink to discover any leftover bits of food from dishwashing.) Next, I spread newspaper pages around the bed using the bed as my hub. My paper radar system alerted me of any invading rodents. Whenever the paper rustled, I'd throw in that direction my shoe or whatever missile I'd taken to bed, and the invasion would be temporarily stalled. Alarmed and frightened, I'd lay awake waiting for the next paper-rustling alarm.

When I rolled onto the floor after being pushed through the transom, I heard rats squeaking around the baseboards and leaping out of the sink. Then I felt something underneath me—something once solid but now squished. I'd hit the floor so quickly and hard that I'd trapped something beneath me, something warm and furry that seemed to have locked onto me.

Too dark to see what I'd fallen on, I lay still, waiting for it to move. It didn't move but looked vaguely familiar in the dark, bulging in the middle and tapering down to long thin shapes on either side. My back tingled from having touched it. My stomach churned at the thought of seeing it, but I had no choice. I had to turn on the light and open the door if I wanted things back to normal.

I ignored the fading screeches of the fleeing rats and pulled the string hanging from the bulb above the kitchen table. And there, exposed in the full light of seventy-five watts of General Electric, above our checkered linoleum floor, lay Mama's rabbit shoulder wrap, the one she wore when she wanted to dress up. Tufts of hair missing from one edge where a rat gnawed on it exposed a blank space of dark hide, ruining her precious garment. Why he pulled it out of her closet all the way to the kitchen I'll never know.

When I let everyone in and Mama saw what happened to her fur, she choked, screwed the heels of both hands against her eyes, lifted her head as her hands slid down her face, and stared at me. She shook her head and said, "Junior, are you alright?"

"Yes, ma'am," I said. Her face frowned, but her eyes looked relieved.

Most women would have been upset having their fur ruined, but not Mama. She said, "Being upset ain't going to get me a new fur," and never mentioned it again. I guess she got that way growing up like she did in Georgia.

MAMA

Mama came from East Point, Georgia, to Cincinnati and brought her soft southern ways north and gifted them to me, her firstborn son in 1946. I am the only child she had by my real father, Big Red, who is just a phantom to me since he left when I was two years old. Mama always handled tough spots well. Where other women might moan and complain, like an experienced gambler she learned how to play the hand she was dealt. She didn't get upset easily. It had everything to do with the way she was brought up. After I turned two, Mama married my new daddy, Lou, and together they had Wanda, Debra, Kathy, Brenda, and Jerome.

We lived on Thirteenth Street for most of my life. There, I knew some of the most loving and colorful people I'd ever meet, and had some of the happiest times of my life. I loved my sisters and brother, but while growing up I never paid much attention to them. As the oldest, I had far more interesting things to do than focus on kids. Born on my birthday, Wanda, the oldest of my sisters, ended my only-child status but not my closeness with Mama. By the time I left Thirteenth Street I felt like an orange with all of the pulp and juice squeezed out, leaving but a torn and misshapen peel behind.

Daddy wore white T-shirts to show off his wide, deep chest. Still holding his WWII Marine shape and wearing a close haircut, he looked ten years younger than his age. Never having shaved, his complexion looked cue-ball smooth. He treated us well and loved all us kids equally, though sometimes I felt like a throw-in, part of a deal Mama made with Daddy before she said yes. "You can't have me without having Junior," she must have said. "We come as a package deal or not at all."

Born in Alabama, Daddy didn't have Mama's soft southern ways. He said he'd seen men hung by the Klan for walking on the sidewalk facing a white woman coming the other way. He smiled often around both blacks and whites, but I watched a vessel in his temple throb when white folk were there.

Mama met Big Red while stranded in the Union Terminal after losing her transfer to Detroit. Like other colored girls in the South looking for a way out, she took the free ticket given by recruiters to girls seeking domestic jobs up north. Even with a free ticket to Detroit, Mama still had to buy her own food along the way. That didn't matter much to Mama since she didn't need much. After she lost her ticket, Big Red met Mama and arranged for her to stay with his cousin on Linn Street until Mama got on her feet. Lots of people knew Big Red, but not many knew about his relationship with Mama. I don't know if they ever married. The only sure thing I know is that he's my daddy and Mama loved him. I don't know if the story about how they met is true—if Big Red "worked the streets," or whether Mama left Georgia seeking work up north. Mama never said anything about her past. I heard this story from Peanut Jim down at Crosley Field where I worked selling lemonade. He knew more about Red than I, but I like my story better.

Mama never recovered from the loss of Red. She didn't tell me why, but he went to prison just before my second birthday. As far as we both knew he died there. The only evidence I ever had of Red's existence is the hand-sewn leather purse he sent Mama his first Christmas away. Mama had no pictures of him, no letters, no friends to keep his memory alive, only a bulky, unstylish prison-made purse and me.

Under better circumstances I could have become a brat. Mama worshipped me, and I adored her and gloried in all the attention she showered on me. We didn't have much money, but when I started school she gave me a fifty-cent tab at Pie Lady's Pony Keg on the corner. All the guys knew that I had a tab and that I didn't mind sharing. Mama wouldn't have let me have it otherwise.

At the top of the hill was a Catholic church on one side and Herrmann's Bakery on the other. I went to Peaslee Elementary School, and on my first day I met Freddie Herrmann. His dad owned the bakery. We walked back to Thirteenth Street together almost every day and became good friends. One day he invited me up to see his dad's bakery. Nearly every day after that for the next two years Freddie and I would run up the hill after school to get first pick of the day-old bakery goods. During those days Daddy used to say I ate enough glazed doughnuts to feed an army.

Born under difficult circumstances Mama learned how to live and let live. Nobody knows who her parents might have been. I sure don't. If you want to know who her parents are, make up your own story. Yours won't be any better than mine. She never spoke of any relatives, and we never went to Georgia to visit as we did with Daddy's mother, Mama Liza, in Alabama. When asked about her parents, Mama always said, "I'm part Indian," and that was it. I believed her but thought it strange that she never talked about going home.

Most everyone in our neighborhood had some kind of story. Dark-skinned guys said they descended from African kings whose grand-children were brought here as slaves. Those with high cheekbones and rawhide-colored skin claimed to have some Indian blood, mostly Chero-kee and Sioux. But most colored people who came from Down South claimed white ancestry. I didn't think it connected them to the people who so dominated their lives, as much as it showed how freely white men had abused colored women—the same way they may have abused Mama.

That's why color is so important. We used it to put each other down, to separate ourselves from each other, and tried to copy white folks by making light-skinned blacks more valuable than those with darker skins. In my neighborhood both guys and girls sang the ditty, "If you're white, you're alright. If you're yella, you're together. If you're black, step back." None of us realized that we were putting ourselves down no matter which shade of black we were.

Mama's friend Miss Jane told Mama, "That uppity high-yella bitch down the street said she ain't having no black babies."

Being closer to Indian than high yella, Mama didn't say much. She just stated, "A baby's a baby, Jane. I guess it ain't got nothing to do with the color."

I usually got special treatment due to my light skin, but some girls said, "I don't talk to no shit-colored niggas like you. Shit-colored niggas think they're pretty. Don't you?"

Color is so important, nobody wins.

This is the rest of Mama's story. I imagine she is the unwanted child of a union between her mother and a white man. Because of her light skin and good hair, it became uncomfortable for her to stay in East Point because everyone probably knew she was a woodshed child. In a town as small as East Point she felt humiliated and discriminated against anywhere she went. She left East Point, erased everything in it from her mind, and never looked back.

After she and Daddy got together, Mama lived throughout the West End, but my best memories are of Thirteenth Street. Mama found happiness among the many characters who, she said, "made Thirteenth Street a real family." I knew what she meant when I started going to Pie Lady's Pony Keg.

PIE LADY

Pie Lady owned the Pony Keg on the first floor of our building. Her store went from the corner of the building back to the hallway and to our apartment, which started on the opposite side. Most Pony Kegs sold beer, wine, milk, packaged lunch meats, dry cereal, cigarettes, and ice cream. Pie Lady couldn't afford one of those big refrigerators to hold milk.

Pie Lady's Pony Keg carried things that Mama didn't have to go all the way to Sonny's Grocery Store to get, like flour, sugar, salt, vanilla flavoring, and Clabber Girl Baking Powder. She also sold cigarettes three-for-a-dime to people who couldn't always afford a pack. But I liked the two-for-a-penny windmill cookies with the Dutch-boy face best of all. I liked them so much that Mama asked Pie Lady to put me on the books for fifty-cents-a-week. We kept it secret between us. Daddy might've said she's spoiling me and making me fat.

Pie Lady was short and skinny, with a long, happy face kissed with smiles. She wore a bandana with the knot tied over her left ear. She didn't wear an apron as you'd expect but wore a dress that hung straight from her shoulders to her bare feet without stopping at the waist.

Mama said Pie Lady was from Down South. "Down South" meant anywhere south of the Ohio River. Most of the other people on our street came to Cincinnati from Down South. It didn't make any difference which state they came from. All Down South people looked, spoke, and acted just about the same to me. Women from Down South liked to wear lots of bright colors and deep red lipstick. That looked more like their African heritage than any white heritage to me. Mama said, "Colored women are sexy without meaning to be. That can be tough."

Nobody knew her real name, but everybody called her Pie Lady because she baked the best pies around. Mama and her friends all baked pies, but their pies couldn't stand in the shadow of one of Pie Lady's. When Mama cooked special meals for guests she always handed me $1.75 to go downstairs and get a pie she'd ordered from Pie Lady. When Daddy asked Mama, "Why are you spending money buying a pie instead of making one yourself?"

Mama said, "I'm cooking. I don't have time to bake." Everybody except Daddy knew that Pie Lady made the best pies.

A tiny bell tinkled as I opened the half-windowed double doors to her store. It was a quiet bell that rang almost as if apologizing for breaking the peaceful silence that Pie Lady created. With no one at the low wooden counter to greet me, I had time to look around before Pie Lady emerged from behind the curtains in the back of the store.

A bulb hanging over the counter gave the rest of the store, big as two of our rooms, the feeling of a warm, dark cave. Sliding more than walking across the smooth hardwood, I looked into the low cases around the walls. With their limited number of items lined up in neat rows, and equal spaces between each item, they resembled crops that Pie Lady may have planted once on a farm Down South.

Saving the best for last, I turned and gorged my senses on the aroma coming from the canisters in the middle of the floor. Windmill cookies, ginger snaps, sugar cookies, baseball cookies, and cookies with white icing were all calling my name. As I looked down through the slanted glass lids into each canister, the cookies seemed to grow bigger and bigger as my hunger for them grew.

So swept up in watching and inhaling cookie aroma I didn't notice Pie Lady emerge from behind the curtains until she stood motionless beside me. She moved so soundlessly across the smooth hardwood floor, I twitched in surprise when she touched me and instantly relaxed when she spoke,

"Umm, those windmill cookies sure look good, don't they, Junior? Want me to get you a couple?" she said, her soft voice sounding like Mama's.

Turning to face her I said, "I'm out of credit and Mama won't have any money till Friday. Can I have a dime's worth till then?"

She laughed, shook her head, and pinched me on the arm. "Junior, I'm gonna go broke dealing with you. Go ahead and take another dime's worth." She picked up a small paper bag from one side of the canisters, snapped it open, and handed it to me. "Here, help yourself, and don't tell your mama."

I filled my bag with twenty cookies as she turned and straightened something on the nearest shelf. Without another word, she walked back to her room behind the curtains. When I turned to go and opened the door to the whispering bell, Pie Lady's presence still vibrated through the darkness behind me. Some say she is a Geechee woman born to know and see things others can't. They said that whether you can see her or not, Pie Lady's presence is always there. I felt it, and it felt good.

With both Pie Lady's Pony Keg and our apartment on the first floor, I passed her store almost every day. Whether I stopped to get cookies or not I always slowed down and waved. Coming home at night I saw her store before reaching our apartment, her single bulb a faint beacon welcoming me home. She lived in the back of the store, never owned a burglar alarm, and never had a break-in.

"You get what you give," she told me one day. "I ain't never robbed nobody, and it'd take a fool to rob me. I know what to do." She didn't sound worried about being robbed to me. We lived on the first floor and didn't have a burglar alarm either, but Daddy didn't have Pie Lady's sense.

THE OPEN WINDOW

I looked out the window, and there he stood: Navigator Jack, a tall, stooped man wearing a captain's hat and a peacoat. His hand rested on a wooden cart with large wooden wheels. Inside were stacks of newspapers with bundles of rags thrown on top. Unshaven, wearing dark pants and shoes with lots of extra space at the toes, he pushed his car to the slope at the bottom of the hill, turned around, and started back down the other side of the street singing his song: "Rags!" "Paypio! Rags! Paypio!" Nobody came out to give him anything that morning. He just kept on his way singing his song. And just before dinner time I heard him coming again, his pushcart moving at a lazy, slow pace and "Rags! Paypio!" bouncing up the street ahead of him to tell the world he's back.

We hadn't lived on Thirteenth Street long before I awoke to Navigator Jack's loud, deep voice resonating off the walls of buildings and sidewalks, wailing "Rags! Paypio!" Living on the first floor of our building meant that I didn't have to climb stairs to get home. Living at street level we could see everyone and talk to people as they passed. Sometimes we'd take the screens out, and Mama would place pies in the window to cool. She often did that for Navigator Jack when he did odd jobs for her around the house. Mama would arrange to leave the pie for him at a certain time, and he'd stop by and pick it up.

Nothing bad ever happened when Mama left the window open for Navigator Jack. Everybody knew that he wouldn't ever cross your threshold without permission. We found out the hard way that living on the first floor with the window open wasn't always a good idea. One night Daddy came home drunk or tired, I don't know which, and for some reason left the window up when he went to bed. We always kept the windows open in the daytime because we had only one fan and it was in the kitchen. At night we moved it into Mama and Daddy's room.

Each night we closed the two windows in their bedroom facing the sidewalk. On this particular night Daddy came home without turning on the light, took his clothes off, and draped his pants over the back of the chair next to the window. He left his wallet in his pants pocket with the window up, and the result led to a change for us all.

Awakened by a scratching sound in the middle of the night coming from the direction of the window, Daddy sat up in bed and saw an arm from outside pulling his pants off the back of the chair and through the window, toppling the chair onto the screen that had fallen to the floor. Someone had forgotten to close the window. Later that night, someone looking for places to break into had seen Daddy's pants through the screen. Taking the chance that a wallet may be in them, he simply pushed the screen through the open window and snatched Daddy's pants from the chair. "Easy pickings," my mama called it. She wasn't too happy about it either, because our rent money was in those pants.

I guess that experience pushed Mama to get Daddy to apply for the third-floor rear apartment when it became open. Mr. Albert, raising his two girls by himself because his wife had died, finally got married again. His new wife didn't like living in the West End so they moved out to Avondale. Daddy said more colored folk were beginning to move to Avondale because the Jews were moving out. His cousin Ted had just moved out there and said it was good for his kids. I asked if we could go out there sometimes to visit Uncle Ted so that I could see Little Ted again. Little Ted had a bike and used to let me ride it when they lived downtown. Daddy said he'd take us all out to visit sometime when he wasn't so busy at work. His company was building the new expressways throughout the city—some even came through downtown—and Daddy got lots of overtime by working late and on weekends. He said he didn't have the time for socializing right now. It made sense to me.

CORNBREAD AND RATS

Before we moved upstairs we could see people on the sidewalk and even touch them if we wanted. The man who stole Daddy's pants proved that. But on the third floor we could see much farther than on the first, which led to my undoing.

Our courtyard was a small, square patch of concrete that lay between our building and the one behind us. We used to shoot marbles and play four square and other games there as long as we had light to see by. On one side of the courtyard stood a six-foot-tall cinder-block wall long enough for six garbage cans to sit side by side. That's where we played my favorite game: rat fishing!

It was almost dark, and me and Leroy, who lived in the building in back of us, retrieved the strong fishing lines that we kept hidden behind the wall during the day. We stacked two cinder blocks in back of the wall, which we used to help boost us up to the top, where we could sit and dangle our feet over the cans. I kept a big hook tied to my line and, baiting it with a thick piece of Spam, cast it over the top of the nearest cans. Always eager sports, the rats struck vigorously at the bait. Leroy lost his balance once before and had fallen off the wall onto the cans, causing all the rats to scatter, whimpering and screeching in every direction. More careful this time, Leroy kept one hand on the wall while holding his line with the other.

The rats made lots of noise squealing, leaping on and off garbage can lids and burrowing down through the garbage like drills through soft wood. They were fun to watch leaping from one garbage can to another, upsetting lids and making a racket. Some slinked around the bottoms of the cans, foraging on whatever fell from the raiding party above. The best of the show were the acrobats who zipped around the rims of cans without losing their balance and made graceful running dives into the hearts of cans without missing a beat. After a few leaps and near misses the rats found something that smelled better or looked easier to reach. The game ended, and another day's circus came to a close. We never really caught any rats that way, but we always tried. And the rats tried, too. I think we all enjoyed playing the game.

We scampered down off the wall, and as I passed a can with the lid almost tilted off, I noticed a hunk of fresh cornbread sticking out from among the garbage. I had already eaten dinner and didn't want the string beans Mama had given me, so I had stuffed my cheeks like a chipmunk, excused myself from the table, rushed to the bathroom, and spit the beans out into the toilet and flushed them away. Before the sound of the flushing had faded I bounded down the steps to join Leroy for rat fishing.

The cornbread must've been thrown out accidentally, I thought. I touched it to see if it was alright. I reached over and moved some dirty-looking lettuce from around the cornbread and felt it. Still soft and moist. It hadn't been thrown out long enough to get dry. It's not that dirty either, I thought, as I pinched off a small corner of the cornbread.

I tasted it. It tasted good. I tore off another small chunk. By then the sun had dipped behind the building and half-submerged in shadow the tiny concrete island that we called a courtyard. The big rats would be out soon and looking for something to eat, so I figured I'd better eat the cornbread and get out of there fast and plucked the last piece of bread from the can.

I didn't know that Daddy had just walked to the back room after an argument with Mama and was gazing angrily out of the window when his eyes locked on me down at the garbage cans. His voice dropped down upon me from above and pinned me to the concrete with jackhammer force. "Goddamn it, Junior, get your ass up here now!"

I choked on that last piece of cornbread but I got it down. With nothing else for me to do, no place to hide and nowhere to run, I had but one choice: go upstairs and face the ironing cord. I knew better than to expect any mercy. I had been caught red-handed, been seen eating the cornbread. What could I say? I'd brought it all on myself.

I turned slowly toward the hallway that went from the front of the building to the courtyard, dragging my feet to reach the hallway as slowly as I could. Tears started leaking down my cheeks the closer I got. I reached our apartment at 3-B, with my shirt cuff wet from wiping my face. Pushing the door open, I saw Daddy standing in the doorway to the back room with the ironing cord held tightly in his hand, his face a thunderstorm of anger. "Come over here, boy. Your mama can't save you this time."

I saw Mama standing near the sink, looking at me the way I looked at someone about to get beaten up at school. Her eyes told me there was nothing she could do to help me. She knew that if she interfered now, it would be bad for us both. I felt like running back down the stairs, but that would only make matters worse when he finally caught me. Trying to control my tears, I wiped my face one more time and stepped inside.

"I didn't do nothing," I cried before Daddy sprang across the room, grabbed me by the arm, and pulled me to him, his grip so tight on my arm that it scorched my skin like a hot dog on a grill. I should have been grateful for that moment because an explosion of blinding pain filled the next. Daddy pulled me between his legs and beat me through my clothes with the ironing cord but couldn't hold me down. I kept leaping and twisting like a rodeo bronc trying to throw him, trying to escape, but he kept holding on. The only consolation I had was that this time I wasn't naked. Maybe this time the welts wouldn't be so deep and the bruises wouldn't show.

I didn't get many whippings after that for a while. I learned to say what Daddy wanted to hear and do what he wanted me to do whenever he was around. Besides, life on Thirteenth Street was far too interesting for me to let a whipping slow me down.

BIKE DREAMS

Many guys in our neighborhood rode bikes. Al rode a Huffy, and Jimmy had a Rollfast, with rear carriers and whitewalls. I liked Jimmy's the best. It looked almost as slick as a car. Bobby rode the only English Racer in the neighborhood. Black with skinny tires and hand brakes, it was the ugliest bike of all and no good for hook-sliding. I didn't have a bike, and Daddy couldn't afford to get me one.

Picking up newspapers from Mama one day, Navigator Jack overheard Daddy say, "Junior, that's enough about a bike. We can't get one right now. That's it."

Pushing his cart up our side of the street a couple of days later singing, "Rags! Paypio!" Navigator Jack stopped when he saw me leaning against the building near the downstairs hallway.

"Hey, Junior," he said.

"Hey, Navigator Jack, you looking for my mama?"

"Well, I'm looking for you if you're still looking for a bike," he said. "I know a place where we could get one if you think your father wouldn't mind."

In one movement I stood up and moved in closer to him. "No, he won't mind. As a matter of fact, he'd be glad to see you help me out. He knows how much I want a bike."

That wasn't entirely true. Daddy might look bad if Navigator Jack got me a bike and he couldn't. It didn't work as easy as Navigator made it sound.

"Okay, meet me down the street tomorrow at the scrap yard around four. After I've tallied up we'll see if we can't come up with something."

"Alright. Thanks. I'll be there," I said, and he went on his way.

I'd always wanted a bike. My cousin Ted and I were the same age, and he had a Rollfast. They lived in Avondale, and he rode his bike to school every day. One day as he pushed his bike through the crosswalk like he was supposed to, a car ran through the crosswalk and hit him. Ted's bike landed ten feet away unharmed. He died the next day. Aunt Alma never did get over it. The odd thing to me was that Ted's bike wasn't harmed. All that remained at the actual point of impact was one of Ted's Converse gym shoes. When he got the news Uncle Ted looked like one of the flattened tires on Ted's bike. Aunt Alma fell to the floor out of breath and cried in a loud silence.

Ted was gone, but his bike was still here. Having my own bike would put wings on my feet. If it were me, I'd be happy to see Ted get my bike. It made sense to me. His mother and father wouldn't be using it. Besides, it might make them happy to see someone get some use out of it. So why shouldn't I have his bike? I was his cousin.

With my bike I could leave Thirteenth Street behind and for a while forget having to return. I could race to Eden Park and back with my own bike, or just ride there by myself and not worry about making it home before dark. If I wanted to earn extra money I could put a basket on the handlebars, a carrier on the rear fender, and be ready to carry groceries home from Kroger for tips. Having my own bike meant much more than just riding. It meant I could go places that I needed permission for but didn't want to ask. There was nothing else like it. That's why I didn't think there was anything wrong about asking Aunt Alma to let me have Ted's bike. I didn't believe that Ted's funeral would be a good place to ask, so I waited until we got home for the repass.

Aunt Alma sat at the first table facing the sliced meat table while people passed by in line shaking her hand and giving condolences. I waited until the line thinned out and stepped up with a sandwich in my hand.

"Aunt Alma, I'm really sorry for all you've lost and miss Ted badly. Do you know when you'll be ready to get rid of Ted's bike? We were so close, I know he'd be happy for me to have it."

For an instant her eyes were flooded with an immeasurable sorrow too vast to plumb, but in the next she exploded with a steely bitterness that burned through my heart. At the same time a hammerlike grip snatched me away by my left arm, pulled me to her lips, and muttered through gritted teeth, "Boy, if you don't get your ass out of here I'll kill you myself."

I managed to maintain a feeble relationship with Uncle Ted for months afterward, but my relationship with Aunt Alma ended at Ted's repass. All my hopes of getting his Rollfast ended with it.

Navigator Jack made most things sound easy. He looked like a bum in his outfit but didn't act like one. Anything you asked him to do, he could do it. If you looked at him, really looked into his eyes like I did, you could see the true Navigator. Looked straight into your heart when he talked. Nobody but him would know what you talked about. He was straight up. I could see him seated next to a pilot plotting a course. The Navigator Jack I saw behind those eyes could do anything he wanted, and at that moment he wanted to be our junkman.

I once asked him, "Navigator, are you really a navigator?"

"Who said that?"

"Nobody really. Somebody said you used to be a real navigator."

"Yeah, I'm a real navigator. I navigate this cart up and down the street every day."

"Okay, I hear you. It ain't my business. We still cool?"

"Junior, we'll always be cool," he said and pushed on down the street.

He didn't have to tell me. I knew. Navigator Jack wasn't no real navigator, but he wasn't no junkman neither. From what I can tell he may have been in the Air Force during the war—smart enough to be a navigator but not given the opportunity. Like Daddy. Daddy volunteered for the Marines to fight and got assigned to the motor pool instead. He said Negroes never made it to combat, "just to keep us segregated from the whites." When I asked him what was it like to be a Marine, he said, "Working on white boys' cars, same as on the streets. That's the only kind of Marine they wanted me to be."

Probably broken and bitter by his Air Force experience, Navigator, whose name wasn't Navigator Jack yet, travelled around the country doing all sorts of jobs. He'd gone to college but lost contact with his family during the war. Wasting all the money he had from service he became an alcoholic, finally slipping down to cheap wine, like Thunderbird. That's when he hit bottom, stopped his slide, picked himself up, and became the Navigator Jack I knew. As Navigator Jack the junkman, no one could put him down.

Regardless of what others said of him or how he looked, I believed Navigator Jack could do anything he said he could. Daddy was always away at work, and Mama trusted Navigator with any job she needed. He fixed the front door that wouldn't close snugly, tightened the leaky pipe under the kitchen sink, and replaced the window weights for the window that wouldn't open in the front room. Not counting all the small stuff he did all year long, when Navigator Jack said he'd get me a bike, it was like saying rice is white. The deal was done.

For years I'd silently watched the other guys turn their bikes upside down, rest them on their handlebars and seat, and start repairing them. I watched with puppylike wonder as they fixed broken bike chains by removing the key link chain and attaching a new link to replace a broken one. It took even greater skill to take the sprocket out of the rear wheel, lubricate it, and make the bike pedal easier and faster, and they all did it. Changing tires, fixing flats, straightening wobbly rims—I watched with the hungry fascination of a starving man looking through the window at diners in a restaurant. All I needed was a bite.

By the time I got to the scrap yard ready to give all of my years of stored-up knowledge and skill to have my own bike, Navigator hadn't come. I stopped at the opened cyclone gate and waited. True to his word, just like when he did odd jobs for my mama, Navigator Jack was right on time. He pushed his cart up to the scale, separated and weighed his haul, then went to the office to get his cash. After what seemed like a long time he returned from the office and came over to where I stood. "Come on," he said, as he lifted the handles of his cart, "Let's go 'round back."

I'd passed the scrap yard a hundred times before and never thought about what went on inside. We all called it the junkyard because everything looked like junk from our side of the fence. I never fully understood how Navigator Jack earned his living by collecting rags and paper that had been given to him or thrown away. "Iron pays the best," he said. He had to be a good scavenger to find iron, but when he did, it was a big payday. Seeing him at work that day helped me understand what Mama said. "Navigator Jack ain't just somebody wearing a junk man's hat. He's a man. And just like the rest of us, he's doing the best he can to make ends meet. That's all that anybody can do."

Navigator Jack knew his way around the scrap yard. He ignored the mounds of rags and paper on our left and turned to the right. We passed cars and pieces of cars, some only skeletons of themselves picked clean of any useful parts by people unable to afford new ones. Other cars were crushed like so many cans of pop by the car crusher and piled up to make a crushed car mountain. We passed numerous small mounds of automobile tire rims and toppled refrigerators scattered like bones throughout the yard.

We walked through an area full of radiators like the one we had in our apartment and kept going until we got to a corner of the yard far away from the office and stopped there.

"This is it," Navigator Jack said. "We can find something for you here," he told me, swinging his arm in a half-circle in front of us. At first I didn't see what he was talking about, but pretty soon I saw a twisted bike frame lying half hidden under a pile of sinks and water pipes. I didn't feel as excited as I had earlier when I'd imagined what a wonderful bike I'd have. I should have expected something like this when Navigator told me to meet him here at the scrap yard. What should I expect to find in a junkyard, a Rollfast? Not hardly.

"Hey, Navigator. What am I supposed to do with this?" I said, pointing to the twisted frame. "That don't look like no bike to me."

"Take care, Junior, just look around. We'll find something good."

I felt disappointed but couldn't risk losing a chance to own a bike. So I took Navigator's advice and started to look around carefully. More bike frames than I could've imagined lay hidden in that scrap yard. But when you got to think of it, bikes are made of metal, and if broken and considered unfixable, then why not get some money for the frame?

After our pulling frame after frame out from under something else, Navigator called me over to where he'd been looking. "Junior, I want you to see something," he said.

He held up a blue twenty-six-inch boys' Huffy frame, with a front fender and no seat. "What you think?" he said, and stood it upright on the ground.

"I don't know, Navigator. You can't ride if you ain't got no seat."

"Junior, the seat ain't nothing. We can find you another seat. It's the frame that makes the bike. Look at those front forks. See how straight they are? Nothing's hit that bike. It's a good one. Now look at the rear and look at its bars. That's how you pick a bike or anything else. Just look at the frame."

He was right. We found a nice wide seat with two wire suspension cushions, like on a motorcycle, that we found on a Rollfast that looked like it had been hit by a car. It took a bit longer, but we found a rear fender that fit but was a different color from the front.

Navigator Jack screwed the rear fender on, attached the seat, placed the finished bike in his pushcart, and walked me back to the scrap yard office. "Bike frames cost fifty cents, Junior. How much you got?" I handed him all I had, a quarter. "Good enough," he said and walked inside. When he came back he handed me a small piece of paper and said, "You've got a bike now, Junior, and you owe me a quarter."

Thanks to Navigator Jack I had a patched-up, blue twenty-six-inch Huffy, with a custom Rollfast seat, and two mismatched fenders. Now all I needed were the tires.

Just as Navigator Jack said, the frame is everything you need to make a bike. When Daddy learned that we'd gotten the bike for fifty cents, he looked surprised. "You know how to go after something you really want, don't you?" he said. He handed Mama enough money to buy two new wheels and tires. "Take him to the bike shop on Freeman Avenue and let him choose some wheels." I bought two twenty-six-inch aluminum wheels with Goodyear whitewall tires. On the way home Mama gave me five dollars and said, "Give this to Navigator Jack, honey. You owe him."

I spent more time away from home with my bike going places I didn't expect before. Like Walnut Hills, where trees and grass seemed to grow everywhere. Some black folk lived out there with nice lawns on quiet streets. Didn't look as friendly as our streets downtown, though. When Miss Betty, the librarian at school, heard I lived on Thirteenth, she said, "Thirteenth Street dances with activity and sways with song. You live in a special place, Junior."

I know. She should hear Navigator Jack sing, "Rags! Paypio!"

DON'T TOUCH THE TV

Before riding away from home on my bike, I rode a magic carpet beyond downtown each time we turned on the TV. Usually we watched TV in the living room after dinner when Daddy got home from work. During the day I'd be outside running around, and Mama would be inside with

Wanda. Our first TV sat on the table in the front room like a small Buddha. Later on we got one with a twenty-inch screen in a blond veneer console with a record player on one side. We all watched TV together, but only the adults could touch it.

Unlike the chifferobe or walnut dresser, the console was not considered furniture. I once bumped into it and knocked the lamp over while chasing my sister Wanda. Mama screamed as if she were dying and scared me so bad I almost stopped breathing.

"Junior, have you've broken it again? Do you know how much it cost to get it fixed the last time you ran into it? You better hope it's alright or you know what's gonna happen when your father comes home."

I bent down to turn the knob to see if it would turn on, but before my hand could touch it, Mama's voice lashed across the room like lightning, jerking my hand away,

"Junior, don't touch that TV!"

The TV wasn't broken or scratched, so when Daddy came home, neither Mama nor I said a word. After his bath Daddy sat down and watched Jack Benny and Rochester go at it. He was at his best then, and I let go of my breath and settled back against the couch with my legs stretched out on the floor. Thankfully, *The Lawrence Welk Show* wasn't on, and I didn't have to watch his tired dancers doing the polka. If I had to listen to singers, I preferred Nat King Cole. Nat oozed cool. When he sang, even "The Christmas Song" was jazz. Nat had his own show, a Negro like me, but his show didn't last long. Other than Frank Sinatra, the only other cool white singer was Dean Martin. I liked listening to Dean and Tony Bennett, too. But watching Perry Como sitting on a stool singing and wearing a sweater was for schoolteachers, not for me.

It was a big deal when I was permitted to change channels. We only had three channels: 5, 9, and 12. Usually Mama got up to change the channels because Daddy sitting in his big chair was tired after working all day and didn't move. With two jobs, one as a mechanic at a car dealership and another as a construction worker, Daddy always said, "I'm due for a little rest now and then. Let me watch TV." I didn't mind. It gave me a better chance to get to change the channels.

The first time Mama asked me to change the channel caught me by surprise. Almost five o'clock and about time for Daddy to come home from work, with Mama still cooking at the stove wanted to see the evening news. "Junior, get *Peter Grant and the News* for me on Channel 12," she said.

The kitchen opened to the living room. Well, not really "opened." Being part of the same room helped her see the TV from the kitchen. I jumped up from the couch as the *Mouseketeers* ended and walked over to the TV. In case you don't remember, the volume knob was on the left and the channel knob on the right.

The big plastic knob, dark in the middle and surrounded by a hard clear plastic circle with evenly spaced brown numbers, 1 to 12, was a combination lock to a magical world of entertainment right in our living room with me as locksmith. Only one problem existed. Strength—not the dial's, mine. The dial was harder to turn than I thought, so I grabbed the center ball as I would a hammer's handle and pulled as I turned. The dial turned alright, but the whole thing came off in my hand. Sticking out from the TV where the knob used to be was a slotted round metal stub. I was stunned. Mama, not hearing Peter Grant, looked my way and saw my hand holding the severed dial. Her eyes were a raging firestorm as her tightly clamped jaws squeezed out the words, "Junior, don't touch that TV."

COLOR TV

Not all my experiences with the TV were bad. When colored folk were on, I was king. "Colored on 5. Colored on 5 at seven," I'd shout as I knocked on the doors in our building. There were six apartments in our building, which was more like a village actually, and whenever colored folk were to appear on television I would carry the news. Like the town crier I made sure every family that had a TV wouldn't miss seeing the colored person who was going to appear that night.

I knew when we'd get the chance to see colored people on TV because I sold the afternoon *Cincinnati Times-Star* for Big Tony. Twelve of us boys pitched papers for him. Big Tony always knew when Nat King Cole or Rochester was going to be on TV. He didn't like Amos and Andy. He said they were clowns and made colored folk look like fools.

"Yeah, *Amos and Andy* is funny to white folk because they're not us. Do you like being made fun of? Well, I don't. To show you how much they think of Negroes, white men played Amos and Andy on the radio. Sounded just like that stupid Amos and that clown Kingfish. Don't get me started about Amos and Andy. They're a disgrace to the race."

Not everybody shared Big Tony's view of *Amos and Andy*. They were a big favorite in our building. Mr. Bill said that Negroes like Big Tony were jealous because they weren't making the kind of money Amos and Andy did. "Don't pay no attention to that stuff, Junior. Big Tony would jump at the chance to play Kingfish if they paid him Kingfish's money."

It was 1957 and we didn't have many opportunities to see colored folk on TV, so it was something to celebrate when we did. Most likely it would be Rochester on *The Jack Benny Show* or *Amos and Andy*. My parents loved Rochester and *Amos and Andy*, but lots of people liked Nat King Cole.

Nat King Cole was the first and only colored man with his own variety show. *The Nat King Cole Variety Show* made Nat the first black to win an Emmy Award. During that same year he had a number-one hit on the *Billboard* chart. Whites and blacks both adored him. I didn't really love jazz at that time, but I liked to hear Nat sing. He was so smooth and cool that I wanted to be like him. When Nat was on, I was locked in.

Aside from his singing, people liked Nat because he was different. When I went to the barbershop, everybody had something to say about him.

"'Bout time real colored people get a chance to do something," said

Joe from Down Below, as everybody called him because he was so dark. People who didn't like Joe or were mad at him called him "the nigger from hell" due to his being coal-black. But Joe didn't mind. He'd just laugh it off with, "Yeah, I'm him, and you don't want to fuck with me."

"Aww, nigger, you just saying that 'cause Nat's black like you. Least he can sing. What can you do?" said Mr. Jimmy John, Billy's daddy.

"It proves you don't have to be light, bright, and almost white, like Lena Horne, to be famous."

"Don't you start talking about my Lena. That's a fine girl if I ever saw one."

"You better believe it," said a new guy I hadn't seen before. "She'll make a man lose his religion. A blind man see and a lame man walk."

"Get outta here," said Joe from Down Below. "The finest black girl in all of Hollywood is Dorothy Dandridge. She can act, sing, dance, and drive white men crazy. They all trying to marry her."

"Well, if you ask me," said Mr. Jimmy John, "they just want to get between her legs and throw her away. That's what white men been doing to black women forever. 'Specially the pretty ones."

"You don't know what you talking about," said Joe. "Dorothy Dandridge ain't no white man's whore."

"Whoa, I didn't mean anything." said Mr. Jimmy John, throwing up his hands. "I'm just talking. That's all."

Nobody said anything for a moment. Then the new guy spoke:

"Getting back to Nat. I know coming up we didn't care much for real black-skinned people, but Nat's changed lots of folks' minds. Don't you think?"

Mr. Jimmy John said, "Yeah, they's plenty of folk, 'specially them high yellas, still wouldn't want one of them to marry their daughter."

"Don't want to darken that white blood, do they?" said Joe, causing everyone to laugh. "Well, anyway, I'm glad to see Nat make it big, and most other Negroes is, too."

"He's a credit to his race," the new guy said. "Yeah, he's a credit to his race."

"A credit to his race," they all chimed in. "Nat's a credit to his race."

Having a colored person on television in 1957 was almost like being there yourself. Jack Benny didn't look anything like us but Rochester did. Rochester had our lips, our eyes, our hair, and most of all Rochester was our color.

Sure, everybody knew about Joe Louis and Sugar Ray Robinson, but how many people had actually seen them fight? Millions saw *The Jack Benny Show* every week, and those millions saw Rochester. In our building everybody with a TV would be sure to be sitting in their living room with the channel on 4 at seven o'clock.

I think seeing colored people on TV made the older people in my building feel proud. "Rochester had some hard times to get where he is. I'm proud to see him up there like that," Miss Louise said. "I know his mama must be proud, too. He's a credit to his race."

Only four of the people in our building had TVs. Miss Louise didn't have one—said the rays from the screen might make her go blind or give her cancer. She went upstairs sometimes to watch TV with Mr. Bill. She said she'd be glad to watch TV with us, but she had promised Mr. Bill.

Mr. Bill was the only person in the building as old as Miss Louise. They used to talk a lot about the old days when they were young, before the war and living Down South. The coach down at the park said they both had "skin that looked like the pocket of an old catcher's mitt, all shiny black and supple." Coach is black, and his people are still Down South. "Skin don't get like that from laying around," he said. "It gets beaten that supple from catching too many of life's hardballs."

Most everyone in our building came from somewhere else. Like Mr. Bill and Miss Louise. Being from Georgia like my mama, Miss Louise knew what hard times were.

"Georgia is a hard place to be," said Mr. Bill.

"And a better place to be *from* if you're colored," said Miss Louise.

Talk was that Mr. Bill killed a white man in Dothan, Alabama, before the war. Nobody knew if it was true or not. Funny thing was, older men from Down South who kept to themselves and didn't talk about their past were singled out as having killed a white man. I guess that made them kinda dangerous and mysterious. Some women liked to think if Mr. Bill ran away leaving everyone and everything behind, it might give them a chance to be his lady. If anybody knew something about Mr. Bill killing a white man it was Miss Louise, and she wasn't saying nothing. It was funny that Miss Louise and Mr. Bill had so much to talk about but didn't meet till Thirteenth Street. Daddy said, "They're two of a kind. Those two together. They're deeper than they let on."

If Mr. Bill did kill somebody, it didn't affect me. "Junior, I want to show you something," he said when he stopped me on the stairs. He opened his door all the way, motioned for me to come in, and pointed. It was an old upright Crosley radio case with a tiny TV screen standing in the middle of his front room.

"Did Navigator Jack give you this, Mr. Bill?"

"No, I found it myself. Down at the junkyard."

"What you gonna do with it?"

"Make it work."

"For real. You can make that work? I don't think so, Mr. Bill. It's too far gone."

"My great-granddaddy helped build one of the biggest plantations in Alabama. My granddaddy kept it running after Juneteenth when they freed the slaves. He could make anything work. I can, too. This TV won't be nothin.'"

The following week Miss Louise started going to Mr. Bill's to watch Rochester. Something must've worked.

For those who didn't have a TV on their floor, or even at their friend's down the street, someone in the building would invite them in to watch Rochester. Daddy never missed watching him.

Mama said, "I saw in a magazine where Rochester is the highest-paid Negro on TV."

"Yeah," said Daddy, "and I hear Jack Benny and him are friends outside the show, too. That's why Rochester can stick it to Jack Benny like he does. Don't any other Negroes do that."

"Did you know Jack Benny moved his whole company from one hotel because they wouldn't take in Rochester? What you think about that?"

"Rochester's his friend, and Benny's no fool. He knows where his money is. They've both got something to protect. When *The Jack Benny Show* is over and Rochester's gone, our sixty minutes of equality ends. Our one hour of standing tall as a colored person is over. You can believe that."

Daddy was right. Life returned to normal after Rochester. The normality of white television with white stars for white people. Of watching Uncle Miltie and Sid Caesar, where coloreds didn't exist—but colored people laughed at their jokes. Of watching Dinah Shore close *The Dinah Shore Show* throwing us a kiss and singing, "See the USA in your Chevrolet, America's the greatest land of all," and our wanting to believe she was singing that anthem to us, yet underneath knowing she wasn't.

"Dinah Shore gets on my nerves," said Daddy. "'See the USA in your Chevrolet.' What country does she live in?"

"Yeah, honey," said Mama, "but what can you do?"

"How many people on this block drive a Chevy? Drive it through Alabama and let a white girl throw you a kiss," he laughed. "That'll be the last drive you'll make."

"Lou," said Mama.

"Well, it's the truth," he said, and leaned back to light another Pall Mall.

Nothing changed. Rochester continued to chastise Mr. Benny and gave us a reason to stick out our chests. *The Jack Benny Show* rolled around at seven each week, and I ran from door to door bringing the good news.

"Colored on 5 at seven. Colored on 5."

GOING TO THE SHOW

I loved going to the show. I didn't have to worry about changing the channels on the TV or Mama screaming, "Don't touch the TV!" Plus, the screen was bigger and I got to see real westerns with real heroes like John Wayne, not Roy Rogers the singing cowboy and his horse, Trigger.

My friends and I went to the Lincoln Theater close to where we all lived. Sometimes we'd go to the Roosevelt, but the Lincoln was closer and had a balcony. I'd get some Milk Duds, a fifteen-cent bag of popcorn, and a Pepsi, and I was down for the count for the rest of the afternoon.

We enjoyed sitting in the balcony, and except for the *tat-a-tat-tat* of the film turning on the spools in the projector room behind us, it was quieter than downstairs. Sometimes we were disturbed by ushers shining their flashlights on people to keep them quiet or to make them put out their cigarettes. Some of the guys who brought their girlfriends to the show sat in the balcony also. The flashlights disturbed them the most.

We didn't have any air-conditioning at home, nothing like the ice-cool Lincoln. We paid seventy-five cents on a Sunday and watched movies over and over all day long. We'd come in at the end of the movie and stay until it ended a second time. There was always another movie and a cartoon to go along with it. Going the movies was an all-day affair for me. Going to the Lincoln on Sunday was better than going to church—and cheaper, too. Mama said to give a dollar in the offering at church, and it only cost me seventy-five cents to see Humphrey Bogart. Now that was a deal.

I saw everyone in our building at the Lincoln at one time or another, except Mr. Jackson, who lived on the second floor. He'd fought in a war, too—the Korean, not WWII like Daddy. Coming home late from the show I'd made too much noise on the stairs, and he opened his door. "Hey, Junior, keep it down," he said.

"Yes, Sir, I will. Just coming from the show, trying to get home on time," I said.

"I know. Just take it easy. Ain't no expressway in here."

"I'm sorry, Mr. Jackson, I'll be quieter. Did I wake you up?"

"No. I'm trying to watch television."

"I just finished watching Hercules at the Lincoln with Steve Reeves. It was alright. No big deal."

"It never is at the Lincoln."

"What do you mean?"

"You don't know? The RKO gets everything first. All the top movies go there. Anything you see at the Lincoln is weeks behind the RKO, sometimes months. And the movies. The Lincoln gets B-rate movies, the kind that can't even make it to the back door of the RKO. The kind that only niggers get to see. That's the kind of movies you see at the Lincoln. I wouldn't go to the Lincoln if you paid me."

The movies were new to me, so I didn't have any complaints. The Lincoln Theater looked like one of those theaters you'd see in those movie posters from the twenties, only more faded and shrunken. I remember a moist, musty smell in my nose each time I entered the lobby. I can't describe the color of the walls because there wasn't any color strong enough to remember. Some of the tiles on the lobby floor were missing and the carpet to the balcony barely there, but I liked the Lincoln.

I liked the Lincoln because it was in my neighborhood and looked like it belonged there with the rest of us. I felt comfortable there. I could wear whatever I had on at the Lincoln and not worry about what I looked like or how I behaved. My friends and other people who I knew were there. From what I'd heard I wouldn't have felt comfortable uptown anyway because I'd probably not know anyone and I'd be the only colored person there. I never wanted to go to an uptown movie anyway because my parents had already tried.

The RKO Albee was everything the Lincoln Theater was not. It flashed all glitter and gold and everything polished and glistened like new, and like Mr. Jackson said, all of the best movies stopped there first. But the most important thing of all about the RKO was its location. The RKO Albee lay smack in the middle of uptown.

Whenever I walked uptown, only seven blocks away, it was like stepping into a sunlit world after emerging from a cave. People, mostly white, wore stylish suits and dresses, and drove new and like-new cars, while unfamiliar aromas from uppity restaurants perfumed the air. Didn't see many black folks there, though. Didn't see any black folk eating in fine restaurants or wearing stylish clothes. Didn't see any driving no big cars either. Floorwalkers followed me whenever I went into a store, so I just stayed outside and started looking at clothes in the windows. The sidewalk was close enough, and I couldn't get accused of stealing from the outside.

Mama didn't know how I felt about going uptown. It wouldn't have changed her mind any. She read in some magazine about Marlon Brando starring in *On the Waterfront* and wanted to see it.

"Lou," she said. "Marlon Brando is in that new movie up at the RKO. You want to see it?"

"Why you want to see it at the RKO? Can't you wait till it come downtown? You know I don't like going uptown," Daddy said.

"If I wait till then, it might be a year from now and I'll know all about it from TV."

"What's the name of it?"

"*On the Waterfront.* You've heard about it."

"Yeah, Cassie, I've heard about it. They say it's supposed to be good. But we can't go."

Mama looked at him without blinking, her head slightly tilted showing just the shadow of a smile, and softly asked, "Why?"

I saw surrender creep into Daddy's eyes and around the corners of his mouth, but he didn't want to give in all at once. "Car's not running right. Might get stuck uptown. That's just what we want, to get stuck uptown."

"We can always ride the bus," Mama said. "It stops right up the street on Freeman. I see people catching it there all the time."

"It's not just that. You know what they say about the RKO. About that prejudice thing. I don't play that game anymore. This ain't Alabama."

Mama stepped up a bit. "I know, honey. They can't give us nothing we can't handle. Plus, it was awhile ago. No telling what's changed since then. I say we go. We got to go sometime."

I rarely saw Daddy lose at anything, but when he did he lost to Mama. She didn't ask for much unless it was important. Maybe that's why he usually found ways to give it to her. They dressed up in their church clothes, Mama in her hat with the flowers in it and Daddy in his suit and no tie. They caught the bus and walked three blocks to the RKO Albee. Except for my parents, no one else in the line going in was colored.

Daddy told Mama, "Don't look good when you the only colored people here."

Mama kept close to his side and said nothing. Daddy reached the ticket booth and said, "Two tickets, please."

The agent looked in Daddy's direction, spoke past him and not to him, looking over his shoulder instead of face-to-face. "The seats reserved for colored people are in the balcony, and the balcony is closed today."

Standing next to Daddy, Mama felt his body tremble and his forearm swell, and she closed her hand around his wrist to hold him still. Knowing how easy it is for him to be the loser in direct conflict with a white man, Daddy stepped back from the window before asking a question.

"Excuse me. When *do* you expect the colored section to be open?"

"I'm not sure," said the ticket taker. "Why don't you check next week?"

"Will *On the Waterfront* still be playing?"

"Yeah, it'll be here." the ticket taker said, getting impatient.

"Well, do you want me to come down here and check, or do you want me to call? I'll need to get your number if I need to call."

Tired of Daddy badgering him, the ticket taker said, "We don't have any seats for colored people, period. Any time, any day. Go. Leave me alone."

"Thanks, that's what I wanted to hear. Just like the Ku Klux. You prejudiced son-of-a-bitch."

While waiting at the bus stop to go home, Daddy's whole body still trembled. He looked as if he'd been hit in the face by someone he couldn't hit back without killing him. When he got home Daddy rushed through the door and said, "I knew it. I knew it. That damn RKO. Ohio is just another Alabama in disguise. All that's missing is the Klan."

Mama said nothing, changed her clothes, and started fixing dinner.

From the way my parents were treated, I was glad there weren't any RKO Albees in our neighborhood. I didn't want to have to dress up to go to the movies. Besides, it was useless. Without all the lights, no one could see me. If the Lincoln Theater moved uptown, I wonder if it would become like the RKO? Would I feel comfortable in it? Could I still get in for seventy-five cents and stay all day? Would it get new paint and get all shiny and smell good, and would I have to be on my best behavior? Or could I just be myself and sit in the balcony because I liked to and not because they made me?

The Alabama sickness followed Daddy wherever we went. Geography couldn't change it. I tried to run away from it with my new bike and couldn't escape. Mama fought the same fight in Georgia and left to start again in Cincinnati. Prejudice existed here, too. Though she and Daddy didn't escape the South's prejudice by coming north they found Thirteenth Street—a village of other runaways making new lives. Some of those people became part of our new family. One of them was Miss Louise.

MISS LOUISE

Mama used to give me fifty cents and a piece of paper with a number written on it and say, "Take this over to Miss Louise and tell her to box it for me." I'd go downstairs, knock on her door, and she'd open it, wearing one of those long house dresses that she liked to wear. "What is it, Junior?"

"Mama said to give you this and to box it for her." I'd hand her the paper, and she'd look at it, fold it over, and place it in a Mason jar kept on a stool by the door. "Alright. Tell your mama I'll take care of it," and she would shut the door with a soft click. Miss Louise lived alone and never failed to lock the door behind her.

One time Mama hit the number, which meant the number she gave Ms. Louise fell as the winning number that day. I didn't know what playing the numbers really meant or how it worked, but I knew gangsters operated it and Ms. Louise sure wasn't anybody's gangster. Mama said that the "numbers man" came around every day and picked up the slips from Ms. Louise and delivered the payoff money to her when anyone won. That's how Ms. Louise earned extra money to make ends meet, Mama said.

The day Mama's number hit, Ms. Louise walked up to our apartment. She sat down at the kitchen table and told Mama the day's number and what it paid. Then she counted out the money and gave Mama her winnings. The numbers man had already given Ms. Louise something extra for bringing Mama's business to him, but that had nothing to do with us, Mama said. Mama took her winnings and gave Ms. Louise some of it for making it all happen. Then, without telling Mama, Ms. Louise took part of her money and bought me a carrier to attach over the rear fender on my bike. "That's for going to the store for me. You don't need to tell anyone," she said. Playing the numbers was a good thing in our neighborhood if your numbers lady was Ms. Louise. The last time I saw her was on a Thanksgiving eve as I was returning from the store with her groceries.

That morning, people had been lined up in the supermarket like they'd heard a storm siren. My feet hurt from just waiting in the checkout line. After walking six blocks carrying two bags of groceries, I turned into our hallway with relief. I barely made it to the third-floor landing when my bags split open, sending groceries scampering down the stairs like frolicking pups. The door to 2-A creaked open, and Ms. Louise's shiny brown face peered out. "Well, Junior, you done done it now," she said in her faint, scratchy voice sounding like a worn LP record.

"Wasn't my fault, Miss Louise," I said, looking her straight in the eye. "The bag boy didn't give me no double bag like I asked. I knew them canned goods would bust through. I knew it, but he wouldn't listen to me."

"*Humph!* Just get them groceries up and in here, boy!" she commanded. "I ain't got no time to listen to no foolishness."

Miss Louise turned back into her apartment, leaving the door ajar. As I hunched down to retrieve the scattered cans, I remembered the first time we'd met. She had dribbled spit and snuff from her lower lip on my forehead when she kissed me and said, "Leave it on, son. The spit will bring you luck."

As I grew older I discovered that everybody knew Miss Louise. She seemed much older than anyone else in the neighborhood, and everyone listened to her. I'd seen her cuss out men who were much older than I, some as old as Daddy, so I tried to stay on her good side. Not that I was afraid of her. With her being so tiny and skinny, Miss Louise couldn't hurt anybody, 'though I wasn't completely sure about that. I'd heard she could do something awful with that cane of hers and was known to pop a head or two.

Whether young or old, male or female, Miss Louise treated all of us the same. She felt we were all errant children, and it was her duty, one she evidently relished, to look after us. In response to her chiding, no one, not even the older boys who had been to the reformatory in Mansfield, sassed Miss Louise.

I took off my jacket, spread it over the landing, and began filling it with the delinquent cans. Retrieving one dented can after another, I carefully placed a can of Bruton Snuff in my jacket. With relief I saw that it wasn't dented because Miss Louise got real upset when anything happened to her snuff. I found two more cans of Bruton, one slightly dented but none of the snuff had spilled. Once I'd added all the snuff to the collection, I knotted the arms of my jacket together and hefted the load onto my shoulder like a knapsack. Heavier than I thought, both bags had ripped through at the bottom. I hefted the load higher and pushed my way through the open door into Miss Louise's kitchen. She wasn't there and had gone to the back room to get something.

I sat my load down on the kitchen table and cleared my throat in a useless effort to rid my mouth of the taste of age and must. I had been going to the store for Miss Louise ever since I'd been able to cross the streets by myself. But no matter how many times I entered her apart-ment, I never got used to the smell. It lingered like a thick finger in the roof of my mouth. Miss Louise nailed her windows shut each fall and stuffed rags into the sills against the cold. She didn't open them again till spring. And with no fresh air circulating in the winter, her two small rooms were hot as the attic in summer.

The smell of old age covered everything in the apartment with an invisible glaze that seeped into the walls and floor. The heat stung tears from my eyes as I rubbed them, trying to see clear through the haze. It wasn't like Miss Louise to go into the back and stay without inviting me. I waited for ten minutes, and Miss Louise still didn't come out or call for me to come in. I started toward the back room and then stopped. *Maybe she's trying to find something special for me*, I told myself, and decided to wait and look around the kitchen again.

Unlike our four-room apartment, Miss Louise had a two-room kitchenette. The kitchen doubled as her living room, and most guests were stopped there and told to take a seat at the table. She lived in the back and only permitted special people to enter that region. I had been running to the store for her for years before she trusted me enough to let me enter it. Now not a week passed without her inviting me into her inner sanctum, and I could hardly wait till the next time.

An open sesame for me, Miss Louise's back room was a treasure trove of her curios, a shrine to her past. I most enjoyed seeing photos of Miss Louise when she looked like Dorothy Dandridge. Seeing her then, you'd never imagine she'd use a cane. Looking at the picture of her with her dead husband, Punching Pancho, I could almost see the strength they gave each other—a strength that Miss Louise seemed to have never given up.

Miss Louise said her husband "wasn't really no Cuban" and that the sportswriters gave him the name "Punching Pancho, the Cuban Hurricane." He was just plain Pete Jackson, a light-skinned black man from Bessemer, Alabama. Pete was a good middleweight fighter but never got the kind of bouts to fight ranked boxers. "Back then, white folks didn't want to see no black man, especially no Alabama nigger, whipping white boys in the ring," she said. According to Miss Louise that was because of Jack Johnson. "He beat them white boys like they stole something," said Miss Louise.

Pete fought at the Cincinnati YMCA when he and Miss Louise met. Both being from Down South, and Miss Louise not knowing many people in Cincinnati other than her cousin who'd sent for her, they eventually married and had two boys: Hector and Luiz. Hector and Luiz both became career Air Force men and sent their Mama curios from airbases all over the world. They were as good as any you'd find outside of a jewelry store. Eagles from all over the world made of crystal, ivory, jade, silver; they roosted on every available surface in Miss Louise's back room.

Her private world first opened for me one Saturday after I'd put down a bag of groceries on her kitchen table and Miss Louise said, "Why don't you come on back, Junior? I've got something to show you," and turned to go inside.

I stepped through the open door to her bedroom. It was so tight I could barely turn around. The bed stuck out from the wall, and the dresser leaned against it on one side. Heavy drapes covered the only window, which faced the alley. A small cane chair fit into one corner, and a small desk sat on the other side of the door. But the most interesting piece of all, the heavy wooden chest that looked like a pirate's treasure chest to me, stood alone at the foot of Miss Louise's bed.

She pulled the chair up to the chest, sat down, and lifted her finger for me to come. I came and stood beside her. "Junior," she said as she leaned over, opening the chest, "I don't always have something to give you for running to the store for me and you never ask, so I want to give you something to let you know how much I appreciate you."

And that's when she did it. That's when she gifted me with my first eagle. She placed something in my hand, a small, bright silver eagle with wings fully spread and "Lackland AF Base" stamped on the bottom. I didn't know what to say or do. So I took the tiny treasure, squeezed it in my hand, bent and kissed Miss Louise on the cheek, then turned and stepped quickly away. Now, with her in the back room I stayed out front, hoping she'd just gone to find a special gift for me again and nothing else.

I lifted a can of snuff from the pile on the table and wondered why Miss Louise stayed in back so long. I stepped toward the half-closed door of her room and called, "Miss Louise, Miss Louise." Nothing. Nowadays I had to be almost on top of her before she could hear me. I stopped and called again, "Miss Louise." Still no answer. I thought, *Mama and I will have to keep a closer eye on her if her hearing has gotten this bad.*

I knocked softly and pushed the partially opened door all the way open. Miss Louise lay with her head at an awkward angle against the headboard. It looked as if she had sat on the bed to dig something out of her cedar chest and had suddenly fallen asleep. I'd seen Miss Addie, Leroy's grandmother, fall asleep like that often. She would sit down and almost instantly fall asleep. I thought Miss Louise might be getting like Miss Addie. I decided to go in and straighten her neck so that she wouldn't wake up with a crook.

When I placed my hand on her head, nothing moved. Not an eyelid fluttered, nor even a sigh escaped her lips. I knew instantly what was wrong but couldn't admit it. Miss Louise was the neighborhood. She still had so much to teach me, so much to give. She was going to show me how to make ice cream out of snow this winter. Who else could do that? When I came home late dribbling the basketball on the landing, who'd be there standing with the door cracked, scolding me, "Junior, don't you know better than to be bouncing that ball upstairs when folks trying to sleep around here? Get your butt on upstairs."

I gently straightened Miss Louise's body on the bed and picked up the contents of her spilled chest and noticed that she was holding something tightly in her closed fist. I placed her hand in my palm and tenderly opened each finger. Inside lay a twenty-four-carat golden eagle. It was one of her favorite treasures, one her youngest son had given her five Christmases ago.

I looked down at Miss Louise once more and this time didn't feel so miserable. She seemed to be smiling, knowing that I had found the gift she'd gotten for me. I straightened out the fold in her bedspread, kissed Miss Louise lovingly on the cheek, and rushed upstairs to get Mama.

Miss Louise was family to us. She spilled snuff on me when I was little to show me her love. I brought her snuff to show her mine. She was my mama when Mama wasn't there. Sometimes she was even Mama to Mama. When Mama needed extra money she showed her how to play the numbers. When I needed to feel extra special she took me into her confidence and introduced me to her back room. Miss Louise brought something to everyone. Our building throbbed with life when she was around. It shrank when she died. We all shrank, Mama most of all.

MAMA LIZA AND SPORT

After Miss Louise died, Mama stopped going to visit other people in the building. "I'm tired, Junior. Let Mama get some rest," she said when I tried to take her to visit anyone. Finally she handed me a quarter and said, "Junior, go ask Pie Lady for some cinnamon sticks."

She loved Pie Lady's cinnamon sticks. Pie Lady emerged from the back of the store as I rushed through the door tingling its bell. With the big floor fan turning languidly behind her, the air in the store smelled like a dusty road after a sprinkle. The edges of Pie Lady's head scarf were moist and her dress sleeves drooped, but her eyes danced when she saw me.

"Junior, sure glad to see you. How's your mama? How's Cassie doing?" she asked.

"She's okay, just a little down."

"What you need?"

"She said for me to get some cinnamon sticks. You got any left?"

"Let me see," she said, as she poked around in one of her bins. "Yeah, as many as she needs. How much you want?"

"If you could let me have a half-dozen, I'm sure that might do it." Pie Lady put six cinnamon sticks in a bag and handed them to me.

"Don't worry about it," she said, and waved me away when I tried to pay for them.

I ran back upstairs and handed the bag to Mama. She looked inside, closed it, placed it on the kitchen table, and went back into the bedroom. She tried, really tried. When I came back three hours later after playing ball, the bag still sat on the table. And she lay in the bedroom, in the middle of the afternoon.

With Miss Louise gone we all felt like punctured tires. Even Daddy. That's when he said to Mama, "The dealership's closing for five days next week and I'll be off. Pack up the kids and let's go down to Selma for a few days. How about it?"

Mama had been to Selma before, and this would be my first time meeting Daddy's parents, Pa Joe and Mama Liza. They sharecropped cotton outside of Selma and raised Daddy's other sons, Joseph, Woody, and Tee. Daddy's second wife, Pearl, left the boys for Mama Liza to raise when she ran off with Big Time when Daddy was overseas. I wanted to meet them but not as bad as I wanted to meet Mama Liza. She sounded like Miss Louise, someone who everybody liked and respected and could pop a head or two if she wanted. Besides, Daddy wouldn't be Daddy to her, and that would be worth seeing.

We had a three-year-old Chevy that Daddy had gotten on a deal where he worked. A large car that could easily seat three, front and back, with a roomy trunk, a radio, a strong engine, and whitewall tires with custom wire rims. But most important to Mama, it didn't have air-conditioning. When Mama saw there wasn't any air-conditioning she asked Daddy to return it, but he said, "I got such a good deal, honey. The first owner didn't have any air-conditioning. We didn't have any in the Dodge. Just roll the window down."

I really didn't care about air-conditioning. I just wanted to go see Mama Liza.

About 6 a.m. the day before we left, Daddy parked the car next to Pie Lady's store and called, "Junior."

I stuck my head out the window, "Yes, Sir."

"Get the pail under the sink, fill it with some hot water and Tide, get some rags, and bring it to me."

You could eat off the floor in any car that Daddy owned, so I knew what to do. I got everything together and ran down to the car. Gave him the rags, put the pail down on the sidewalk, and ran back to the apartment to get my stuff.

"Bring the wax, polish for the dash, and upholstery cleaner. And find the carpet brush."

"Yes, Sir," I said, returning almost before he finished talking. I liked cleaning the car. Daddy treated me different then, almost like an equal. He didn't have to force me to do anything or explain something. He didn't like to explain. He knew that I wanted what he wanted and that I knew how to get it. Washing the car made us one.

Daddy did the outside, and I took care of the inside. No putting your feet up against the back of the seat with him. He didn't want any fingerprints all over the windows either. And don't, don't get any peanut butter on the upholstery. If you felt like throwing up and he couldn't stop, put your head out the window. Vomit could be washed off of the outside of the car easier than it can off the inside.

By the time we finished, both inside and outside looked spotless. Most people wouldn't know whether it was new or not. Daddy threw out the dirty rinse water I'd brought to replace the soapy pail, put the rags and wax and stuff in, looked at me, and said, "Pa Joe and 'em gonna love it. Good job, Junior." He didn't say that often.

Daddy would rather have driven a Pontiac or an Oldsmobile but couldn't afford one this time. Maybe the next trip south he'd have one. His Chevy looked as fine as any Pontiac you'd want to see, with its whitewall tires and custom wire rims. The blue and white Naugahyde interior looked almost too clean to sit on. The matching blue and white body, so deeply hand-waxed that insects couldn't stick . . . new cars cringed when they saw us.

Standing admiring our masterpiece together, Daddy shook his head in silent approval and said, "This car is me. Mama Liza and Pa Joe are gonna love it. I ain't going home in no beat-up car. Everybody coming around to see me, and they all want to know how I'm doing."

"If your car is in good shape, you're in good shape?"

"It's more than that, Junior. My cousin Pig, my uncles, all live in Selma. But I left. I came to Cincinnati. I didn't have to come to Cincinnati to be poor. I could've stayed in Selma and been poor."

"Yes, Sir," I said, beginning to understand.

"Every time I come, I come in a different car."

"Like the Chevy?"

"Yeah, like the Chevy. It ain't new but it looks new, *and they ain't never seen me in it.* So it's new to them even if it ain't. Pig and everybody will love it. Pa Joe and Mama Liza will be proud. Me and you can feel good."

"Why us?"

"It's our car."

We left at first light on a Sunday morning, stopped just across the bridge in Newport, Kentucky, and gassed up. Gas is cheaper in Newport than in Cincinnati and a good place for Mama and Wanda to use the restroom. Daddy said the farther south we went, the less chance they'd have to use one. We hit the road and settled in, the big Chevy engine humming and lullabying Mama and Wanda to sleep. I stayed awake watching the scenery and watching Daddy drive. Our new-looking used car stood apart in its showroom shape.

When we crossed over into Tennessee Daddy said, "We've got about five hours to go so just hold your horses and we'll be okay." By that he meant we should be able to hold off going to the bathroom unless there's an emergency. But it wasn't okay. I had to pee. We were driving on a two-lane highway and no other cars were in sight. Daddy stopped near a clump of trees, and I got out, ran behind them, and peed. When I got back in the car Wanda whined, "Mama, can I pee, too?"

For Wanda to pee, Mama had to go with her and Daddy had to watch out to make sure that no one saw them or came too close. They were behind the same bush that I'd visited when we spied a black pickup truck coming up toward us on the opposite side of the road. Before it could get within hearing distance Daddy told me to go and warn Mama to get back to the car because someone was coming.

I rushed to the bush, stood beside it, and told Mama what Daddy said. I heard her tell Wanda, "Hurry, honey, we gotta go. Daddy's waiting." Before we could return to the car I saw the pickup truck come clearer into view. Its hood rattled and the cab tilted like the bill of a newsboy's cap. How they rolled the windows up and down is still a mystery to me. The tires were unrelated. The two front wore memories of treads, the left rear was bald, and the right rear looked like an orphan. The whole contraption lumbered opposite us, trembled, and with brakes screeching, stopped.

Two white men inside—one with a lean, Stan Laurel face and gray hair, the other bald and round, a two-dollar Oliver Hardy, who may have been his son. Their grim eyes and mean faces made them poor lookalikes for Stan and Ollie. Hard faces and big hands made them look more like farmers or bootleggers. They talked low between themselves as if deciding what to do. Daddy said, "Driver's eyes don't stop blinking when he talks—a liar or a fool."

Looking up and down our car like a wolf at a pork chop, Stan leaned out the driver's side window and said, "Hey, you having trouble with a car like that?"

I could almost hear "boy" struggling in his throat.

Daddy looked up, smiled, and said, "No, sir, just taking a break."

"There's some coloreds live about two miles down the road and a mile to the right. Why don't you take your break down there? *This ain't the place for you to be taking no break.*"

They looked at each other for a long moment in silence. Finally, Daddy said, "Thanks, I appreciate it."

Daddy's smile disappeared as the pickup's engine started. Stan's eyes watched us in the rearview mirror as he pulled away. I tasted tension on my tongue. Both the men in the truck and Daddy acted as if they had been strung together by invisible cords, cords that imprisoned them in a unique familiarity. All three were afraid of what might happen should those cords break. As he later explained it, "Poor whites. You never know. One moment they're your friend, in the next they'll kill you."

About fifteen minutes later we found the colored people the man in the truck had mentioned: Mr. Josh Franklin and his wife, Ruth, who had lived there before the war.

"Our family worked for the Bensons for years. Bensons been here forever. Going back to Reconstruction, they say. Anyway, we got a nice piece a land from 'em that was passed down to my daddy, most of which is gone now. Some sold, some stole. Thank the Jacksons for that."

Mr. Josh and his wife were colored, not like high yellas with light skin. Their skin was white with faded sepia undertones. They say eyes tell something, too. Joe at the barbershop said, "You can't hide them wood-shed eyes. Ain't no nigger got no blue eyes." Both Mr. Josh and Mary had light, strangely colored eyes. Didn't look blue to me, but it didn't look like most colored folks' either. I guess in olden times they might have been called mulattoes.

They welcomed us with sandwiches and provided a private outside toilet for Mama to use, and Daddy, too. Daddy asked about the men in the pickup truck. "Yes, we know them," Mr. Josh said. "The Jackson brothers. The oldest looks like the daddy but they're brothers. Don't worry about them. They used to be strong with the Ku Klux, but it's moved farther south. Just don't come through here and stop late night. They might mess with you, take your money, steal your car. But they ain't never kilt anybody . . . not that I know of. Just be careful if you see them again."

We discovered that the Franklins were a well-known stop for colored people going south on that route. Daddy tried to pay them when we left, but Mr. Franklin held up both hands and pushed Daddy away.

"We ain't got much, but we got enough and it's here for any of us who need it. We lost our son in the war. We ain't got no people now and nobody to leave it to, so might as well put it to good use."

"Take care of yourself," Mr. Josh said as he waved us off. "See you on the way back."

As we pulled away Daddy said, "They lost their son in the war and they've got the Jacksons to worry about. They're some strong people, strong people."

We reached Mama Liza and Pa Joe's about four hours later. Driving into their big hard-packed dirt yard—with chickens running free, a small shed, and a pigpen farther down—I knew I'd finally arrived in real country living. Supported at each corner by concrete blocks, their wood frame house stood about three feet off the ground with an open space underneath. Mama Liza stood tall on the porch as if she could see all the way to Ohio and will her baby home.

Pa Joe was about six feet, heavy chest, dark and somber face, and eyes that concealed a joyful nature that only Mama Liza could ignite. He was much darker than she, with a complexion that had never been profaned by a razor. His head, topped with dark, wiry hair, not nappy, lay smooth on his head with a short razor cut.

Mama Liza was light-skinned, stood tall with long hair and eyes that twinkled when she smiled, and she smiled a lot when she saw Daddy. Mama Liza always looked like she had just come from the kitchen making something good to eat. A "tea towel" dangled from her closed right hand, her left gently squeezed the knuckles of her right as she held both against her stomach. When she looked down and saw Daddy standing there wearing a goofy grin I'd never seen before, she rushed down the three steps from the house, pulled Daddy to her, and said, "Sport, you sure look good. Come give your mama a kiss."

From that moment till the day we left, Sport was the best daddy anyone could ever have. Mama Liza released something in Daddy that made us all feel better, but most of all it seemed to free his spirit to be Sport, the fun-loving, softer man Mama Liza raised him to be. I couldn't help from crying after discovering that the daddy that I lived with every day was the same Sport that Mama Liza and Mama knew and loved. Mama Liza was a magician and as special as Mama said she was.

Mama stayed in the kitchen with Mama Liza until the rest of the relatives arrived. "Cassie, each time you come I love you more. Sport don't know how lucky he is to have you." Mama smiled like a little girl and looked down when Mama Liza talked like that.

Most of the women gathered around Mama Liza to meet Mama again. She knew many of them from before. The men came to see Daddy and his car. Each one looked at it, talking among themselves. Everyone except Pa Joe, Daddy's father, and Pig, his cousin and closest friend.

"Musta cost a fortune, Sport," said Pa Joe, as he walked around our car. "What happened to the one you drove down here last time?"

"Traded it in," Daddy said.

"Get a good price?"

"Yes, Sir."

Everybody said "Sir" to Pa Joe, even Daddy. Pa Joe didn't play.

Pa Joe always said, "Play with a dog he'll lick your mouth. Play with a child he'll sass you out." He meant it.

That was it for Pa Joe. Our new car must have cost a fortune and the old car was traded in. Saving money on the purchase meant something. Daddy had done everything right. He'd passed the test.

Pig was a different story. Pig was Pig: short, fat, with a large head on narrow shoulders, but that's not why they called him Pig. His nose tilted back in his face like someone had hit him hard in the nose with the heel of their hand. Appraising the car with small, squinty eyes, his nostrils stared straight at you almost like a snout. Admiring the blue and white interior, matching body color, custom wire wheels, and flawless body, he said, "Sport, this car so big must remind you of that tractor you and Pa Joe used to drive."

Daddy said, "Pig, when you get a car like this, you don't know what a tractor even looks like."

"Nice ride," Pig said with feeling, "Nice ride."

And that was it. After all that work, washing and waxing and primping, "Musta cost a fortune" and "Nice ride." A few choice words from one who counts when it counts is all it takes. Nothing, nothing is said if your car doesn't make it. The silence says it all.

The next night, eating fried catfish, cornbread, and collards from a paper plate on Mama Liza's porch, I nearly died listening to Daddy and his cousins laughing in the front room. It started when Daddy asked his cousin Man, "You still peeing in poison ivy patches, Man?" Man nearly choked on his beer. Daddy wouldn't stop. "Looks like you had a baseball bat with warts on it." Man, spitting laughter, said, "That ain't the half of it. Try peeing with that thing in your hand without scratching it."

Most people think Man got his name to keep white folks from calling him "Boy."

"His name could be Jesus," Daddy said. "He'd still be called 'Boy' if he lived in Alabama."

Truth is, Aunt Mae called him "my little man" from the first moment she saw him. He looked the perfect image of his daddy, Uncle Little Joe, who'd disappeared or died after beating a white man uptown. Some said the man was a member or related to someone in the Klan. Who knows? Anyway, "little man" became Man, the one who kept his father and her husband alive in her heart. Uncle Little Joe was Pa Joe's nephew, Aunt Mae's husband.

Woody said, "Pa Joe don't take no mess. 'Specially when it come to family. He found out Little Joe was killed by a man in Lowndes County, owned a gin. We missed Pa Joe for about a week. When he come home we heard the man in Lowndes County got his head bashed in, both legs broke. Don't know if he'll walk again. They say some stranger did it. It wasn't Pa Joe. That's what Mama Liza said."

Pig teased Daddy about Mama Liza's catching him smoking under the house and sending him out to cut a switch. Trying to mimic Mama Liza, Pig said, "'Sport, I done told you about smoking. Now go get me a switch, and it better be green. Don't make me have to tell Joe.'

"I guess they run outta switches where you went," said Pig, "'cause you didn't get home till the next day." Daddy laughed so hard he couldn't stop. Words erupted from his throat like beer popping from a shaken can.

"I wish I'd found that switch. Pa Joe grabbed me before Mama Liza could get to me, and you know I didn't want any of that."

I heard them fall to their knees laughing. Mama stayed in the kitchen with Mama Liza. Daddy's Aunt Babe and his sister, Lillie Mae, keeping the catfish coming. We stayed three days, and in all that time Daddy never cussed once, not once. I think Mama Liza would have popped him one.

I loved Sport.

My new brothers, all older and bigger than me, were easy to talk to and fun to be around. Joseph, the youngest—hardest to understand and quick to fight—had Daddy's smooth, brown complexion, short hair, and constantly roving brown eyes. Joe punctuated every sentence with a laugh. Tee, the oldest—about six feet, square head, deep-set eyes under a large forehead, the tallest of the three—talked the most but said nothing. Woody, the quietest, looked most like Daddy and had his same quiet self-assurance. He smiled a lot and spoke softly with conviction. When he spoke we listened. As adults, they all later joined the military during Vietnam—Joseph the Marines, Tee and Woody the Air Force. But when I met them, they wore bib overalls and no shoes, just like in the movies. I'd never wear bibs but it looked natural on them, or anyone picking cotton. The cotton field lay behind the house, exploding with white puffy balls on slender stalks. I'd never been that close to a cotton field before, and it felt strange.

"You ever picked any cotton?" I asked Joseph.

"Yeah, but I ain't the one. Mama Liza can pick."

"Yeah," said Tee. "You just pick at it. Mama Liza can pick."

"If Mama Liza can do it, it can't be that hard," I said. "I bet I could do it."

Woody said, "Mama Liza been pickin' cotton since she was a little girl down in Sardis. She pull two bags a row, one on each shoulder. That's slavery-time picking. Cain't nobody else do that."

"I bet I could do one bag," I said.

"Even if you could, we don't pick on weekends," said Joseph.

"Why?" I asked.

Tee said, "Mama Liza said."

"Junior, you want to pick some cotton?" said Woody, with authority.

"Sure, ain't that what I said?"

"Okay, Mama Liza don't need to know everything," said Woody.

They took me to a shed closer to the field and pulled a bag from the pile on the table. "Here, this should fit," said Woody. "Joseph used to use it."

I took it and put it on. The gray cotton bag hanging on my shoulder was heavier than it looked. I felt like a slave in a movie with it hanging on me.

"How much cotton fit in a bag like this?" I asked.

"'Pends on who's doing the picking," Joseph said. "Little Belle down the road pick twenty-five pounds. Man pick thirty. You probably do twenty since you new."

"That's too much," said Woody. "Twenty pounds a lotta cotton. Junior, what you think?"

"Don't sound like much to me," I said.

"Alright," said Woody.

We headed for the field.

The cotton field ain't like no movie. Those puffy white balls on the screen must be painted 'cause real cotton is gray, and it ain't puffy, it's sticky. Gloves work better than hands.

"Start here," Woody said, stopping at the head of a row of sickly looking cotton about three feet high."

"That ain't too tall?" I asked. "I'm gonna have to bend."

Tee said, "I've picked shorter than that. Boy over in Sardis picked on
his knees. That's short."

"No shit," I said.

"No shit."

I cut through the first cotton like Tarzan through the jungle, snatch-
ing balls left and right as if they were something good to eat. Coming
back up the second row, my back bent lower and my pace got slower.
Better off Cheetah than Tarzan for picking at that height. But my bag
would be dragging the row. By the fourth row I'd almost given up. Rows
look shorter standing than walking, and cotton is softer seeing than
picking.

At the end of the fifth row I stood up. Head throbbing, fingers bleeding, pain shooting along my spine like in those TV commercials, thighs
knotted like tug-o-war ropes, and my bag—my bag not even breathing.
Where had all the cotton gone? I thought it would be overflowing by
now. I could pick more than ten pounds with my hands tied behind my
back. Little Belle could pick twenty-five and look at her, didn't weigh half
as much as me. Ten pounds is nothing.

I looked down at my bag. It looked dead hanging by my side. Feeling
sorry for me, a few balls of cotton chose to stay, to stick. Others escaped
through the bag's unstitched bottom. The harder I pushed, the faster
they fell. What could I do? I looked back down the row and saw Woody
waving, Joseph and Tee holding their stomachs laughing. They had me.
They were older and knew I wasn't supposed to pick cotton on the weekend. What would Mama Liza say? What would she do? I was stuck.

Seeing my hands at dinner that night Mama Liza said, "Son, what
happened to your hands? Look like you been picking cotton."

I couldn't lie to Mama Liza. I just shook my head and said nothing.

"Didn't your Mama Liza ask you a question?"

"Yes, ma'am."

"What happened to your hands?" she asked again.

I didn't say anything and looked at Woody. She leaped right in.

"Woody, what y'all been doing to Junior?"

"We ain't did nothing, Mama Liza. He asked to pick some cotton and we let him."

"You *let* Junior pick cotton. Woody, this boy don't know nothing 'bout picking no cotton. Look at him. And you did it on the weekend when I told you not to."

She turned back to me, laughing. "Junior, you a real butcher boy to take all this mess standing up. Let Mama Liza work on those hands. Woody, I'll deal with y'all later."

From then on everybody Down South called me Butch. It meant something to me. I was part of them, a special part. Sometimes I wish we could have stayed in Selma forever—me, Mama, Wanda, Mama Liza, and Sport.

In Selma I picked cotton, met a whole new family with Mama Liza, Pa Joe, and the boys, and most of all found Sport, the man who lived inside Daddy. The thread running through it all, the one that I'll always remember, is Mama Liza standing there in her dirt yard with arms wide apart as we were leaving and saying, "Come here, Butch. Come and give your Mama Liza a kiss before you get away." I hugged tight as she pulled me close and kissed me. Her strong, moist arms encircled me, leaving memories of sweet, warm sweat and tea soap—two scents of Mama Liza's together, making hers the purest scent of all.

She laughed, "Don't nobody drink it, Butch. Just 'cause somethin' smell good don't mean it taste good."

I think I know what Daddy feels. Whenever I see something that doesn't feel right or make sense, I think of what Mama Liza said and my doubts disappear. I know just what to do, and I am in Selma again.

By the time we reached the Ohio River, Sport was flattened out. Daddy still smiled at Mama and pointed out how smooth the car climbed Kentucky's grades to the river, but when we crossed into Cincinnati through downtown and so near the RKO, I could almost feel Daddy reject Sport as he tensed. It was like witnessing a free-spirited bird wilt at the sight of his captors and then steel up when entering its cage.

I believe Daddy wanted to hold onto Sport, but he needed support. Needed Mama Liza and everyone he left behind. I don't think Daddy ever found Sport in Cincinnati. Sport didn't fit.

MAMA'S DEATH OPENS NEW WORLDS

We visited Mama Liza's three other times after that. Each time Daddy drove a new car with more of us in it. My new sisters, Debra and Kathy, made four of us kids. For that last trip Daddy had a big Buick. Wanda, Debra, and I sat in the back fairly close together, and Kathy, the smallest, sat up front. Mama, Daddy, Wanda, and I folded right into our Selma family as if we'd never left. Debra and Kathy, both less than five years old, found themselves surrounded by older cousins with kids their own age to play with. Mama Liza embraced us all, found a special nook for everyone to sleep in, and fed us well.

Wanda, the oldest of the girls and the most willful, trailed Mama Liza wherever she went. She absorbed everything and everyone she met, and they adored her. If we hadn't left Cincinnati together, I'd have sworn she'd been living in Selma all the while.

The night before we left on our last trip with Mama, she and Mama Liza spent time alone just walking and talking across the yard out back away from the rest of us. Whatever they talked about stayed between the two of them. When they rejoined us around front, Mama glanced around to see that the girls were all in bed, walked up the stairs to the porch, kissed me on the head, and said, "Better go to bed, honey. Getting up early tomorrow."

I got up as she turned to Daddy sitting in Pa Joe's chair, who was inside asleep, placed her hand on Daddy's shoulder, wrapped her other arm around his neck, and lay her head aside his cheek from behind and stood there holding him and saying nothing.

Standing at the bottom of the stairs, Mama Liza looked at Mama, and her eyebrows briefly knotted together as her eyes showed a deep concern before she was herself again, "Sport, let Cassie get some sleep. She ain't got all night to stand out here keeping you warm. Get yourself in the house and take Cassie with you."

"Alright, Mama Liza," they both said. "Good night," and that was the end of that.

Home again on Thirteenth Street and things returned to normal, almost. Dr. Sheldon came to see Mama for her usual visit. She had high blood pressure and often got headaches that Dr. Sheldon said could be controlled with the right medicine. He was still adjusting her medicine and had scheduled to see her about it after our trip.

Dr. Sheldon had been our doctor for as long as I could remember. He took care of us, and we took care of him. When we couldn't pay on time he'd just say, "You're not going anywhere, and neither am I. Take your time." Dr. Sheldon had curly black hairs on the back of his hands and arms. One time a fly got caught in the hairs on the back of his hand and he hardly noticed. It would've taken me lots of nerve to sit there like that. Sometimes he and Mama liked to talk about photography. Before she had Wanda, Mama worked for a while as a darkroom assistant for a photographer downtown. Mama used to say, "Mr. Sheldon's not a big man or the handsomest, but he's one of the kindest and smartest you'll ever want to know."

Daddy said, "I don't know what I'd do if we had to go to someone else."

I liked Dr. Sheldon because he always brought something good for me and my sisters. Usually it was some sort of hard candy, something to suck on to keep us quiet or out of the way while he worked. One time I was downstairs when Dr. Sheldon was going upstairs to see Mama when Rich, one of the guys from the top of the hill, said, "Ain't that that Jew doctor, Junior? Can't you afford a real one?"

I said, "I can afford your mama," and it was on. It was no big deal, neither one of us really took it seriously. He punched me in the chest and I punched him back, then we sat down on the sidewalk together. "Lighten up, that's Dr. Sheldon. He's cool, man. Really. Give him a break."

"Alright," he said. "I really didn't mean nothing. Just wanted to mess with you. Talking about my mama wasn't cool."

"Yeah, man. I know, but you shouldn't have talked about our doctor. We still cool?"

"Yeah. We're alright."

I didn't know it at the time, but Mama Liza and Mama had been talking about what Dr. Sheldon said when we were last in Selma. "What do you mean, Cassie, you can't have any more children?"

"Well," Mama said, "my doctor thinks I could have a cerebral hemorrhage if we have another baby."

"Is that the same as a stroke?" asked Mama Liza.

"Yes," said Mama.

"Have you told Sport?"

"He knows, but we don't really talk about it. We're just trying to be careful," said Mama.

"Ain't no being careful unless you plan on stopping," said Mama Liza.

"It takes two," said Mama.

"Well, you better come up with something, 'cause halfway just won't do."

"Don't worry, Mama Liza," said Mama. "We'll come up with something."

My youngest sister, Brenda, never went to Selma because Mama couldn't travel. She was pregnant with my baby brother, Jerome. He would be her fifth child over eight years. I accidentally overheard a conversation between Dr. Sheldon, Daddy, and Mama when he visited her after Brenda's birth and told Daddy, "If your wife has another child, it could be very dangerous for her."

Daddy knew what he meant but asked anyway. "She seems okay. What's wrong?"

"She's had four children in seven years. Her high blood pressure increases her chances of having a stroke with each succeeding birth," said Dr. Sheldon.

"We didn't plan for this to happen. This is the last one," Daddy said.

"Let's hope so," said Dr. Sheldon.

One year after Brenda was born, Mama went to the hospital to deliver her fifth child in eight years, my little brother, Jerome. She was thirty-two years old.

I don't remember much about her leaving for the hospital other than Daddy rushing her out the door with a small bag packed like he'd done many times before. The girls were all standing around not saying anything, just looking scared and excited all at the same time. But I remember everything that happened later.

The day that Mama and Jerome were supposed to come home, I stood, body tensed, listening at the door for their footsteps. Like radar my ears picked up steps coming down the sidewalk, but it sounded like one person instead of two. My muscles relaxed. In the next instant the footsteps stopped at our door and my insides tightened. The door opened, and Daddy stood there alone. His proud, muscular frame looked as if it had been trapped in the car crusher down the street at the junkyard. He shuffled through the doorway, and Daddy never shuffled. He pulled out a chair, painfully sank down at the kitchen table, and moaned softly.

"Your little brother won't be coming home. He's at the hospital in an incubator." Then, in a cracked, froglike croak he added, "And your mama won't be coming home either. Ever." It was the way he held his head between his hands and plunked face down against the table that let me know he was too hurt for tears. Irresistibly moved by his anguish, I reached out, gently touched him on his shoulder, and cried.

I turned and blindly stumbled to the refrigerator where I tried to stuff my face between the back of the refrigerator and the wall, where I inhaled lungsful of spiderwebs, dust, and dirt, choking and sobbing, trying to breathe. I came to on the kitchen floor silently crying—hands balled into fists, neck throbbing, bottom lip bleeding—and willed myself to sit up, wishing that somehow something Daddy said would change, go away, and never be said again.

When we went to the funeral, I sat in the front row unable and unwilling to believe she was gone. It was only six days before my twelfth birthday. I knew Mama wouldn't leave us without warning. I could see her breathing as she lay in the casket. Why didn't anyone else notice? She wouldn't just walk out the door going to the hospital and not come back.

Lying there in the casket she didn't even look like Mama. They'd shaved her head for the operation, Daddy said, and bought the wig for the funeral. Part Indian, Mama used to wear her hair in long, heavy braids down her back. I didn't like seeing her in that stiff, shiny wig. It made her look like some deacon's wife, all prim and proper, not my mama. I stood up, turned, and walked shakily out of the room, scared and angry. Angry at Daddy for killing her and scared for how my life would be without her. I am still angry.

BOOK TWO

THE JACKSONS AND RESPECTABILITY

Daddy and I hadn't gotten along well before Mama's death, and we got along even worse afterward. He couldn't work and care for six children by himself. Five months after Mama's funeral, Daddy and the County Children's Services placed us in a foster home with Bertie and Aaron Jackson. The social worker said we were lucky to find foster parents willing to take us all in. It made no difference to me. Without Mama around I didn't care who I lived with. We stayed there for four years, long enough for me to find an escape route from life in the West End. The Jacksons owned the house we lived in, plus some rental properties, and like many middle-class Negroes, they were highly, almost fanatically religious.

I didn't care very much about religion, and neither did my parents. I guess they got their cues from Pa Joe and Mama Liza. In Selma, their religion served as a refuge from the daily rhythm of their lives as cotton sharecroppers. It was convenient at Christmastime and Easter but mostly at funerals. Funerals occurred frequently in their large extended family and served to renew old friendships, meet new offspring, and catch up on the successes and tragedies of returning relatives. Their worship started every evening at sundown when they came in from the fields. All religions have rituals, and theirs were eating supper together and just being with family and friends.

Saturday they packed everyone into the truck and drove to town. Once in town Pa Joe went to his house of worship: the Chicken Shack. Daddy says it was a juke joint where Pa Joe drank white lightning and gambled with his friends.

Mama Liza went to First Baptist Antioch Church where she sat in the sanctuary with nine other women, caught up on the latest gossip, and stitched patchwork quilts. Left to themselves Daddy and his sister Lila Mae wandered in and out of white folks' stores, chased their friends, or just sat on the wide wooden steps of First Baptist fascinated by the world passing by.

By the time Daddy married my mama, he worshipped the same way he'd been taught in Selma. He spent all week working hard and the weekend worshipping at the Pirates Cave—a stand-in for the Chicken Shack, where he had more than a few drinks with friends and sometimes other women. He sent Mama and me to church at Christmastime and Easter, prayed when others prayed at funerals, and generally left me to my own devices when it came to religion. Still none of us, including Mama, were allowed to begin any meal without first saying a Bible verse. I usually said, "Jesus wept," because it was the shortest one in the Bible. I never gave much thought about God, but I often thought about the devil. After all, Daddy kept reminding me of how the devil was going to catch my ass and take me straight to hell if I didn't straighten up.

Aside from being middle class and living in the suburbs, the biggest difference between the Jacksons and my parents was the Independent Missionary Baptist Church. Mr. and Mrs. Jackson lived in the church. Mama had taken me to church on most holidays and funerals, but Daddy was always too tired to go. The Jacksons never seemed to get enough of church—Wednesday, Friday, Sunday all day, and Mondays for Mr. Jackson's Deacons' Prayer Group. It didn't take me long to figure out that the best way to stay in their good graces was to adopt their zeal, and what better way to get it than to seek the Holy Ghost?

Under Mr. Jackson's care I attended church three times a week. Our minister, Elder Saunders, became my shining knight and I his squire. As other boys my age dreamed of becoming basketball stars, I dreamed of becoming a preacher like Elder Sanders. Through my participation at Independent, reading seemed more connected to real life than to anything at school. I learned to read from the Bible as if it were a novel. Mr. Jackson—or Ace, as we kids called him, because he was as "black as the ace of spades"—held Bible study sessions at home with me, his niece Alma, and sometimes his wife. But more often it was just the two of us.

Elder Sanders began each sermon by calling out book, chapter, and verse from the pulpit of his text, and whoever located it the fastest was given the privilege of reading it aloud for him. I became so adept at locating the given text that the church soon looked upon me as Elder Sanders's official reader. When I stood reading from my Bible in church, nothing else mattered.

Located in its quiet, warehouse neighborhood surroundings, the storefront Independent Missionary Baptist Church was home to about forty adults and fifteen children. Despite our surroundings we filled the air with singing, Holy Ghost shouting, hot organ riffs, and jangling tambourines every Wednesday, Friday, and Sunday. Every service was packed, and the congregation completely immersed in the service. No "Miss Jane" trying to outdress "Miss Judy" or spying on who dropped the biggest offering in the basket. Some people called them the working poor. They were hardworking and stable and gave me something solid to hold on to after losing Mama. Most of the women came to church looking like they'd applied a hot comb to their hair the night before. The men were square and old-fashioned in their wide ties and suits with Humphrey Bogart lapels. But most important to me they were supportive, dependable, and very predictable. I always knew exactly where I stood with them, and they could be relied on to give me guidance and support.

The church had a small pulpit with a covered pool in back that was used to baptize new "saints." Most of the members were saints. They had received the Holy Ghost and were "sanctified and filled with the spirit." To stay in the Jacksons' good graces, I decided to get some of that spirit for myself. But I had to give up all my sins before the Holy Ghost could fill my soul.

It was a sin "to be in the world," according to Mr. Jackson. That created a problem because I didn't know where else to be. It was a sin to dance, a sin for a woman to wear tight clothes, a sin to listen to the kind of music that I liked, a sin to eat hamburgers because of the people who frequented hamburger restaurants, a sin to go to the movies and a sin to masturbate. What was left to do? As much as I liked the movies, dancing, listening to music, and hamburgers, I could find a way to give them all up, except masturbation. Masturbation felt too good to be sinful.

No one was surprised when I began to tarry for the Holy Ghost. I loved to read and always took the lead in my Sunday school class. Tarrying for the Holy Ghost was the church's way of separating the sheep from the goats, and only those strong enough to withstand its demands could expect to be saved. We tarriers went forward after each altar call, fell on our knees, and cried, "Save me, Lord," until we were hoarse or filled by the Spirit. After our shouting and "speaking in tongues," the saints would gather 'round beating tambourines and praying us on to glory.

The night I started tarrying, four chairs were placed in front of the pulpit and I knelt at the last one. I arose an hour later, the seat next to me empty, and Joseph, who had been sitting there earlier, had fallen to the floor in a spiritual swoon. Six months later my knees were as sore as a scrubwoman's, and I was the only one of the original four still unsaved.

DANCING BREASTS

Margaret Jones had breasts. The Jacksons entered me in Hoffman Elementary School within walking distance from their house. Margaret Jones went to Hoffman, and Margaret Jones had breasts. I had seen breasts before, but they were all on grown women. This was the first time I'd seen a woman's breasts on a girl, and Margaret Jones had them.

I first saw Margaret at the school dance that was held once a month in the gym. It cost a dime, and we got an octagonal plastic tag to get in. The money was used for the recreation program to help needy students buy gym supplies. Everyone in the sixth grade went to the dances, especially the boys. Any boy who had confidence in his manhood wanted to dance with Margaret Jones.

Coming from downtown I felt more experienced than my middle-class classmates who'd grown up in the suburbs. The moment I saw Margaret standing across the floor I became a sinner in my heart. The Jacksons had forbidden me to dance because it was a sin, but it would have taken more than a pitchfork to keep me away from her. She had a Hershey chocolate–colored face with light brown eyes and lips that twisted when she smiled. But it was her sweater that held me captive.

It was winter, and she was wearing a green, woolen V-neck sweater over a yellow-collared blouse. The sweater wasn't meant to be tight, but it clung to Margaret Jones's breasts in what looked like a losing battle to keep them from bursting through. Until seeing her in that sweater I hadn't paid much attention to women's breasts. Mama had used hers for feeding my sisters, and I was used to having them around. Actresses dressed to show off their curves and deep cleavage, but that was in the movies and out of touch. I'd seen Jim's older sister, Betty, wearing a tight sweater over her breasts, but never as closely as I was seeing Margaret Jones's.

I crossed the floor and asked her to dance, leaving the other boys standing like children behind me on the wall. She said okay and stepped toward me. Margaret didn't just look like a woman, she moved like one. I offered my hand, and she took it and stepped in close and full-bodied against me. I wrapped both arms around her. She was soft and firm and warm. A fire passed through me from head to toe from our being pressed so close together. Nothing that anyone could see—just a quick movement, a momentary unexpected intimacy, an effortless engagement that left me scalded. I knew we couldn't continue like that. Challenged by our closeness to maintain a semblance of innocence, we stepped back in unison without a word. I kept one arm around her waist, took her other hand in mine, and started dancing to the Shirelles. Yes, Margaret Jones had breasts, and she knew how to use them.

After fourteen grueling months, the Holy Ghost finally arrived. Feeling that I had no legs below the knees and seeking relief from my throbbing pain, I flopped backward and, whether by intent or passion, started speaking in tongues. No one understands what's being said when someone is being "taken over by the spirit" anyway, so anything I'd heard others speak was good enough for me.

After ten minutes of intense thrashing and jerking about, someone offered a hand to lift me up. Someone else produced a chair. Elder Sanders anointed my head with oil while praising God for my salvation. With my possession of the Holy Ghost I was now a "saint." All I needed was to be baptized to make it official. Mr. and Mrs. Jackson standing in the circle around me looked as proud as two angels with a fresh cherub to raise.

ONE THIN SLICE

Once I had the Holy Ghost life, began to feel more comfortable at the Jacksons'. Besides having my own room with a window that I could climb in and out of unnoticed, I had more time to focus on Mrs. Jackson's pies and cakes.

Mrs. Jackson loved to bake. She made fancy rolls that I'd never seen Mama make—the kind that sat out all night on top of the sideboard waiting for the yeast to rise before being put in the oven. Fresh hot out of the oven with a tender crust, they were so soft and buttery I could never get enough. But she only baked them on holidays or special occasions when we were having Elder Sanders over for dinner.

She baked pies often, which later proved that thieves are made and not born. Mrs. Jackson's pies couldn't beat Pie Lady's, but they sure left the rest of the world behind. Apple, lemon meringue, and sweet potato were her favorites, but her tastiest and my favorite were her sweet potato pies. She was very strict about when her pies should be eaten. "I don't want anybody eating any of this pie for a snack. There's too much sugar in it. Do you hear me? It's for dessert. Don't let me catch you eating this pie for a snack," she commanded.

After having sweet potato pie for dessert at one Sunday dinner, the remaining half was put away. Later that night I went downstairs to get some water, opened the refrigerator, and saw the pie sitting there covered with wax paper. Mr. and Mrs. Jackson were in bed, my sisters were upstairs, and it was just me and the pie. As I stood there with the door open, despite Mrs. Jackson's warning, I just had to have another taste of that sweet, sweet potato pie.

I kept the door open with my right hand and took a knife out of the silverware drawer with the other. I knew that a large missing piece would be easily noticed, so I carefully measured a slice that would be undetectable. I pressed the knife firmly along in one smooth stroke that made a cut as tailored as if a machine had done it. That was the beginning and the end of my career as a thief in Mrs. Jackson's house.

The next day no one noticed that the sweet potato pie was a finger's width less than the day before. That night we had sliced peaches for dessert, and the next night nothing. Each night I'd taken another thin slice of the sweet potato pie, thinking that no one was the wiser. By that time my three thin slices added up to a very visible missing portion of what once had been a full half pie.

When we sat down for dinner on the fourth night after my thievery began, Mrs. Jackson brought the sweet potato pie to the table for dessert. She cut big slices and passed them around to everyone except me. When she got to me, the pie was gone. I looked up with innocent expectancy. She looked at me stone-faced and said, "Oh, I thought you'd already eaten your sweet potato pie, Junior," and walked away smiling, ending my pie-thieving career.

Ace found me in my room the following day. I thought he was going to ask me about the pie when he said, "Junior, musta taken some pie when you weren't supposed to. Am I right?"

"Yes, Sir," I said. "Miss Jackson tell you?"

"No, she didn't have to. You've been taking it along. She just confirmed it at the table. I wasn't going to say anything, just to see what you were gonna do," he said.

"I'm sorry," I said. "I won't do it again."

"That's not what counts," he said. "What counts is you think you're fooling people all the time. Like you did in church the other day. You didn't fool anybody."

"What you mean?" I said, trying to look hurt.

"The Holy Ghost. I bet you think Elder Sanders thought you got the Holy Ghost? You better wake up, boy."

I didn't know what to say. I thought I had gotten away with slicing the sweet potato pie and I hadn't. Ace and Miss Jackson had known all along. He said that he and Elder Sanders knew I hadn't been filled with the spirit or spoken in tongues. I felt like I'd been a fool and made a fool of.

"If you didn't think I had the Holy Ghost, then why didn't you say something? Why did you stand me up in front of everyone and call me a saint?"

He said, "Junior, you think you're the only one ever faked getting saved? You're a fool if you think that. Elder Sanders knows everybody ain't saved just cause they roll on the floor and speak in tongues. You did it, you know how easy that can be. But some people are serious about getting saved, some people really believe in the Holy Ghost, so there was no need for him to call you out to them.

"Elder Sanders didn't call you out because they don't need your disbelief exposed for them to believe in the Holy Ghost. The Holy Ghost is real to them, it's real to me, and it's real to the rest of the church. The Holy Ghost ain't nothin' to play with, Junior. You just ain't ready for it. By accepting you into the church Elder Sanders gave you another chance to get ready instead of running you away by calling you out. Straighten up or straighten out. It's up to you."

"Yes, Sir, I didn't know." I said. "I really didn't know."

"Junior," he said, "just because you're book smart don't make everybody else no fool. Now stop playing games with the church, and stop messing with Bertie's pies. I ain't talking just to hear myself talk. Okay?"

"Yes, Sir," I said, as he turned and walked out the door.

MANGLING

After the pie incident I stayed out of the refrigerator and chose not to get baptized in order to regain some of my self-respect with Elder Sanders and Ace. I knew Mrs. Jackson took in ironing, and I figured I could get back in her good graces by sticking close to her ironing business.

I know why they call it ironing. Your arms feel like iron after you've finished ironing twenty shirts. Mrs. Jackson took in laundry from white families—shirts, sheets, skirts, and blouses. She got more sheets and white shirts than anything else. She kept a big Mangler in the basement where she ironed the sheets. I'd never seen anything like it in the cleaners we had downtown. The first time I saw Mrs. Jackson working with it, she was sitting on a short padded bench facing a desklike machine. On top of the desk was a large, round padded cylinder with a metal cuff underneath it. The cylinder was open on one end to slip the sheet onto the cylinder. Mrs. Jackson fed the sheet onto the cylinder and, using a foot pedal, pressed the sheet against the cylinder with a heated metal cuff. She continued feeding the sheet through the Mangler until the sheet was completely ironed. She did this twice a week every week and still went to church three times a week. Mama would have said Mrs. Jackson wasn't afraid of hard work and that I could learn something from her because she was doing the best she could.

IRONS, BOARDS, AND SHIRT MAPPING

I hadn't watched Mrs. Jackson run sheets through the Mangler more than two weeks when she said, "I've got more sheets than I can handle, and the shirts keep piling up. If I show you how to do it, Junior, do you think you can iron shirts?"

"If you show me, I can," I said.

"Tell you what," she said. "If you get it right I'll pay you. How about fifteen cents a shirt to start with, but I have to inspect it first. Is that okay with you?"

I said yes, and my lessons began. The first step to any ironing, said Mrs. Jackson, is to set your ironing board up. "It's got to fit you all by yourself," she said. "It's like you are sitting down standing up. You're going to be in that spot for hours, so make it yours."

She took an ironing board, set it up to about where my waist would be, and then told me to stand up next to it. "Alright, Junior, place your palms on the board and stand up straight. Now, relax and stay like that while I raise the board."

She adjusted the board until my arms were almost perpendicular to it. "Now let your whole body straighten up till your elbows are above the board and hold it. Okay? She made one more slight adjustment. "You can iron all day now if you have to, and you won't get tired, 'cause the board fits."

After getting my board set up I was ready to iron. Miss Jackson said you can't iron shirts until you learn how to use the shirt map. Yes, there is a shirt map. I didn't know this until Mrs. Jackson taught me.

"Junior," she said, "you don't just throw a shirt on the ironing board, plop a hot iron on it, and call that ironing. To iron a shirt, especially a white shirt, you got to watch out for three things: no scorching, no scorching, and no scorching. The second thing to watch out for is ironed-in wrinkles, and the third is no pinching around the cuffs, collars, and plackets."

I was beginning to feel that maybe I could earn some extra money doing something else. She went on:

"Everything depends on the temperature of the iron, whether it's steam or dry. I only use steam and how you position the shirt. Start with the back, the biggest part of the shirt, turn it face down, spread it out tight, smooth it with your hands before you put the iron to it. Then do the same thing to each of the front sides, using the neck of the board to get up close to the shoulder, smoothing everything out before putting the iron to it. Next take the yoke below the collar that's connecting the shoulders and spread it smooth, using the neck of the board. Follow that up with each sleeve, careful to get the crease at the elbow. Iron the cuffs around the neck and not flat against the board. No respectable man wants creases in his shirt cuffs. Finally get the collar. To do it right, lay it out flat against the board and iron it till the tips turn up. Pick it up, fold the back of the collar over, and then iron again, using the neck, leaving the collar to fit round on the neck. Once that's done, bring it to me and we'll see how much you've learned."

It didn't take long for me to learn, and after about a month I was a real help to Mrs. Jackson. She trusted me enough to throw more white shirts my way. More business was being sent to her because of her quick turnaround and the first-class job she did on shirts. I got so that I could whip out a shirt in fifteen minutes, a starched shirt in twenty because of being extra careful to avoid making wrinkles. Mrs. Jackson started paying me twenty-five cents a shirt once her business picked up. I never forgot what Mrs. Jackson taught me, and I still prefer to iron my own shirts. Not everyone knows the shirt map.

MR. WRIGHT'S WORLD

I entered a part of Cincinnati that went beyond anything I'd imagined on Thirteenth Street when I went to work for Hoffman's principal, Mr. Wright. Mr. and Mrs. Jackson had unlocked the safety and security of the Negro middle class, but we were all in new territory with Mr. Wright. Never having taken art before, I was surprised by the skills I found waiting in my fingers to be released on a canvas, a sheet of paper, or wallboard. Our art teacher—David, as he asked us to call him—wore California-blond hair that hung to his shoulders, wide sideburns, and blousy-sleeved Cavalier shirts. He showed me what it meant to use perspective, how proportion made figures come alive, and how different mediums are used to express emotions. Were it not for David, I'd have never gotten the chance to work for Mr. Wright.

Mr. Wright wanted a mural hung in the main corridor to celebrate Hoffman's thirtieth anniversary. Two other students and I from David's class were chosen to do it. Three large sheets of construction paper were taped to the wall, and Mike, Paul, and I were each responsible for one. I had the third one, where the first principal and teaching staff were shown entering the new school, so mine involved most of the figures. Each of the figures were challenging, and I sometimes stayed after school to complete one. Mr. Wright's office wasn't far down the hall, and he'd often stop on his way out to see what progress I'd made. When we were almost finished with our mural, Mr. Wright stopped at my station, and instead of commenting on my work he said, "Junior, if you'd like to earn some extra money, I've got some yard work you can do, if it's okay with your parents. I'll pay you ten dollars. How about it?"

"Yes, Sir, I'd like that a lot. What would you like me to do? My parents won't mind."

"Cut my grass. Our regular man's sick. It shouldn't take long," he said.

"Okay. What's your address? When would you like me to come?"

"Saturday morning around nine. I'm on Eden Park Drive. Give me your address. I'll pick you up," he offered.

"Thanks, Mr. Wright. Number 4 Crescent Street. I'll see you Saturday."

When Mr. Wright came to pick me up, Mrs. Jackson was at the door to invite him in. He thanked her and turned back down the stairs with me trailing behind, saying he'd have me back by lunchtime. She said, "We're not worried, Mr. Wright. Take your time. Junior will be alright."

Eden Park is close to the center of downtown Cincinnati and is an oasis of peace and beauty. It sits high on a hill, creating a postcard view that overlooks the Ohio River into Kentucky, while far below, Central Parkway zooms traffic into and out of the city in apparent silence. Eden Park is also the home of three of the city's top tourist attractions: the planetarium, the conservatory, and the Taft Museum. One of the city's reservoirs is also located there. Many said the park's most popular spot was the Duck Pond where lovers sat on benches or strolled along the winding paths that encircled the pond. Caught up by its charm, they tried suspending themselves for a moment that stretched longer than a day. This was the area of town in which Mr. Wright lived. This was his neighborhood.

Mr. Wright drove a beige and dark brown Ford station wagon. Although it looked and felt like new, my experience with Daddy suggested that it could be two to five years old. When we got to his home on Eden Park Drive, a twisting, two-lane, canopied road leading uphill to the park, I was already dazzled by the houses we'd passed. I was just as dazzled by Mr. Wright's two-storied structure with wings on either side. The windows started closer to the floor and rose higher than any I'd seen before, even at the Jacksons, and definitely not on Thirteenth. The slates on the roof were lined up so neatly that no human could have placed them there. The bricks were a pale pinkish, almost white, giving an appearance of both firmness and softness at the same time. The entire effect was one of cleanliness, like Mr. Wright himself.

A funny thing about the house though: Mr. Wright said he'd gotten it power-washed just last week and was surprised by how white it looked. I didn't say anything because I couldn't see anyone wanting to get their house washed in the first place. Daddy would have laughed till his head ached if anybody had asked him to wash the outside of our apartment building. Mr. Wright had to have money to throw away to pay someone to wash his house. I knew people who didn't clean the insides of their homes for days and couldn't imagine anyone wanting to clean the outside. I guess it looked nice, but as Miss Louise used to say, "It wouldn't put any food on the table."

The lawn, softened by splashes of red and yellow flowers closer in, embraced the house like a huge horseshoe, its two ends stopping at a tree-lined berm in back. Mr. Wright said the whole affair was about two acres but not to worry because "it's only one-half acre to cut, and I've got a mower you can ride."

It didn't take all morning with such a mower, and I finished before noon. Since I had gone straight to the garage when I started, I couldn't tell if anyone else was at home. Mr. Wright came out the side door and motioned for me to drive the tractor to the garage. When I got there, a slender woman about five-feet-six with mixed-gray hair, a pageboy cut, and blue eyes invited me to join them for lunch on the deck. I washed up in the garage and joined them on the deck.

It wasn't much of a lunch, just tuna sandwiches, grapes, cantaloupe, and cheese, with lemonade and tea to drink. Nothing really to sink your teeth into. Just healthy stuff. The real lunch was the setting. Sitting in the back of Mr. and Mrs. Wright's house—embraced by the surrounding trees, seeing no other houses beside us, and hearing no one talking but ourselves—transported me to a place that hadn't existed for me before. I felt some of the peace, security, and confidence that Mr. Wright brought to school every day. The peace and security represented there hooked me like a bass caught mid-leap by a perfect cast. The Wrights existed in a special world, a world apart from all the Negroes I'd ever known, even the Jacksons. It was a world that I wanted for myself.

When the meal was over I thanked Mrs. Wright for her great lunch, and Mr. Wright drove me home. He stopped at our house and, before paying me, asked if I would cut his grass next week if his regular man couldn't come. I said yes but didn't get the chance to go back again. I figured his regular man must have returned.

At the end of my year at Hoffman we were all tested to determine which high school we'd be eligible to attend. When the scores were returned I learned that I was slated to attend the city's prestigious college prep school at Walnut Hills. I hadn't expected it and wasn't planning for it. Nobody on Thirteenth Street imagined themselves going to a school like Walnut Hills High. Scared and excited by the challenges, I figured I would do the best I could. Like Mama used to say about Navigator Jack, "He's doing the best he can and that's all any of us can do."

WALNUT HILLS HIGH / WEST END AGAIN

Walnut Hills High was *the* academic high school in Cincinnati. Most of its students seemed to have been born with a college catalogue in their cribs. Its graduates were admitted to virtually any college of their choice. And if you wanted to be somebody and didn't go to Walnut Hills, you were already behind. When I first became a student there, the idea of my attending college was as foreign to me as having a full stomach or money in my pocket.

I attended Walnut Hills for three years, and for two of those years I had to attend summer school in order to pass Latin. I didn't feel college bound at all. In comparison to my fellow students I seemed to be playing a constant game of catch-up. If my test scores had predicted brightness, my performance seemed to indicate the opposite.

Whether I'd ever get to attend college or not, going to Walnut Hills High was everything I'd imagined a college might be. First, it looked like a college. When I walked onto its rolling green campus, I entered into a dream that I didn't know I had. It smelled like success, and standing there surrounded by its buildings I felt successful.

Sitting majestically atop a hill overlooking Columbia Parkway, Walnut Hills High dominated the area's landscape. A replica of Monticello, it looked like it would still be there one hundred years from now. Stepping onto its campus opened a slit that let me peek into a world I'd only heard of before. It was a world like Mr. Wright's, where I could live in a beautiful, quiet place—a clean place where even the outside of my house was clean—where I could relax without hearing traffic outside my window and welcome my sisters and friends to a peaceful, happy home. Being a student at Walnut Hills wouldn't be enough. To make my transformation complete I had to graduate.

In addition to looking like a college, Walnut Hills High was structured like one, a private one. Instead of classifying grades seven to nine as junior high, those grades were known as the "Lower School" at Walnut Hills. When I arrived in the seventh grade, an "Upper School" student was assigned as my Big Brother to help me negotiate my first year. With his help, by the eighth grade I was acclimated enough to survive its academic rigors on my own.

My Big Brother's name was Ben. His family lived in Avondale, a suburb where many Negro professionals lived. Ben and I first met at the school counselor's office, where Big Brothers were matched with their Little Brothers. He didn't stand much taller than I, not so big for a Big Brother. He wore a gold sweater with two letters on it, one on his chest and another on his sleeve. Basketball and track. I liked him right from the start.

"Ben, this is Junior Johnson," Miss Harrison, the counselor, said.

"Hi, Junior," said Ben as he stuck out his hand.

It started as simply as that, a handshake and a friendship that would carry me safely through the next two years.

Ben didn't dress sharply by downtown standards, but he must have been campus sharp because everybody knew him. Madras button-down shirt, khakis, letter sweater—the only thing he didn't have were Pat Boone's white bucks. Short haircut with brushed curls on top of an open face with smiling eyes, Ben looked as happy as other people wished they felt. I know he made me feel happy. Ben managed to do all of this while being dark-skinned like Nat King Cole, and not high yella like you'd expect someone as well liked as he.

The first time Ben took me to his house, I discovered why he had such confidence in himself and others. Before we left school he said, "Junior, my father's a professor. He teaches journalism over at UC. You love to write, and it might be good for you to meet him."

"You mean the University of Cincinnati?" I said. "Yeah, it would be better than good."

He laughed.

We walked over to the parking lot, got into his car, and left. (On Thirteenth Street, hardly any adults had cars, but Ben already had one. I wonder what Daddy would've thought of that.)

Meeting Ben's father completely shattered my previous impressions of being black. Before I was born, Avondale was an almost exclusively Jewish suburb of professionals with large houses on big lots. As colored folk moved into Avondale, most of the Jews moved farther out, leaving their large homes to be sectioned into apartments. Some of the houses remained and their properties parceled off. Many owners of the new homes lived graciously downstairs and rented their second floors as apartments for extra income. That's how Ben's family lived.

We drove up a long circular driveway and passed two houses before reaching Ben's at the end. Their two-story redbrick home had a wide full-length porch with white Doric columns on each side of the door. Draperies instead of curtains hung from the windows, and two cane chairs sat at one end of the porch with a table in between. The two other houses were similar to Ben's but each was uniquely different from the others.

After parking the car in the garage under the first floor, we walked upstairs where for the first time I saw his father.

"You must be Junior," he said and threw both arms around me. "Thank you so much for coming to our home. Ben has told us so much about you. Please sit down."

Before I could say, "Thanks," or "Yes, Sir," my mind was in a spin. I smiled, nodded my head, and sat down.

Everyone always called Ben "Ben Guzzi," and I thought that was his name. He never told me anything different. I didn't know what to call his father.

"Thanks, Dr. Guzzi," I said.

"Ben, why don't you take Junior down to the basement while I get something for you two to eat and show him your project? I think he'd like that."

"That's alright, Father," said Ben. "He just wanted to come over and meet you and mother and then we have to go."

"Your mother's not here yet. She'll be late. There's some sort of meeting at the hospital and will hate to have missed meeting Junior," said the professor.

Ben's mother was a nurse at General Hospital. All the while I'm in a fog listening to Dr. Guzzi talk. Suddenly it hit me. He talked like an Englishman. He's dark-skinned like his son, a little taller, voice deeper, and he didn't look English. It was kind of like going to a James Brown concert and hearing Pat Boone's voice come out of James Brown's mouth, except Dr. Guzzi had an entire country coming out of his. Dr. Guzzi said, "Where are you from, Junior? Did you grow up here?"

"Yes, Sir," I said. "Born in General Hospital and have stayed here all my life."

"Ben, why don't you tell Junior where you're from?" said Dr. Guzzi.

"I was born in Nigeria and came to America before I was two when my father went to Case Western," Ben said. "Didn't I tell you that, Junior?"

He must have told me but I had forgotten, so I said, "Yeah, I remember, but I forgot."

"Everybody calls me 'Guzzi' at school because my real name is Nguzi. Benjamin Nguzi. Guzzi is just easier to say. Oh, Dad's a PhD, but we don't call him 'doctor.'" Confused, Junior continues to call him "doctor" out of respect.

Just from meeting Dr. Nguzi I could see why I felt so relaxed and at ease around Ben. Ben radiated a casual, easy confidence that made those of us around him feel better about ourselves. Consequently, we all felt good about Ben. Ben's father exuded that same casual confidence.

"Junior, Ben has researched all sorts of things for a book on Nigerians in America, and he keeps most of it in the basement near my office. He told me you were thinking of being a journalist, and I thought maybe you'd like to see what he's done so far."

"Father," said Ben, "Junior and I can't stay but for a moment. I just wanted you to meet him, and I knew he'd want to meet you and now we have to go."

"Wait," I said. "What kind of stuff is it?"

"We can do it the next time you come. Okay?" he said. Dr. Nguzi stepped over, placed both his hands over mine, and said, "I like you, Junior. Please come back when you can meet Ben's mother."

He walked us to the door, patted Ben on the back, and said, "Be careful, son. Good-bye, Junior."

Throughout the next two years I visited Ben's home often. His family fascinated me, especially his father. Dr. Nguzi knew everything I wanted to know about journalism, how to interview a subject, how to write an article, how to write a headline, how to edit, how to use a light board, and even how to set type with a California Job Board. He was better than Elder Sanders, for with Dr. Nguzi I could live my dreams, and with Elder Sanders I had to die first.

The most remarkable thing about Dr. Nguzi and about Ben was that Dr. Nguzi never seemed to notice anything different between himself and white folk. I'm sure he noticed their different skin color, but unlike most American blacks it had no effect on his opinion of, nor how he carried, himself. Ben had that same ability. It seemed that Nigerians like Dr. Nguzi and Ben didn't feel ashamed of having dark skin like we did. Maybe it was because they didn't have any high yellas who wanted to be white always putting them down.

I remember Dr. Nguzi treating Ben and I to a dinner at one of the fancy restaurants uptown where I had stood outside like a starved puppy staring through the window at the diners inside. I had never seen or imagined any black folk going there.

Due to his English accent Dr. Nguzi had reserved a table for three in a VIP section of the restaurant. When we arrived at the hostess's desk, Dr. Nguzi asked for his table and the hostess didn't know what to do. She summoned the manager. The manager arrived and saw Dr. Nguzi calmly standing there with knitted brow. He asked again for his table and set off walking as if he'd been there a hundred times before. The manager quickly caught up and led us to our table. Without a word of protest, anger, or threat, Dr. Nguzi assumed the same privileges that white folk thoughtlessly took for granted. It would have never occurred to him to be inconvenienced over such an inconsequential matter, and he would have never allowed it.

Years later when the guys in the West End were jumping up and down about Black Power, I thought of Dr. Nguzi. He had Black Power to spare.

The first time I brought Ben to Mr. and Mrs. Jackson's house he was a big hit. Mrs. Jackson loved how he talked, his quick smile and easy laughter, and his effect on me. My speech improved greatly, as did my desire to attend college. "Ain't" didn't cripple my conversations as often anymore, and I tried to "speak distinctly" by modeling Ben. Everything was fine until Mr. Jackson invited Ben and his family to go to church with us. It was fine with Ben, who was Methodist and could sit though one of our services. Ben was actually Muslim by birth and was permitted to practice Christianity because Dr. Nguzi wanted Ben to assimilate more easily into US culture. Dr. Nguzi was Muslim and a member of the Ibo tribe from northern Nigeria. He had experienced a bloody conflict between Muslims and Christians when he was younger. Those groups were forced to live together in the same region, inside a political border drawn by others. It was one of the reasons he'd immigrated to the

United States. Dr. Nguzi was liberal, but he wasn't about to come to the Independent Missionary Baptist Church to worship. Ben was polite and kept giving excuses about why his parents couldn't accompany him on a visit to our church. As we finished eating one of Mrs. Jackson's fantastic sweet potato pies one Sunday, Ben decided to stop making excuses and tell why his parents couldn't join us at church.

He turned to Mr. Jackson and said, "I'm grateful for your letting me join you at church and have enjoyed worshipping with you, and I regret that my parents can't come with us."

"Well, we're truly sorry because we'd counted so much on having them. It's their choice, and everybody has their own reason. Do you know why they can't come?" said Mr. Jackson.

"They're Muslim," said Ben.

That stopped all conversation for a minute. Muslims not only weren't "saved," but in the eyes of Mr. and Mrs. Jackson of the Independent Missionary Baptist Church they were also Godless.

"I don't know what to say," said Mrs. Jackson. "I'm glad you've told us. I hope we haven't embarrassed you or anything by asking."

"Nothing to be embarrassed about," said Ben.

The rest of the evening was spent circling around Ben's shocking revelation about his parents. Sound, responsible, and upright as they wanted to be, the Jacksons just couldn't get around their discomforting ignorance of Islam. After Ben left, they sat me down to straighten me out.

"Junior, how long have you known about this?" said Mrs. Jackson.

"About Dr. Nguzi, almost since we first met. His wife much later," I answered. "Why? What's the big deal?"

"What's the big deal? You've seen those Black Muslims on Peebles Corner selling those papers. Dressed all in black, wearing those weird hats and talking 'bout the 'White Devil,'" said Mr. Jackson. "You don't need to be hanging around anybody like that. I don't want you over at Ben's house no more, and I don't want him over here."

I was stunned. I knew they were scared of the Black Muslims, but how could they connect them to Dr. Nguzi and Ben? They knew Ben. He'd come home with me many times. He was no Black Muslim. They liked Ben. Why do this to him? To me? What was going on?

As calmly as I could I said, "Ben's family are true Muslims and don't hate anyone. There are white Muslims, too. The Black Muslims are nothing but a hate group trying to cash in on black folks' fears, Dr. Nguzi said, and no real Muslim would ever go near them. He's one of the smartest and most honorable men you'll ever meet, and Ben is just like him. If being a Muslim means being like them, then that's what I'd like to be." And swiftly, like a knife thrown silently through the air, Mrs. Jackson's calloused hand slapped me solidly to the floor.

"Talk like that again in this house and the Children's Service will be here so fast to get you that you won't know what happened. Now get upstairs till I tell you to come down," she said.

That was the beginning of the end of my wanting to please the Jacksons by trying to get the Holy Ghost or anything else that mattered to them.

At the end of my second year at Walnut Hills, Ben graduated. He went to Columbia University in New York because of their journalism school. His father had quietly pushed him toward Harvard but claimed to be delighted at Ben's choice because it was his decision. I hated to see him leave but felt so proud to have been his Little Brother. He was a real Big Brother to me.

Before Ben left for Columbia, he and Dr. Nguzi gave me a gift that only they could give. Having been my academic mentor during his junior year and quasi-adopting me into his family in his senior year, Ben helped clarify what I really wanted to get out of Walnut Hills. Even though I didn't want to admit it, Ben knew that I needed someone to map it out for me.

"Junior, I'll be leaving soon and will really miss you, and before I leave I want us to sit down with my father. He has something we'd like to share with you," said Ben. "What do you say?"

"Sounds good. When do we go?"

"By the end of the week," said Ben. "Let me take you home."

We jumped in his car and were gone. I let him drop me off just before we reached our house, claiming that I had to pick up something at the neighbor's.

After school on Friday we drove directly to Ben's house. "This shouldn't take long," Ben said. "I'll have you home before dinner, and Mrs. Jackson won't be upset."

"She'll be fine," I said. "Don't worry about it." At this point I didn't care if she was upset or not.

Dr. Nguzi called from downstairs when he heard us arrive. "I'm down here, Ben, in the office. Bring Junior down."

His dark-paneled basement office with its large desk, stacks of newspapers, and textbooks was my first glimpse of a home office of any kind. An Underwood typewriter reigned supreme on a small rolling table beside his desk. None of his many academic degrees were displayed in his office. They were probably at school. Instead he had a painting of a beautiful black Arabian stallion prancing in a lush meadow behind him.

Dr. Nguzi said, "If you're serious about becoming a journalist, as Ben says you are, I've got something you ought to think about."

I looked at Ben, who said nothing and just smiled. My breathing got faster. "Yes, Dr. Nguzi, journalism is the only thing I think about."

"Would you be interested in working in the summertime with some real journalists?" said Dr. Nguzi.

"Yes, Sir. How can I do it?"

"Ben has set it up," he said. "Tell him, Ben."

Ben said, "Father helped me develop something that we felt would take what you've done at school into a complete learning environment. Something you could use in the real world. You know where O'Bryonville is, right?"

"Yeah," I said. "It's right up from where I went to Hoffman School in the sixth grade. Old Horace Mann used to be up there, too."

Unlike most high schools, Walnut Hills offered an internship program reserved for juniors and seniors. Ben graduated with honors from the Walnut Hills curriculum. Dr. Nguzi was a noted author and professor of journalism, and I, the little guy with high hopes, had the good fortune of being mentored by both.

And then Dr. Nguzi stepped in. "And I know you know how to write, but you haven't gotten a chance to interview yet, have you?"

"No, sir, I haven't, but I'd like to," I said.

Ben said, "I spoke to my internship chair and told him about the work that you have done with Father and me. He said that even if you were qualified he couldn't find anyone who'd take you at your level. The school couldn't risk sending someone as young and inexperienced as you to represent them. That's when I came to ask Father for help."

"Junior, a former student of mine operates a monthly community magazine and is willing to give you an opportunity to learn as much as you are able whenever you are ready to work," said Dr. Nguzi.

I didn't know what to say or do. I just lowered my head and held my hands over my face. I uncovered my face and spoke, "What can I say? Thanks isn't enough, Dr. Nguzi. You and Ben are just too much. I've wanted something like this, something real. How does it work?"

"The magazine is *Your Space*, published and edited by Kenneth Nese. It covers Madisonville, O'Bryonville, and Walnut Hills—areas you should know," said Dr. Nguzi. "Everything is done in shop, typesetting, light board, headlines, photos, artwork, magazine covers—everything except binding. Anything that you want to learn you can find it there. Kenny is willing to take you as long as you're willing to work hard and do what he asks you to do. What do you think about that, Junior? Can you do it?"

"Yes," I said, shaking my head in wonder. "What about school?"

"Dr. Caldwell, the internship counselor," said Ben, "is willing to give you internship credit for next year based on the evaluation you get from

Your Space at the end of the summer. Until then he can't credit it as a school-approved internship. That's the best we could get."

"More than enough for me," I said. Before summer was over I knew what I wanted to be. I wanted to be a journalist, and as a matter of fact, I'd already become one.

Despite having to attend summer school to bring my Latin grades up, school ended at 1 p.m., and I was able to reach *Your Space* by 1:30 p.m., where I stayed until dinner at 6 p.m. During that time Kenny put me to work setting type. When the magazine was set I watched him at work on the light board, fitting images in the right "holes," cutting each to fit and leaving a border to make them pop. I watched as he cut columns and photos on the page, and finally he said, "Junior, put the back inside cover together for me. I've got to run downtown. Take care of it, okay?" And from that day on I was his go-to guy.

We did local news, real estate, obits—things local papers would have done were there one, except for one thing: our local newspapers didn't offer features on the area's history. Those gave me my first chances for interviews. My first interview was with a woman in her seventies who lived in a row house built in 1892 on McMillan Street in Walnut Hills. Mrs. Kamner kept an attic full of trunks with photos and paraphernalia that had been passed down from her ancestors. She had plenty of stories to tell. Talking with her was like talking with Miss Louise, except that she was German. Cincinnati was heavily settled by Germans, and many who lived in the Walnut Hills area had gotten wealthy from their interests in the pork, beer, and packing house industries. The name "Porkapolis" may have derived from the industry that Mrs. Kamner's grandfather and others had fostered. The answer to the question, "Do pigs fly?" is "Yes," if you were born in Cincinnati.

When I wasn't doing history pieces, I got the chance to polish the lives of people who'd died, most of whom were black and poor. Like Mrs. Hattie Jones.

Mrs. Hattie Jones of Cincinnati died last week in her home at 310 Ridgeway Avenue. She was 72. Services will be held at 7:30 p.m., May 16, at the J. C. Battle Funeral Home, and the viewing will take place at 3:30 p.m. Mrs. Jones, the centerpiece and founder of the Usher Board at First Baptist Church, the largest church in the city, was well known for her spiritual leadership and guidance. She was respected by all who knew her for her kindness to others. Her leadership at church was reflected in the love she showed to others in her neighborhood and throughout her community. She lived by the Golden Rule we all espoused. "We will miss her morning walks through the neighborhood. She made it seem like we were just one big family and she was looking after us," one of her neighbors told *Your Space*.

Mrs. Jones worked at the Cincinnati General Hospital for twenty years, where she trained more than forty-five orderlies before retiring. After retirement she worked as floor supervisor at the Rose Sanctuary Rest Home for twelve years. She received the Special Letter of Commendation for Twenty Years of Commitment and Service from the chief operating officer at General Hospital that was reserved for its top employees. Mrs. Jones was the beloved wife of Mr. Aaron Jones, switchman for the Baltimore and Ohio Railroad and member of the Elks. Both from Alabama, they met in Cincinnati and were married for fifty years. Mrs. Jones was preceded in death by two children, Albert Jones and Shirlene (Jones) Bales. She has four grandchildren, Frank, Louise, Diane, and Betty Bales. The Jones family requests that you please send any donations to the Colored Orphanage of Walnut Hills.

I wrote lots of obituaries, and the families seemed to appreciate the extra time I tried to give each one. The obits were like interviews to me. Although we were often given biographical data, I loved talking to family members if I could. Many times people told me that they'd cut out my obituary to save in their Bible, to honor the person they'd lost. I felt I was a real journalist whenever someone told me that. I had painted a picture of someone's friend or loved one that presented them as a full person and not just another one of the many who had died. Mama would have loved it. I was doing the best I could.

Daddy was also doing the best he could, and it ruined me.

BOOK THREE

GEST STREET

My escape from the West End closed like a clam when Daddy entered the picture again. He wasn't the same person he was before Mama died. Each time he visited us at the Jacksons', part of his old self was missing. My sisters couldn't finger the loss because they were younger. It became clearer to us all when he brought home his new "wife," Nellie. Almost twenty years younger than Daddy, she was just a few years older than I.

Being that much younger than Daddy and raising six of us was trouble enough, not counting the trouble younger men might bring. Coupling that decision with Mama's death and his growing alcoholism, it looked as if he'd fallen full-speed down a coal chute into a molten furnace.

We moved deeper into the West End sewer into Daddy's new apartment on Gest Street. South of Freeman Avenue, Gest Street is littered with broken-down houses, broken people, and vacant lots. It is a conduit, a pass-through to go somewhere else, a neighborhood in permanent transition with transitional people stuck in place. Throwaways in the Laurel Homes and Lincoln Court projects warily watch would-be victims pass through to the Union Terminal and Crosley Field farther south. It is a neighborhood of streets and numbers that makes it easier for outsiders to define poverty by branding its offspring as drug addicts and criminals. The numbers were there for anyone to see, and those of us inside those numbers were crippled by them.

Very few women worked, and the men were underemployed or unemployable. The lucky ones, like Daddy, worked on construction sites during good weather and other jobs in the off-season. Farther south on Carr Street, the same useless derelicts huddled in groups in front of the same tired-looking, overcrowded, decaying buildings from sunrise till dusk, seeking handouts from construction workers on their way home. Men in knots of four and five stared vacant-eyed at passersby as if they expected the dope man to arrive at any moment. Young children scurried among them up and down the sidewalks as if trying to outrun their fates.

I never saw a cab on Gest Street while we lived there. Cabbies knew the neighborhoods those numbers represented and chose not to go into areas they termed dangerous, areas in which they had little opportunity to make money and a greater chance of being robbed. They don't consider it discrimination against the people living there. When I asked one why he wouldn't pick me up when I called, he said, "Nothing against you, my man. It just business."

I tried not to speak to Daddy when I first moved into the apartment with Nellie. I caught the bus across town to Walnut Hills High every day at 7 a.m. and got home close to 5:30 p.m. After my first quarter ended, we talked about my staying at Walnut Hills. Daddy said it was too expensive to continue paying bus fare to go across town when I could go to Oyler Junior High. It was too hard on me to have such long days when he didn't have those hours at work, "and I get paid every day," he said. "It would be easier all around if you went to Oyler where you could walk to school. Junior, it just makes more sense."

It may have made sense to him, but for me it meant giving up my way to get out.

"Okay, Daddy," I murmured. I hung my head, turned, and walked quickly away before my eyes said too much.

———

Oyler was an all-white school in the all-white ghetto of Price Hill. The families that lived there were poor like ours, and their kids were as tough as us. They were prejudiced as a matter of course and hated "niggers." The only learning that took place there was how to get by without getting suspended. In order for me to get to Oyler, I had to cross an overpass that was the dividing line between blacks and whites. I could cross it going to the school in daylight hours but not after school was out, and it was just as dangerous for the white guys to be caught on our side after hours.

Once the black guys had learned of my going to a college prep school in a middle-class neighborhood, whenever I felt challenged or threatened I'd growl, "Just because I went to that white boy's school don't mean a thing. I'm still from the ghetto, and unless you've got a death wish, don't fuck with me." I'd already lost some black authenticity when I told a group of guys on the basketball court at Lincoln Center that I had played for the basketball team at Walnut Hills. I went on to tell them that I was the only black guy on the team and was the second-string guard. It took awhile for me to live that down. As Jim, who later became my friend, said, "How can the only black guy on a white basketball team play second-string guard to a white boy? Man, you blow my mind." He laughed it off, but it took me awhile to get back on track.

The unexpected jewel of Oyler was far from being college prep but became the symbol of everything I strived to become. Shop class isn't the most likely place I'd enroll for college-prep training, but under Mr. Barfield's teaching, my compass was righted.

When I first saw Mr. Barfield I felt let down. I was still judging people from the outside, by the clothes they wore and how they wore their hair. He didn't wear a dashiki or even a beard. From the way people talked about him, I expected to see a Leroi Jones or a Stokely Carmichael, someone with power and presence—someone who white folks respected, and sometimes hated or feared. Instead, I got a man in a tie.

After returning to Gest Street from Walnut Hills my glimpse of college began to fade. Under the rigors of surviving in the atmosphere of the West End I focused on the present. A key part of that present was attending ninth-grade shop class at Oyler Junior High.

When I enrolled at Oyler all of the instructors were white. Even at all-black Samuel Ach Junior High, most of the instructors were white. I'd only been there for five weeks when a guy sitting at our segregated lunch table announced, "I hear we've got a black teacher, man." Joe, a short guy who was always angry, answered, "Yeah, he's probably some Uncle Tom."

The rest of the lunch period was devoted to the new black teacher. Everyone's opinion was strongly based on their own needs. We all wanted a black teacher who could fulfill roles beyond any we'd expect from a white one, needs beyond any that Mr. Barfield should have been expected to fulfill. Our needs were often greater than we could identify or name, but we knew we had them—needs that our education or our parents should have met. Now that Mr. Barfield was here, those needs could be filled.

Despite Joe's negative pronouncement, none of us believed that Mr. Barfield was an Uncle Tom. No Uncle Tom would be aggressive enough to seek a job at Oyler or have the guts to keep it. All of us knew that Mr. Lynn, the gym teacher from West Virginia, probably wouldn't speak to Mr. Barfield. He certainly wouldn't sit with him at lunch. We also knew that he wasn't the only one who felt that way.

Shop class wasn't at the top of my things-to-do list before Mr. Barfield came. Under Mr. Monroe I learned how to plane wood and the difference between hard woods and soft. That wasn't much use to me in the concrete streets and alleys of Gest Street. I had no dreams of becoming a carpenter. Before he left I had learned how to make a corner shelf for our living room. It never really fit in the corner, and Nellie didn't attach it. Yet it was always available in the closet, right there on the floor. That was about as useful as shop class was for me. Until Mr. Barfield came.

The second Thursday after Mr. Monroe left, I walked into shop class and didn't see Mr. Barfield. The saws were quiet, sand belts shut down, and the overhead exhaust fans barely hummed. Even the dripping faucet from the third sink had stopped dripping. The shades were lifted as high as they could go, and the whole room shimmered under light. Something in shop class was about to change. The paneled glass door to the office at the end of the shop pushed open, and Mr. Barfield stepped out. My first impression was that of a man with a preacher's stature and a post-man's face. His smile rained confidence all over us. He was an imposing regular guy.

Light-skinned and tall, but not as tall as a basketball player, Mr. Barfield could look anybody in the eye. He had a smile in his eyes that tempered the serious expressions he sometimes used to keep us in line. He told us a little about himself on that first day that made me like him from the start.

"I'm from Dayton, Ohio," he said. "I used to teach both phys ed and shop. When we moved back here with my wife's family I chose to teach shop alone. I enjoy making things, learning how to fix broken ones, and figuring out what makes things tick. I hope that's what each of you are here for, too. Or at least you can discover what it's all about."

Next he talked about what interested me most. "Like most of you, I grew up in the city. And I'm not trying to turn anybody into carpenters here. What I would like to do, and I'd like for us to be able to do this together, is to develop skills that will help you outside of this classroom. Skills that can help you develop into the person that you wish to be."

I didn't know if he could deliver on that promise, but as I looked around the classroom almost everyone seemed to be open to his challenge, even the most prejudiced guys. Mack, one of the toughest, asked, "What if I'm already the guy I wish to be?" Without missing a beat Mr. Barfield said, "Good, then maybe you can show the rest of us how to get there." That was the end of that. Mr. Barfield had lit a fire inside me, and I worked steadily throughout the year to unleash my skills. I didn't feel I'd made much progress until four weeks before ninth grade ended and I could leave Oyler behind. We were all in shop when Mr. Barfield came out of his office with the test papers. Everyone had completed their work projects previously, and the written test supplied a narrative of the planning, materials required, and manufacturing of the finished product. With my project out of the way, a small three-drawer chest for our hallway, I looked at Mr. Barfield handing out the test papers as if I'd seen him for the first time. Mr. Barfield wasn't wearing a tie.

It never occurred to me until that moment that I'd never seen Mr. Barfield without his tie. Mr. Monroe, our former shop teacher, never wore one. Neither did Mr. Lynn, not even on parent-teacher days. Mr. James, the principal, wore a tie. His assistant, Mr. Franklin, as Miss Louise might have said, wouldn't know a tie if it bit him. Whether his colleagues did or not, Mr. Barfield always wore a tie. Always.

When I asked him what happened to his tie, he smiled his friendly postman's smile and said, "Thanks, don't worry about it. I spilled some coffee on it, and it's drying in the office. It will have a stain on it, but I'll deal with that some other time. It's ruined now, and a few of you have been asking about my ties. When the tests are over next week, why don't I hold a session for anyone who's interested in learning about ties? Sound like something you'd be interested in?"

Of course I was interested. None of the men on Gest Street wore ties, except Jim's father, and that was because it was part of his uniform. He parked cars at the city parking garage in the heart of downtown. Mr. Abraham, our rent man, didn't wear a tie, and he owned the building. Sonny wore a tie but never closed it. Our postman wore a tie because he had to. In the summer he kept it open until he returned to the post office. The only people I could count on wearing ties were ministers, policemen, and funeral home directors. Most people thought it best to stay away from all three of them. Altogether, ties weren't a big hit in my neighborhood. Ties represented something that our neighborhood didn't have and often yearned for: respect. Educated people wore ties. People with good-paying white-collar jobs wore ties. People of a different class than those of us on Gest Street wore ties. There were other examples, and almost all of them were white. Imagine how powerful it felt for me to see Mr. Barfield in a tie.

The following week, about nine of us met in shop after school to learn about ties. Mr. Barfield said the history of ties began in the 1600s in France and we didn't need to delve into it for our purposes. Today's necktie developed from basically four forms: neck cloths, bandannas, bow ties, and ascots. Each reflected the period in which it was developed. Ascots, for instance, were used when shirt collars were worn high and wrapped loosely around the neck. Today's ties were primarily made of silk, cotton, and polyester, and the material sometimes determined which knot to use. When asked what kind of knot he used, Mr. Barfield said, "I thought someone would ask that question, so I came prepared. You've got to pass the test though before I'll sign it." He held up sheets of gray scalloped paper with a gold tie embossed on the right hand corner of each one. Each name was written in fancy script across the center. Printed underneath that in large black letters a line read, "**Certified Four-in-Hand, Windsor, and ½ Windsor Knot Specialist.**" A signature line at the bottom read, "Approved by Samuel L. Barfield, B.A."

My sisters had always teased me about being too emotional. To counter their arguments, I tried to maintain a stoicism when around the guys on the street. The whole thing hit me too quickly, was too soft, too kind to be expected. I quickly placed my palms over my eyes, and by the time I pulled them away, the redness around my eyes was the only evidence of my tears.

He brought each of us in turn to the front of the room and placed a tie around our neck. "We'll start off with a basic knot, something easy, something smooth, something that you can tie quickly. Something that will look good no matter if your tie is cotton or silk."

We learned to tie three common knots that day: the four-in-hand, the Windsor, and the half-Windsor. He wore the four-in-hand to work every day and the Windsor with the pinched front on special occasions. "Those two are all you really need to know," he said. "One for work and another for dress, and you'll be okay." At the end of our training he sat down at his desk and signed our certificates as he called us up to receive them, one by one.

I lost my tie certificate a short time after leaving Oyler, but I never lost my respect and affection for Mr. Barfield. He taught me a lot more than how to cross the fat end over the slim end of the tie to get a four-in-hand. He filled the emptiness that I couldn't define when I first met him. By tying the knot of a tie, I had learned why I felt more confident when he was around. He would have still been himself without wearing a tie, but he couldn't have done what he did for me without one. For someone like myself who judged people from the outside, that tie on Mr. Barfield said, "Stop, look, and listen. I believe in myself, and you better believe in me, too." I believe it said the same thing to everyone he met. It certainly said that to me.

———————

Walnut Hills had given me an edge over the so-called academics they taught at Oyler, so I let the guys from my side of the overpass see the answers on my tests. It paid off, too, because their grades were going up. One of the white guys saw me, informed the teacher, and that was it. I got a one-hour detention. Detentions aren't that bad if you've got something to read to kill time. But the black guys walked over the overpass together after school. If you weren't with them when they left, you were on your own.

When my hour was up and I had to leave the school building, I opened the door just a crack and peered out without showing my head. At one end of the yard a bunch of guys were playing basketball. Another group was standing along the fence as I passed, smoking cigarettes and laughing and pushing each other around. I figured I could stay close to the building and break out running when I reached the corner. I could have been out of the schoolyard before anyone noticed, except for one thing. One guy stood away from the others holding a transistor radio to his ear. He wouldn't hear me, but not being distracted by anyone close, he might be looking my way when I made my run. I checked everything out the best I could, and without another thought opened the door just a little wider and slipped out, hugging the wall.

Pasting myself onto the building and staying in its shadow, I was almost at the corner when the guy with the radio looked my way. Not waiting for him to focus, I zipped across the bare cement yard and headed for the open cyclone fence. At that same moment the cry went up, "Look, look! There's a nigger on the yard! Get 'im, get 'im before he gets away," and the race was on. I reached the fence and jetted through it in a flash, but like a flash they were almost on me. I was out of breath and nearly in their hands when I reached the destination. I was aiming for and ran straight into the firehouse across the street. A fireman standing inside the open bay saw me coming and stepped out to catch me as I fell.

"Whoa . . . what's going on here?" he asked as he pulled me inside.

"They're after me," I said. "I had detention and all the black guys are gone. Now the white guys are gonna get me."

"Let's slow down for a minute," he said. "Where do you live, son?"

"'Cross the overpass at the lower end of Gest Street," I answered.

"Do you think you can make it home without getting hurt?" he asked, eyeing the vibrating crowd of angry white faces behind me.

"I wish I could," I answered shakily.

"Alright then," he said and turned to face the crowd. "Okay, boys, step back. Leave the kid alone before I have to call the police."

They slowly shuffled back and set up camp across the street. The biggest one stepped forward and said, "You can't tell us what to do. You're just a fireman. We're gonna kick his ass if we have to stay out here all night."

The fireman didn't trade any words. He told me to stay put and went back into the firehouse. I heard him tell someone, "Get the car, Frank." When he returned to me he smiled and said, "How'd you like to ride home in the chief's car?"

The way my face lit up said it all.

The sun was just beginning to pitch long, dark shadows into the street as we backed down the driveway. My detention had been for sixty minutes, and I had just spent over an hour at the firehouse. Now I would be nearly two hours late getting home, and Daddy was gonna kill me—first for getting the detention and second for getting home so late. I could already feel the welts from his belt on my back. As we turned up the street past the threatening group, words spat out of their mouths hitting the sides of the chief's car like gravel, "You can run now, but we'll get your ass tomorrow, nigger!"

Those words helped me make my decision: I'd leave home for school every morning, but I damn sure wouldn't be going there. Those 'necks needed time to cool off, and I needed time to get some help. I'd go to my best friend, Jim, tell him to get T-Baby and his brother, Bop. Nobody would mess with me then.

When we pulled into Gest Street, Jim noticed the chief's car but didn't see me in it. When I opened the car door and hopped out, you'd have thought I'd come home from Vietnam or something. Jim whistled and called out, "Junior!" like he'd just seen James Brown instead of me. Bettie, Jim's younger sister, the one I was going with, jumped up like she'd been struck by the Holy Ghost and just stared at me. Jim's other sisters and his baby brother, Lazy Eye, started talking all at once. "Look at Junior. Coming home late, and being brought home by a white man. *You know what that means?*"

I turned to the chief to thank him and he asked if I wanted him to speak to my father. Daddy, a refugee from Alabama, always said he wouldn't give a dime for all the white men in the world—unless they played baseball for the Cincinnati Reds—so I told the chief, "No thanks."

I stood in the street and waved good-bye as the chief's car disappeared around the corner. Jim and his sisters were all over me the instant his car was out of sight. Each one wanted to be the first to find out what had happened for me to come home this late riding in a fireman's car.

"What did you do? Did you get caught doing something wrong? You get in a fight with those white boys?" they all asked.

Before I could answer, a woman's voice called down from our third-floor window: "Junior, your father says get your ass up these stairs now!"

It was Nellie, Daddy's common-law wife who played stepmother to us six kids. She'd been perched in the window as a lookout for the past hour and had silently watched the scene below. So without Daddy even seeing it, I was busted coming home late and for being driven home by a white man in an official car. In our world, any white man other than the rent man and the mailman spelled trouble. I knew my ass was grass as soon as I hit the door.

I ducked inside the first-floor hallway without saying a word, and Jim was right behind me. I quickly explained what had happened, and as expected, he stood right by my side. He promised to get T-Baby, Bop, and Eddie-B, who'd just come home from the reformatory, to "go 'cross the overpass and kick some ass." In the meantime I had Daddy to worry about.

I dragged myself upstairs, and before I reached our landing I could hear Wanda, the oldest of my four sisters, schooling the others. "Nellie says Junior's been brought home by the police and Daddy's gonna get him!" She'd picked up the tone of Nellie's voice and was certain I was going to get crucified. She was almost too excited to breathe. The moment I stepped through the door of our four-room apartment, I knew things were deadly serious. My sisters immediately scurried as far away from me as they could get, not wanting my fate to spill over onto them.

Nellie entered through the living room doorway. "Your father's waiting for you in the bedroom," she said, with the air of an executioner directing the victim to the gallows.

For one brief instant I thought, *One mad dash, one leap back down the stairs, and I can outrun this. I can beat this. I can escape this whipping.* But where would I run? Who would I run to? I had no money and nowhere to go. I had no other choice than to face Daddy. I tried to squeeze back the tears that had formed behind my eyelids, but failed. I passed trance-like through my sisters' bedroom and crossed the threshold through the doorway into his and Nellie's.

"Hi, Daddy," I said in my best little-boy voice. Standing there with his belt in his hand he said, in a cracked voice, "Get your ass in here, Junior," and reached out and pulled me into the bedroom. As the first bite from his belt hit my back I mentally shut down to escape the pain. I asked myself, *What good was it to escape from one beating only to run into another?* And then it came to me: *Maybe I couldn't escape the beating.* I just had to choose which beating take . . . or not take one at all.

DANCING IN THE DARK

The move to the West End came a lot easier than expected, as easy as picking up the phone and talking to my brother in Selma, Alabama. The moment I hear his voice I start using the same familiar dialect we spoke years ago. Moving to Gest Street had that same familiar feel. I hated having to move there, yet I couldn't break free of its hold on me. Even with one foot planted in my promising new world, Gest Street felt as comfortable as an old shoe.

Gest Street received a lot of through traffic, some going to the Reds games on game day and night traffic looking for another kind of game. It wasn't my first exposure to "tricks" in the black neighborhood but my first one up close. As part of the larger ghetto, we were familiar with three types of white men: the rent man, the mailman, and the policeman. Most other white faces dealt with something illegal or dangerous, like the "cruisers."

Cruisers drove slowly through the streets at night close to the curb so that they could stop and ask someone to find a girl. After a while we got to know each cruiser by his car and how to deal with him. Everyone knew about Gus. One night just as the streetlights came on, Gus cruised through Gest Street, saw me standing by the corner, stopped near the alley, and called me to his car. "Hey," he said, speaking low, "think you could find me something tonight?"

"Sure," I said in the same low tone. "What you looking for?"

"You know, someone nice and clean to have fun with. A nice colored girl."

I knew right away what he wanted, and it wasn't someone nice and clean.

"I'll give you twenty dollars if you can do that for me. Think you can find one?" he said, as if ordering a steak.

This wasn't the first time I'd been stopped by Gus cruising the neighborhood looking for girls. He always wanted the same thing: a nice, clean colored girl to have fun with. Why couldn't he find himself a nice, clean white girl? I didn't know any nice, clean black girls who wanted to have fun with a man in a car for money. Gus thought he was invisible in his green four-door Chevy sedan with blackwall tires that looked like an insurance man's car. He parked near the alley so that I could bring someone to him without his being seen from the street. He knew it was safer that way. Gus had been set up once and had gotten out of his car to meet a girl. Baby Stone pulled him into the alley and robbed and nearly beat him to death. After that he stayed in his car and let the girls be brought to him. He was pathetic in the way he set himself up time after time. Girls despised him, and men hated him.

"Gus actually believes he can hide from us by driving that so-called insurance man's car, and we live here," said Baby Stone. "What's worse, he thinks that damn car is his protection. That car can't hide who he really is. A blind man could see that. That's why I kicked his ass. He thinks we're too stupid to see through his shit."

The first time Gus stopped me, I didn't know who he was. He was sitting in a dark blue Ford parked around the corner from the Downtown, a juke joint where he could find girls, drugs, or anything else he'd want.

Just as I walked out of the alley Gus rolled down his window. "Hey," he said, and motioned for me to come over. I kept on walking like I was deaf. He motioned again.

"Hey, I just want to ask you a question."

I kept on walking.

"I'll pay."

I wasn't fully convinced yet that he wasn't a cop, but I walked over.

"Listen, I don't mean any trouble. Can you help me out?"

"I don't know, man," I said, waiting to see what he'd say.

"I heard I might be able to find some smoke down here. And maybe a girl? Do you know where I could find any?"

"Sorry, man. You got the wrong information," I said, and turned to go.

Just as I was leaving, Baby Stone stepped out of the Downtown. He saw Gus's car and me walking away from it. He moved in closer and saw Gus sitting behind the wheel.

"Junior," he called. "Who's this? You know him? What's this motherfucker doing here?"

"Told me he's looking for some smoke and a girl. I don't know where he came from."

Baby Stone turned and looked at Gus and Gus looked away. Gus tried to say something but changed his mind and made a quick move to start his car. It wasn't quick enough. Baby Stone sprang to the car and nearly pulled Gus through the window by his head alone. Gus squirmed and tried to pull Baby Stone's hands away.

"Get your hands off me, motherfucker. Looking for some smoke or a girl. Ain't you a bitch. You a narc or a trick? Or just some damn fool looking to get killed? You better get your ass out of here, motherfucker. I'll give you what you're looking for."

"I didn't really mean no—" Gus started. Baby Stone stopped and hit him with his stone-right hand to the face—the same stone-right he'd used to bust up Artie Crumb, a black cop we all hated. Gus collapsed with his bleeding face on the steering wheel and his arm dangling loosely down the side of the car.

"Now, go find some girls with your punk ass," said Baby Stone. He turned to me and said, "Junior, watch him leave."

"Okay," Gus whined. "I'll give you twenty-five dollars. See what you can do." He handed me a new twenty-dollar bill and a five out the window of his car. I took it and left.

When I peered from around the corner of the alley about thirty minutes later, Gus's car was gone. He never learned. Gus risked losing his money or worse each time he came. Yet he always came back, same time, same station.

Living on Gest Street generally meant learning how to go with the flow and staying above it. People passing through always wanted something. Some, like Gus, wanted to buy girls. Others had something to sell, like Frankie, who sold stuff in the beauty parlor and at Bodel's Barber Shop that he'd boosted from uptown. Most people bought his goods without asking where they came from. If I bought anything hot at the barbershop, I wouldn't have been able to take it home. Either one of my sisters or Nellie would have told Daddy, and that would have been the end of it, and the end of me.

I put some money in my pocket working at Sonny's Grocery Store. Sonny's was on Freeman Avenue about four blocks up Gest and two blocks over. It was the biggest store in our neighborhood, kind of like a supermarket and a butcher shop combined. Mama sent me there to buy whole chickens and have Sonny cut them up. Sometimes he'd cut center-cut pork chops right off of a cut of pork while I watched. He sold collard greens, Mustards, and all kinds of vegetables that we didn't have to walk all the way up to the Eighth Street Market to get. Like Pie Lady, he let us buy stuff "on the books" till Daddy got paid. Sonny wasn't a regular white guy. He was Italian like Dean Martin, and had curly hair like Dean. If you couldn't pay your book off on time, Sonny always gave you some slack.

From time to time I worked in the alley in back of the store stacking pop bottle crates. Sometimes Navigator Jack, Cee-Cee, and Big Milt would build a fire in an empty barrel and stand around out back drinking Thunderbird or Wild Irish Rose. I never drank with them, though they offered once and I turned them down. Not because I wouldn't have taken a taste or two, but I didn't want to drink out of the same bottle they were sharing.

"Watch those winos," Sonny used to say. "Don't let them burn down my store."

I knew them and knew they wouldn't do him any harm. As a matter of fact, because I worked there and Sonny had left them alone at their barrel, if anybody had tried to burn his store down they'd have been the first ones to try to stop it. All decent guys in a pinch, but one I could always depend on was Navigator Jack. I could fill pop bottle crates pretty fast: Coke, eighteen holes; Nehi, twenty; Pepsi, eighteen; RC Cola, eighteen. I always stacked RC Cola on the bottom because it was the tallest. Whenever I had lots of bottles and needed to make taller stacks, Navigator Jack was there to help build them. The truth is, Navigator Jack never stopped helping me build things up. Even after he died. Whenever I needed him, he has never failed to help build me up. I never said it to him and never really acknowledged it to myself, but Navigator Jack was the kind of man I've always wanted to become.

BILLY GOAT HILL

On ice cream delivery day, the MeadowGold truck parked on Freeman Avenue in front of Sonny's. The routine was the same. The driver lifted up one of the side panels, took out his hand truck, and started rolling tubs of ice cream into the store. He came in and out four times to complete his delivery, settled with Sonny, and pulled away. And each time he went into the store, he pulled the side panel down. Every time he came back, he pulled it up again to get more ice cream. He'd done this ever since I'd worked there. I hadn't paid much attention because he had never changed his routine. It was almost like he wasn't there. But he was there for Jim, and Jim had something up.

I first met Jim when he was in my homeroom class in Oyler Junior High. He didn't have the sharpest clothes and didn't wear Edwin Clapps or Florsheims on his feet. He wasn't the most popular guy with girls either, but could he wear a topper! Jim looked better in a hat than Frank Sinatra.

Most of the time Jim wore a snap-brim wool fedora with a silk band. Sometimes he switched it for a wide-brim Dobbs felt with a feather in a silk band. He wore a Panama straw in the summer with an extra-wide brim in a leather band. His Panama cost the most, but he wore it the least. I asked him once why he paid more for the straw that he couldn't wear as often as his others.

Jim used to say, "You can put straw on your head for nothing, but if you want a straw *hat* on your head, there's only one Panama. It's not how much a hat costs or how often you wear it, but how it makes you feel that counts. If you look good, you feel good, and I feel great in a Panama."

Watching Jim put on his hat was like watching a magician at work. He said if I wanted to become a real hat master like himself and not just a hat wearer, I first had to master hat placement. Placement is the key. He said it makes a twenty-dollar hat look like a hundred dollars and the wearer look like a millionaire.

Jim learned to spot-clean his hats himself, by mixing baby powder with water and dabbing it with a cloth to dry. For general appearances he brushed each hat every time he took it off and before he wore it again. But he couldn't block his hats. That had to be done professionally.

When he could afford it, Jim took his hats uptown to Batsakes. It was one of the few shops in the country that still blocked hats and catered to both locals and celebrities. Pavarotti and Frank Sinatra had their hats blocked there. A picture of Pavarotti wearing one of Batsakes' hats stood in the window to prove it.

I bought my hats down the street from Batsakes at Adams Hats. Adams sold some Stetsons and Dobbs hats, but you had to choose carefully to find quality sky pieces among the rest, Jim used to say. When we worked at Crosley Field selling lemonade, I spent most of my money on clothes to impress the girls. Hat money came afterward. Jim, however, put almost every penny he earned on buying hats. Besides, Jim had eleven brothers and sisters. If he bought clothes, sooner or later his mama would hand something down to one of his brothers. Jim said his head wasn't going to change size and felt his hats were a safer investment. Later, when Black Awareness grew stronger in our neighborhood, Jim's hats came under fire. Many of the brothers wore dashikis and Afros. Though less numerous than the others, brothers wearing skullcaps or tarbushes elicited the strongest reactions. Of the few hat wearers left, only a small group of them wore hats with wide brims.

Big hats with wide brims received a short reprieve through the Blaxploitation film *Super Fly*. Super Fly was one of our heroes in the West End. A black hustler who came from the ghetto like us, played by his own rules, and earned his money by his wits, Super Fly beat the system for us. Not many of the hustlers in our neighborhood had Super Fly's success. Most of them had done time in prison or were doing time. I guess when we compared our lifestyle to his, we needed to believe that we could live like him—that we could be him.

It took Jim and I three years or more before we gave up our big hats. The Super Fly mentality spread throughout the black community like an illness. Wide-brimmed hats and those wearing them became symbols of a drug- and crime-riddled lifestyle. The Black Awareness movement wanted to eradicate that symbol. Ready for any sort of change I easily embraced the new thought, put my hats away, and got me a mean tarbush with red, black, and green stripes woven into it. Jim thought otherwise.

"You look like some kind of militant," he said, when I showed up at his house wearing my tarbush.

"I know," I said, "but I'm tired of people taking me as some kind of pimp or drug dealer when they see me wearing my hat. Super Fly just won't fly anymore."

"Well, my hats cost too much for me to give 'em up for any tarbush or skullcap-wearing brothers. Others can wear 'em if they want to. That's their business. I ain't no pimp and I ain't no dealer. I ain't never seen a hat pimping. So I'm keeping mine." And that's what he did.

Jim was one of the last guys in the neighborhood to give up wearing a big hat. He walked around with it cocked ace-duce over his right ear and right eyebrow as he always had. And nobody ever said anything to him about it, because Jim was Jim.

———————

Jim's house was across the street from mine, and we'd walk out the back of his building, across the alley, and through an empty lot till we came to a mound of crabgrass and dirt that we called Billy Goat Hill. It had never been built on or used as a dump, so there were still some trees around—the kind of dirty, twisted city trees that never grow tall and spout sickly, pale leaves. Summer is hot on concrete, so Jim and I wasted time on Billy Goat Hill sitting on dirt-strangled grass. It was just a little cooler than sitting on concrete and a whole lot softer. It was a good place to hide stuff, even clothes that you didn't want to bring home right away. I once bought a pair of Florsheims that Daddy would have wanted me to take back because they cost too much. I hid them in a secure place on Billy Goat Hill and wore them when I was going to a party or someplace special.

Jim was out back helping me stack bottles one day when the ice cream truck pulled up to the curb in front of Sonny's. I heard the side panel slide up and told Jim, "The MeadowGold truck's outside. Let's go check it out."

I don't know what we expected to find, but for the first time in my memory the MeadowGold man broke his pattern. For his first three trips it was the same as before: side panel up, load ice cream onto hand truck, side panel down, take ice cream away. It never varied: side panel up, load ice cream, side panel down, take ice cream away. But today the MeadowGold man was in a hurry. On his fourth and last trip into the store, the side panel went up, the hand truck was loaded, the load pushed into the store—and the side panel stayed up. Jim and I couldn't believe it. It was like throwing a handful of marbles up in the air, and one stayed up while the others fell. It just wasn't natural. But it was natural to me, because that's the way things happened when Jim was around.

Jim and I looked at each other. There was no need to speak. He eased over next to the truck and stood motionless by the open bay. Moving just his eyes, he peered lazily inside, like an alligator motionless in the water peers at a tasty zebra on shore. Before anyone could react, he reached into the bay, snatched a tub of ice cream, and lobbed it my way. I was standing against the wall at the corner of the store, out of sight near the alley as the tub tumbled toward me with Jim racing behind.

Jim was running so fast he could almost catch the ice cream himself. I couldn't let it fall to the ground. The ice cream would be left behind, just a blob on the sidewalk, not doing anybody any good. I stuck out my hands and caught it like it was a football, turned, and ran down the alley like a split end avoiding garbage cans as if they were tacklers. Jim was at my back. We ran four blocks and stopped in the alley in back of his house to get our breath. I sat with my back against the building, holding the ice cream tub between my legs.

Jim, standing, said, "We can't take this inside. Mama's home, and she'd want to know where it came from. What about your house?"

"That'll be the day. Daddy's at work, but Nellie's there and she will *know* where it came from. She knows I work at Sonny's .... I know!

What about Billy Goat Hill? This will be melting pretty soon, and we've got to find someplace to eat it where we won't be seen."

"Yeah," Jim said. "Billy Goat Hill is the place. But we can't eat the ice cream with our fingers. I'll run in and grab a couple of spoons without anyone noticing it, and we'll be on our way."

Jim came back with the spoons, and we were gone.

The sun was dazzling atop Billy Goat Hill in the middle of the afternoon. Other than at night it was never comfortable up there in the summer. In winter we would nearly freeze to death. That's why it was such a good place to hide things, because even the bums didn't want to stay on Billy Goat Hill. Jim and I had found enough places to make comfortable shelter from the weather among its stunted trees and mounds of dirt and crabgrass where no one could see us.

We reached our favorite spot just short of the top where the trees were thicker, the ground hard and smooth. The trees behind us higher up the slope served as our back wall and had branches hanging forward, creating a roof that left an opening for us to crawl under like a cave. It was a safe spot for eating ice cream. The two-gallon tub of strawberry ice cream was getting soft by the time we settled down, and the sun started poking its fiery fingers into our cave. We had to get to work quickly or the ice cream would be gone.

I loved chocolate ice cream and strawberry was alright, but Jim had to get what was available, so today I loved strawberry. All we had were spoons—no bowls, no napkins to wipe our mouths, no water to wipe the stickiness off of our hands, nothing to take the drippings off our clothes. Just the ice cream, spoons, and us. I had never tried eating a gallon of ice cream before. That's the way we divided it, one for Jim and one for me. We hadn't thought about eating it when we took it, or that it wasn't ours to take. I guess for Jim it was the thrill and challenge of getting away with something, and for me it was the thrill of being a part of it. It was a game with no thought of the endgame.

We started at a fast pace, dipping our spoons almost in unison one behind the other. As our pace slowed and the ice cream got softer, everything got sloppier. Spoons were harder to hold onto, and our hands and chins were thick with stickiness. About halfway through, my stomach felt as if it were a washtub with too many clothes being sloshed around in it. Made only of thin cardboard the ice cream tub was collapsing inward at the middle, and ice cream was seeping out of the bottom and dripping through the seams. It ran like pink water from our spoons when we tried to scoop it up and soaked the front of our shirts. With our hands clutching our stomachs, we both stood up and looked at each other.

"That's it for me," Jim said, looking like a five-year-old who'd eaten without his bib. "If I could, I'd whip myself for doing something so stupid," and he started off down the hill, walking slowly toward the alley.

I didn't want to wait until Daddy got home and chose to take my chance with Nellie. By the time I'd walked upstairs to our apartment, my stomach was a volcano about to erupt. I knocked. Nellie opened the door and I flew to the bathroom before her mind could react to the swoosh that zoomed past. When I returned with a clean face and hands, faintly stained shirt, and a calmed but still knotty stomach, I looked almost normal. Always suspicious of my behavior, Nellie asked, "Some crazy stuff went on up at Sonny's today. They said two guys took off with a two-gallon tub of ice cream. Can you believe it? It would take a real fool to do something like that."

"Yeah," I said. "It would take a real fool to do something like that."

UP MY ALLEY

To be respected on Gest Street I had to know how to fight, shine on the dance floor, dress sharply, and know most of the girls in the area. My status increased with the number of girls I knew. More girls meant increasing my chances of meeting another one to take to bed.

I wore Florsheim shoes and tailor-made pants when I could afford them. Without questioning it, every man in the area wore a hat. Whenever I left the house, I wore my hat. Always. Boys wore caps. Guys in my group favored Dobbses or Stetsons. I preferred a Dobbs, because of the way the brim looked when I snapped it over my brow. Even with all of those other attributes, I still had to be athletic to belong. Being tough sometimes trumped everything else, but it didn't necessarily make you popular or cool. I never aspired to be tough, but the girls didn't mind.

For our own peace of mind, we refused to compete with the world around us. We didn't feel capable, or we lied and said it wasn't worth a damn. So we didn't try. Instead, we fiercely competed against one another in everything, big and small. While competing, I couldn't just beat my opponent. I had to annihilate him.

One of the more competitive challenges at school was the three-standing jump. Some guys could jump sixteen feet in three jumps. Others only twelve. Your success with one jump predicted how well you'd do with three. I've seen guys jump six feet from a standing jump. My best was five and a half. The three-standing jump became one of the challenges that fit our competitive natures and could be blended into our competitions at home.

Jim and I used to jump the alley between his building and the one next door. We both jumped about the same, landing on the farthest sidewalk away in turn. Mr. Frank, who worked for the city, said the standard alley widths were sixteen or twenty feet. The buildings on Gest Street were so old I doubt if their alleys were that wide. Nothing on Gest Street was standard.

Barely wide enough for a garbage truck, Jim's alley looked like a dungeon. The cobblestone bricks and sidewalks just wide enough for garbage cans left spilled and rotten garbage for the roving rats. The sun, on leave from the alley both night and day, concealed any activity within. Anyone desperate or foolish enough to respond to "Meet me in the alley" was definitely from far away.

All but one of the windows in Jim's house faced the street or the wide alley out back. One side abutted the building next door, and the other side faced the dungeon. Withdrawn into a darker world, the alley-side bricks wore coats of mold. Some were wounded, scraped, and full of grime. Others were waiting for an excuse to tumble out of the wall. Lift the window in either of the apartments' bedrooms, and you could look down into that dungeon. The fire escape was a staircase to hell or life rope for survival, depending on your direction.

Fire escapes, anchored into the building under the windows, criss-crossed the alley like dinosaur skeletons. Those box-shaped platforms were death traps. Only items that you didn't care about or were too toxic to stay inside ended up there. With little sunlight and tainted air, the fire escapes weren't fit for sleeping outdoors or growing flowers. Just something solid to hold onto when running away from a fire, though I've never seen any used that way.

Miss Addie, who lived on the third floor, told me someone once tried to get into her apartment from the fire escape. I helped nail her window shut and said, "If there's a fire, Miss Addie, break the window to get out."

She said, "I'm too old and weak to break that window. If a fire's up this far, ain't no use in my running away."

I couldn't understand why anyone used the fire escape. Fire escapes were too noisy and dangerous. Sometimes the ladders came loose from the platforms. At others, they dangled perilously from the wall, waiting to fall under the slightest touch. I was thinking about all of this when Jim asked, "Junior, how far across the alley do you think you can jump?"

"We've jumped it before. You know I can jump it."

"But that's not it. How *far* can you jump over it?"

"Well, if I make a good run I can probably land in the second square standing up. What about you?"

"Let's try it and see."

Jim tried first. He backed up to the line of the third sidewalk square, ran as hard as he could, and jumped. He got up laughing and scraping off his butt from where he'd fallen when he landed.

"I almost made it to the third square."

"Yeah, if you count the part of you sliding on your butt."

"I'm talking about in the air. I landed on both feet. Let's see what you can do."

I backed up to the line of the third sidewalk square just like he did, ran as fast as I could, jumped, and landed just over the line into the third square on the other side.

"You barely made it."

"Yeah, but it was all air and that's what counts."

"You know, if we can jump the alley like this, we can jump from my building to the next just as easy."

It sounded feasible to me.

"I'm game. Let's try it." Without another thought we headed for the roof.

I remembered how Jim's rooftop looked before we'd climbed the stairs. The flat tar and gravel–covered roof resembled a telephone line graveyard. All the families in the building stretched their clotheslines on the roof. Jim's mama said it was so hot up there that her clothes flash dried. The hot tar and gravel rooftop wasn't an ideal runway for our jump. It was the only runway we had.

I knew better than to look down before taking my jump. When Jim and I were younger, we had peeing contests off the roof. Standing as close to the edge as we could, we'd see who could pee the farthest out and last the longest. Nobody ever passed through the alley while we were peeing. It already smelled so bad nobody would have noticed. Jim usually won those contests because he cheated. He lived right downstairs and drank lots of water before we went up to the roof. From four stories away, the bottom of the alley looked as deep as the Grand Canyon.

Right away we saw we had a problem. Though Jim's building was shorter than the neighboring by half a story, its roof was surrounded by a low wall. It couldn't have been more than two feet tall—just a safety marker—but it didn't spell safety for us. Any advantage we had by jumping from a higher to a lower roof looked compromised by that wall.

Talking like an engineer, Jim said, "It's still lower than this roof, but not as much as we thought. We'll just have to jump higher and longer. I can do it. I know you can."

"Alright, once we clear it, we've got the surface to deal with. Did you know the surface was gravel like this? We might slide."

"Yeah, and we might not. It's the same as that we're standing on and what we're going to use for a runway. It better not be slippery, or your daddy won't recognize you when it's over."

Jim let me jump first. I lined up about fifteen feet from the edge and started running. Like a jet taking off, I picked up speed the farther I went, and by the time I reached the edge I expected liftoff. All along my feet had been spitting gravel like a mower throwing stones. Pieces of tar stuck to my shoes like discarded chewing gum, but I kept going for two feet before sliding off the edge. I shot up into the air and hung there for just a fraction of a second, like a basketball player making a dunk. But like a pole vaulter in the Olympics at the crest of his jump, my momentum burst through the pause and thrust me across the alley, over the wall, and onto the roof of the building on the other side. I fell, landed on the gravel of the roof, and slid like a spatula scraping tar. After I stopped rolling, I jumped up, looked back at Jim on the other side, lifted my arms like a prizefighter, and yelled, "Get some of this with your bad ass."

OVER THE BURGERVILLE WALL

Despite everything else it represented, Gest Street was my throughway to baseball heaven. Crosley Field, the home of the Cincinnati Reds, was less than ten miles from our building. Consequently, everybody on our street had baseball fever, including Daddy. Before we had a TV we used to listen to the Reds' announcer, Waite Hoyt, a Hall of Famer and former Reds pitcher, call the game on the radio. Every sound of the ballpark came pouring vividly through Waite's description. When you heard the sweet crack of Big Ted Klusewski's bat against the ball, the next sound was Waite's trumpeting tenor pushing the ball "Up, up, up, and over the Burgerville Wall." You could feel Hoyt leaping up out of his seat and pushing the ball over the wall with his every breath. Daddy and every other man and boy on the street would puff his chest out a little farther, smile, and say, "Big Klu did it again."

Gest Street gave me baseball, the Reds, and Mark's Drugs. Six blocks down the street from our building, Little League and neighborhood teams played in a full-size ballpark in the Gest Street Park. Our neighborhood team regularly played teams from other parts of the city and usually won. Mark's Drugs, the biggest drugstore in the area, sponsored a team each year, and their team always won the neighborhood championship. One summer our team met their qualifications, and Mark's Drugs chose to sponsor us for the season.

Playing for Mark's Drugs was like playing for the Reds. When I played for Mark's Drugs I played right field like Frank "Robby" Robinson on the Reds. Mark's Drugs not only had the winningest teams in our league each year, but also paid for those orange and blue uniforms that looked just like the pros. They gave us everything: hat, shirt, pants, and even the cleats. *Even the cleats.* When I tied on the cleats it was like tying on the whole baseball field. The scrunch and grinding bite of the cleats into the grass transported me into Crosley Field. Once I tied those cleats on, I was gone.

To top it all off, I put on my uniform at home, walked down the three flights of stairs to the hallway, stepped out of the hallway onto the street, and slung my cleats over my left shoulder to walk the six blocks to Gest Street Park. I felt like a hero going off to battle. Along each side of the sidewalk, Jim's sisters and other girls on the block, but especially Jim's sisters, worshipped every step I took toward the field. I could have marched to the field and back all day long, and never even lifted a bat, just to see their eyes each time I passed. Gest Street had its good days.

When Jim and I got jobs working for SportService at Crosley Field, things got even better. Only sixteen years old at the time, we had to get our parents to sign a permission slip before we were officially hired. Daddy thought giving me permission to work might straighten me out, so he jumped at the chance to sign my slip. Jim's mother was happy to see him make his own money because she needed help feeding her other eleven children.

With our permission slips signed, Jim and I were free to go to work at Crosley Field. We couldn't believe we had gotten inside so easily. Crosley Field was the Emerald City, our Nirvana, Mount Olympus—the place where baseball gods lived in the flesh and we walked their hallowed ground.

Underneath the stands, SportService was king, and our entry into Major League Baseball and its kingdom behind the magic began. Under age and too young to make top money as beer vendors, Jim and I were given jobs selling lemonade, the lowest on the totem pole. We didn't care because we earned some money and had the chance to see our baseball gods in person, playing up close and live. What could be better than that?

On that first day, I walked out of the tunnel carrying my tray of ten cups of lemonade on a strap around my neck. When I looked up and saw that manicured field so deeply green it shone like an emerald, Waite Hoyt's vivid descriptions on the radio faded into shadow. The sand of the infield was brushed so smooth that a caterpillar's passing would have been a profanity to its perfection and a curse to my baseball dreams.

I walked up and down the steep stairs between the rows of seats calling, "Lemonade, lemonade, lemonade," and made a few sales that way. It didn't take long for me to jazz it up to "Lemonade, lemonade, lemonade, the best in the West, the most from the coast. Have fun, have a lemonade." After that, hands shot up and people began calling out, "Lemonade, lemonade here," and the money started rolling in.

I made twenty-five cents for every cup of lemonade sold, and SportService made seventy-five. Each tray meant two dollars and fifty cents in my pocket. Ten trays meant twenty-five dollars. On most games with a full house I averaged nine trays, and on doubleheaders sixteen. It was hard to average ten trays due to people leaving after the seventh inning or my checking out before the game ended. Between games or at the seventh-inning stretch, Jim and I ate hoagies in the bowels of the stadium with the other vendors. After the third inning, when everyone had an idea of how their sales were going, we'd order hoagies from Judy's Hoagies, the best in the West End. I've never eaten a hoagie as juicy or tasted better than those I ate sitting under the stands at Crosley Field on dirty benches with Jim and the sounds of the game echoing throughout the tunnel.

After the game we'd all line up at the supervisor's window, turn in the day's chits, one chit for each tray sold, and get our cash. Then we'd go to the locker room, take off the blue and white SportService uniform—still stiff from having lemonade slopped onto it—throw it into the laundry basket, and change into our clothes.

I felt good going home with money in my pocket. I could stash some away for emergencies and still have enough to show Daddy in case he asked me how much I made. Piece by piece I added items to my wardrobe so that they weren't noticed immediately or at all. I never wanted to admit how much money I really made. Daddy may have thought having too much money of my own might make me too independent and more difficult to manage. I loved working at Crosley Field because of that independence. My stint there lasted for two seasons before the price of my independence came due.

PEANUT JIM

If Crosley Field had a mascot, it was Peanut Jim. Before you got inside to see Robby, Big Klu, or Pete Rose, you saw a tall, dark man wearing a stovepipe hat and tails. He stood behind a cart with two big metal wheels in back and two smaller ones in front that rested on stalks that folded up like those on a card table when not in use. His coat and hat were black, but everything else about him was colorful. He wore a red shirt, blue pants, and brown shoes. If you went to Crosley Field to see the Cincinnati Reds, you saw Peanut Jim.

Peanut Jim didn't just sell peanuts. He *was* peanuts. You smelled Jim's peanuts before you saw him. The smell of roasted peanuts hovering around the stadium's front gate embraced and caressed you as you approached and forever linked you, Peanut Jim, and Crosley Field. His big roaster was always roaring, trying to keep Jim's customers happy. Rain or shine, his customers were there. Peanut Jim bought an awning and attached a frame to his cart to hang it on just for them. He took no days off. If the Reds played, the fans wanted Peanut Jim there. He was part of their experience, part of their game.

When I left Gest Street, Peanut Jim was famous. The *Cincinnati Enquirer* printed an article about him that showed a picture of Jim with his cart in his usual spot outside the stadium. He still looked spry to some, I guess, but I had worked at Crosley Field and had spent some time with Peanut Jim. He was okay, but wasn't as spry as he'd like folk to believe, and he hadn't always been the Peanut Man.

Peanut Jim said he knew who my daddy was, my real daddy. Even before I started selling lemonade at Crosley Field, I had bought peanuts from Peanut Jim. When I started working there I bought a bagful almost every day. One day after a group of customers left Jim and me alone, he looked at me quizzically and asked, "Who's your daddy, boy?"

"Lou, works over the river in Newport at the Chevrolet dealer. You know him?"

"Naw. Go on. Take your peanuts," he said.

Three days later when I was back at Peanut Jim's cart again, I asked for a bag of peanuts. He gave them to me, took my money, and said, "Stand over there by the side. I'll give you your change in a minute."

It was longer than a minute, but after he'd taken care of everyone else he called me over and said, "Is your mama's name Cassie?"

I really didn't want to talk about my mama with Peanut Jim, so I said, "My mama's dead, Jim."

"I'm sorry. If your mama's named Cassie, maybe you Big Red's boy. Must be somebody else."

"Must be, because I don't know no Big Red."

I wasn't surprised to hear that Peanut Jim and my real daddy were in prison together. Nearly everyone I knew had a relative who was either in prison, going to prison, or out of prison on parole. Mama had already told me that Big Red died in prison, and we all knew you were sent to the Ohio Penitentiary to do "hard time." The following day during the seventh-inning stretch I ran out to Peanut Jim's cart again.

"You remember the last time we talked?" I asked. "You said you were in O.P. with Big Red. Listen, do you know what he was in for?"

"Wasn't my business to know. All I know is he was doing six to twenty-five years. What for, I don't know."

"Thanks," I said and turned to walk away.

"Wait, maybe he ain't your daddy. He died in the joint. They say he had some kind of fit, fell, and broke his neck climbing stairs. He had one when I was there, too."

I nodded my head in thanks and walked back toward the stadium. As I thought about it later, I didn't have any feeling of loss or anything. No hatred either. Mama talked about him before, and I hadn't remembered until now. About a month before she went to the hospital, she'd shown me a brown, hand-tooled leather purse that she kept in the bottom of her dresser. "Junior, your real father, Big Red, sent me this purse when you were two. I want you to know that Lou has been good to us, but he's not your real daddy. Lou doesn't have to know I told you this, but I want you to know. He already thinks I pay too much attention to you and not to the girls because you look like Red. Your sisters are your sisters, you just have different fathers. Okay? Now keep it to yourself. You may need it someday."

My sisters never knew that we didn't have the same father. Mama never told them, and neither did Daddy. Unlike most other kids in the neighborhood with different fathers and the same mother, we didn't think of ourselves as half- or stepbrothers and -sisters. We were all one and the same as far as we knew or cared. When we met Daddy's eight other children from three previous marriages, they also became our brothers and sisters. Step-relations had no place in our family. I kept it so hidden from myself that I had forgotten it until I'd talked to Peanut Jim.

Thinking back, I owe Peanut Jim for clearing up something I'd been wanting to find the answer to for quite a while. If Peanut Jim was right about Big Red having fits, that proved he was my real father because I also had fits. Maybe my father did die in prison, as Jim said. At least it was an accident. At least no one killed him, and I was glad to hear that. I felt more connected to Big Red now because I had something that was passed down to me through him. Big Red was my father, and I was his son.

I didn't have fits, or seizures as the doctors called them, until I moved to Gest Street. That's where I started partying. At first Jim and I went to dances on Thursdays at the Lincoln Court Community Center on Clark Street. Many of the girls from the Laurel Homes projects would also come down. Between them and the girls we knew from our neighborhood, Jim and I were invited to more parties than we could handle.

Many of the house parties were held in basements and cost twenty-five cents to get in. Apartment parties were usually free, but regardless of where they were held, Jim and I would find our way there—Jim with his big hat, and I was dressed to kill. Once inside Jim knew what to do. He would unscrew the lightbulb and stack 45s on the record player, all slow dances. His favorites were Jerry Butler, Smokey Robinson & the Miracles, Sam Cooke, and anything else we could grind by. Sometimes it got so hot it was like doing it standing up.

Jim always said, "It's best to slow dance with girls we know and safest when the dance is in our neighborhood. Ain't either of us going to a dance someplace else without the other. Bet?"

"You better know it," I always answered.

I felt fairly safe the night that I went to the dance in the Lincoln Court without Jim. Though it was in the West End like us, the Lincoln Court with its one thousand apartments in fifty-three buildings was large enough to be considered its own part of town. Growing up in the projects was almost like being in prison. To stay alive, you either beat someone up or got beaten up yourself. With the buildings standing so close together and most the same color, the Lincoln Court resembled prison blocks. Its concrete playground hemmed in by the tall buildings was a smaller variation of the prison yard. Mix all the noise and filth with the wired balconies resembling tiered prison cells, and the setting was complete. Living in the Lincoln Court made being sent to prison a farce. Going to prison from the Lincoln Court wasn't leaving anything. It was coming home. As a matter of fact, one of the guys I met said, "The only difference between prison and the projects is that in prison there are no women and dogs. Other than that it's all the same." I'd heard all that before. To hell with that. I had been invited to a party by a girl I'd wanted to get closer to for weeks. Tonight was my chance.

I told Jim about it, but he couldn't go. His mother was in the hospital, and with his father at work Jim was keeping an eye on his younger sisters and brothers.

"Be careful, man," he said. "Don't give them any excuse to start anything. They'll mess you up."

The party was on the third floor, and I could hear the music before I reached the second-floor landing. When I reached 302 the door was open, so I walked right in. It was jam-packed. I wore my black Ban-Lon sweater over tailor-made Denato pants with Kangaroo Florsheims on my feet. Squeezing my way through the crowd I heard someone call, "Junior, you came."

I turned and saw Pearl, the girl who'd invited me. She waved for me to come over. Her black hair was newly pressed to just below her ears. Eyes so dark the sun couldn't touch them, and her lips outlined the whitest teeth I'd ever seen. She wore a white blouse over a tan knee-length skirt that was so tight I could see every muscle in her hips move as she walked. After reaching me she hugged me and said, "I didn't think you'd really come. Let's dance."

We danced one slow dance after another. We didn't change partners, didn't look at anyone else, just danced. I was breathing like a locomotive on fire and felt as hard and flexible as galvanized rubber each time Pearl and I twisted our bodies into each other to the music's beat. I didn't know what time it was, but it was late when I heard someone say, "Yeah, Big Otis ain't gonna like this shit one bit. Just wait till Big Otis gets here."

I didn't know Big Otis and if they were referring to Pearl or to me. As good as I felt, I didn't care one way or the other. Big Otis didn't come and Pearl hugged me as if she didn't want to let go, but the party had ended and I had to leave. Nearly everyone else had left when I started back down the stairs. When I reached the second-floor landing all the hallway lights went out. Total blackness swallowed me whole. In that same instant, someone pushed me down the concrete stairs into the first-floor hallway. I hit step after steel step like a punctured bouncing ball. A pain so intense it tried to outrun itself jetted from the bottom of my feet to my head and back again, and for a moment I died. In the next instant, sound pressed against my head like smothered voices underwater. Then I heard a voice from upstairs say, "Here he is, Big Otis. This is the motherfucker who was dancing with Pearl."

Another voice shouted, "Stupid motherfucker coming over here to dance with my woman," and jackhammered me in the ribs with his foot. "Fuck him up," he commanded.

And they did. There must have been four or five of them, because it felt like I was being kicked and stomped by a herd of frenzied beasts. Everyone was cursing and shouting. The sound of their kicks hitting my body was like a ram's head slamming against rock. It felt like my stomach was about to split open and squish its contents through my navel. The ones at my back ruptured the darkness with blinding lights with each kick to my spine. I took all of this without calling for help, for who would help me, an outsider in the Lincoln Court? Besides, I was stupid enough to believe the street life propaganda. If I could survive this beating, I'd have a rep and nobody would mess with me again. I rolled around trying to protect my neck, tried unsuccessfully to get into a fetal position to protect my genitals, and tried to protect my face. I cursed, spat blood, and swore I'd get even, but I never begged for them to stop. Anyone could get beaten up, but only a coward would plead for them to stop. Chili, one of the toughest guys in our neighborhood, had gotten stomped once in a fight out in Millville. He wouldn't stop fighting and kept trying to get up while the Millville guys kept kicking him. Finally, Smitty, their leader, said, "We'll have to kill this stupid motherfucker before he quits. I ain't going to jail for his stupid ass. Let him go." After that nobody wanted to mess with Chili. Nobody, unless they were prepared to kill him. I was thinking about Chili as I was having my ass kicked. To get beaten up and beg, too, that was something I couldn't live down. I was holding my own and they couldn't put me away when two things happened almost simultaneously. Someone wearing pointed shoes kicked me in the balls and I screamed so loudly in pain that it woke the whole building. As I learned later, at the same time Big Otis kicked me violently in the back of the head and my lights went out.

When I awoke at General Hospital all bandaged up, tubes in my arm, and smelling like a toilet, the nurse said the gang had peed on me before the police arrived. A woman on the second floor called the police after hearing me scream. I stayed in the hospital for two nights. No serious injuries, nothing broken, just lots of bruising and swelling.

When Daddy saw me he said, "You really messed up, Junior. I'm not going to do anything to you this time. They've already done more than I could do. Just keep your ass off the streets and you'll be alright."

Two weeks after that I had my first seizure.

PUNCHING MY TICKET

Condemned buildings held treasuries of window weights. They were full of blank windows concealing two iron sashes in every frame. Each window sash weighed ten pounds. Navigator Jack, who sold more scrap iron than anybody I knew, said he got ten dollars for every one hundred pounds of scrap iron he sold at the junkyard. Jim and I needed five windows to make ten dollars.

Ten o'clock on Sunday morning I met Jim on the sidewalk near his house on Thirteenth Street. As we walked toward the condemned building on Boone Street just two blocks away, Jim asked if we weren't wasting our time digging rusty window weights out of old window frames.

"Well," I said, "broken windows don't need window weights. Someone has already taken the radiators out of the building, and they weighed a ton. Imagine how much money they got. Those sashes are about all that's left, and we've got to get at least ten windows if we want to make anything. After all, it's a condemned building. Everything will be gone if we don't move now."

I got there first, stepped high over the stoop, and pushed past the door into the first floor. The mustiness was so overpowering I could almost chew it and spit it out. I felt woozy holding my breath while going up the shattered stairway. When I reached the third floor, I looked through an open door in front of us and saw an empty window frame.

After reaching the wall together, we split open the sides of the window frame with claw hammers. Everybody in our neighborhood had a claw hammer, like in some neighborhoods everybody had a gun or knife. Daddy had a claw hammer and crowbar that he kept in the trunk of his car. "Don't touch my crowbar," he told me once. His once was enough. Not willing to die I never touched his crowbar.

Jim and I got thirty window weights out and stacked in the downstairs hall before noon. I stood guard while Jim ran home to get an old wooden pallet with wheels attached that we'd use to load the weights. Afterward, we'd hide them in the alley behind his house till the junkyard opened on Monday.

When Jim returned we loaded the weights onto the pallet and covered them with his little brother Jesse's bedspread. Jim took a serious risk taking Lazy Eye's spread. Lazy Eye's left eyelid drooped over a rheumy yellow thing that rolled from side to side. None of us who knew him ever made fun of Lazy Eye. A guy from Boone Street almost laughed when he first saw Lazy Eye. Jim and I stopped breathing and tried to look away, not wanting to witness what might happen. Lazy Eye walked over to the guy and jammed his bad eye into the other's face. He cupped hardened palms around each side of the stranger's face and pressed. We heard a soft clap as if Lazy Eye's hands had come together through his face. It wasn't a clap we heard but the soft snap of a fractured jawbone muffled by skin. None of us ever called him Lazy Eye to his face, not even Jim.

Jim and I hadn't realized how noisy we had been for a Sunday morning. Sunday was really nothing special in our house. Even when Mama was alive we didn't go to church regularly. Jim had eleven brothers and sisters. His mama seldom had time for church, although she did take some of the younger kids now and then. Evidently, someone else didn't go to church either, because that must've been who called the police. The police stopped us before we could get the pallet to the alley.

Jim and I were arrested and taken to the Juvenile Detention Center at 2020 Auburn Avenue. We were told we'd be there overnight until we could see a case worker on Monday. Our parents were notified. Jim's mother came to see him, but our phone was out of service because last month's bill wasn't paid. Jim's mother said she'd tell Daddy, which only made matters worse for me. Daddy got upset because his "personal business was out in the street," and she found that he was behind on his bill.

Monday the Juvenile Court judge sentenced Jim and me to thirty days in the Detention Center: one week for trespassing and three weeks for destruction of private property. The judge said she was lenient with us because we were both sixteen years old and hadn't been in her court before. Jim and I accepted the sentence chins up.

"2020" was who you were once you'd been there. It was a place you didn't want to go, and once you'd been there it was always a part of you. In our neighborhood, 2020 meant making the grade.

We shared a common dayroom and tried to find ways to waste time and wear the clock down with about thirty other juveniles. We ate tasteless food three times a day and spent the rest of the time in our cells, called "rooms," with a bed, dresser, chair, and no mirror.

Having to spend so much time alone in my room gave me lots of time to read. Our time alone was supposedly a time to think, to reflect on what brought us there. I think its real purpose was to minimize our time spent together and to keep us from causing trouble. Someone had decided that a library might help achieve both of those ends. I agreed. I often got into trouble for reading at home. "Stop reading at the table," Daddy would warn at dinner. "Turn out that light, Junior," he'd yell from his bedroom. "Don't you know how late it is?" Yet while locked up in my room at 2020, I read almost nonstop. *The Man in the Iron Mask, The Count of Monte Cristo, The Three Musketeers*, and my favorite, *Treasure Island*, with wonderful illustrations by Andrew Wyeth, helped carry me through. *The Call of the Wild* and *White Fang* often left me misty-eyed. Even though Jim knew I liked to read, I didn't want it spread throughout the unit. My being a book lover wasn't the kind of impression I needed to make.

We were told what to do and what not to do. We had restrictions for everything: no loud talking, no rough-housing, no being out of place, and no reading in your room after ten o'clock. And worst of all, no visits if caught breaking any of those rules. Jim and I had heard about 2020 for most of our lives, and we were only there for four weeks. Our futures were mangled by those weeks.

Twenty-twenty Auburn Avenue wasn't exactly the Ohio Reformatory at Mansfield, but it was close enough. On the road to the Ohio Penitentiary, 2020 enrolled you into elementary crime school. It put juvenile offenders like Jim and me on the conveyor belt to jail. The Boys Industrial School—BIS, as we knew it—imprisoned juveniles with serious offenses in an industrial learning center for longer periods. Given enough time you could easily graduate to BIS from 2020. Mansfield Reformatory, the prison for convicted felons under twenty-one, was the crime college where most BIS graduates ended up. Road's end—the Ohio Penitentiary—was the place where criminal studies ended due to advanced age. Occasionally, freshmen from Mansfield started new studies based on their past failures. As the portal to a series of steps designed to lock us into a lifelong system of imprisonment, the specter of 2020 hovered over the West End like a hawk ready to swoop down and devour every male alive.

Once a person had done time in Mansfield, nothing worse could happen. It was a pre–Civil War prison with five-story-high cellblocks housing thirty two-man cells per tier. New prisoners from small towns seldom made it through. They were chewed up by the violence shortly after they arrived. Even prisoners from larger cities did their best to survive. Guys our age after returning from 2020 tried to assume the Mansfield air. Coming home from 2020 was like riding our bikes for the first time without training wheels. We weren't bona fide felons, but we had certified criminal records. Surely that counted for something.

Most girls in our neighborhood would love to have a boyfriend who'd been to Mansfield. Often their mamas would, too. They believed that any man who had survived Mansfield could protect them from the dangers on the streets. No one cared why someone was sentenced to Mansfield. His survival alone said enough. Everyone knew that anyone who'd been to Mansfield wasn't supposed to be afraid of anyone. Some were even dangerous. When it came down to it, a girl with a boyfriend who'd been to Mansfield knew that her abusive father would get hurt if he laid a hand on her again.

Jim and I knew many of the guys who went to Mansfield before they had gotten sentenced. We liked hanging out with them almost as much as the girls, but for other reasons. The guys from Mansfield demanded respect from most other guys and were girl magnets. We got invited to the best dances just from being around them.

But not everyone who went to Mansfield came home a girl magnet. Jim's cousin Ted joined the Black Muslims while he was there and changed his name to Ted X. He didn't go to dances anymore, wore a suit and tie, stopped eating pork, and talked about the White Devil. Another guy who'd been with Ted in Mansfield said that Ted prayed in Arabic a lot and scolded them for selling out to the Devil. Nobody challenged Ted because of his previous reputation for unprovoked violence and were afraid of what he might do. When Ted came home, most people stayed away from him. We certainly did.

If 2020 was small potatoes compared to Mansfield, it was often a stepping-stone along the way. Twenty-twenty started you off with a record and entered your name into the criminal justice system. And once you were in the system, you were in it for life. It crushed your adolescence and ravaged your future. Best known for its networking, 2020 introduced you to other juveniles throughout the city. You learned how to shoplift, where to fence stolen goods, and in which beauty parlors and barbershops to sell them. If you didn't already know, you learned how to steal cars. Posing as a juvenile detention center, 2020 Auburn Avenue was known throughout the city as the expressway to Mansfield.

When Jim and I returned to Gest Street after just thirty days in 2020, the guys on our block listened to us with more respect. A few even looked at us warily, not sure of how we would behave. When one of us made a hard foul on the basketball court and knocked someone down, no one jumped up itching for a fight. Three days after we were home, Jim and I walked upon Eddie-B and a group of guys huddled together in a circle behind Sonny's store. The circle opened for us as a bottle of wine was being passed around. Before passing it to me, one of the guys looked at Eddie-B. Eddie-B wiped his open palm across his face, paused, and said, "Give Youngblood a drink."

Jim and I were part of the circle now. Our ticket was punched. We were riding the express train to prison and had no way of knowing whether this train would make it to the station or jump the tracks.

HITTING THE STREETS

It was late October. Winter was stalking the alleys but not yet in the sunlit streets. I got home late from playing basketball at the center, and Daddy was mad because I was past curfew without letting him know. When I walked upstairs and stepped into the kitchen I knew immediately that something was wrong. No light was on in the living room, the TV was off, and the house was quiet. It was after eleven o'clock, and after basketball I had gone over to Jim's house to see his sister Barb. The eleven o'clock curfew had come and gone, but I was only down the street. What difference could it make? Well, it made a big one.

My stepmother, Nellie, and my sisters were asleep when I came home, but as soon as she heard me, Nellie got up. "You're lucky you came home when you did, Junior. Lou's out in the streets looking for you and says wherever he finds you, he's gonna whip your ass all the way back home. How many times you going to keep staying out like this when he's told you to be in? He's going to kill you this time. I don't know 'bout you, but if it was me, I wouldn't be here when he gets back."

I'd been looking for an excuse like that ever since I'd gotten out of 2020, so I didn't waste time talking. I grabbed a sandwich from the refrigerator, got my heavy coat from the closet, went through the front room and into Daddy's bedroom, opened the window, and climbed down the fire escape. I didn't want to run into him coming up the stairs while I was going down. Somebody might get hurt.

Summertime is the best time for running away. The days are longer, nights warmer, people are outside, and it's easier to blend into a crowd. I made a fool's escape in my running away. The night was king except for the streetlights. Anybody with any sense was inside at this time of night, and the cold was pinching me all over. For relief, I made a beeline for the first place that popped into my mind: the White Castle.

I slept anywhere that offered warmth and shelter. The White Castle was up on the hill on Reading Road, and it took me twenty minutes to get there. From outside it looked warm and cozy, but after I got in and sat down, I found the lights were almost too bright for sleeping. It was open twenty-four hours a day, and things began to slow down when the late shift started at eleven. There were only two workers instead of the daytime four, and the heat was turned down. There, amid the morguelike whiteness of the restaurant's starkly bright interior, I sat at the booth farthest from the counter. I bought a cup of coffee for a quarter that rented me the booth for an hour. I sat in the darkest part of the room, sipping it slowly so that I wouldn't be thrown out as a vagrant in case the police walked in. To warm myself I held both hands around the cup and let its heat radiate through my fingers. In moments, I felt the heat needling up my arms, but it didn't last long enough to warm me any further. The temperature in the restaurant seemed stuck on low, and I got up to leave.

I had to use the bathroom before I left and didn't want to chance peeing outside. So I walked to the back, put a dime in the slot in the toilet door, pushed it open, stepped inside, and shut it behind me. Because of addicts shooting up in its bathrooms at night, White Castle locked its doors to keep them out. But no locked door could keep addicts out if they needed to get inside. They slid through at the bottom despite the filthy floor. Locked doors barely slowed them down.

Relieved after peeing, I pulled my collar tightly around my neck, left the White Castle, and headed south toward the Laundromat on Vine. I remembered seeing it a couple of days earlier when going to the center there to play basketball. It was about two in the morning by then, and the only people on the streets were hustlers and bums. The bars would be closing at 2:30 a.m., and this was a bleak time before that group hit the streets. I wanted to be careful not to be seen. Hustlers might try to rip me off or the cops might pick me up, and either way I'd be the loser— a hustler taking whatever I had, or the cops throwing me around and then locking me up for being out so late. Worse yet, they'd call my daddy to pick me up. Staying out of sight was the best way to go.

Walking hunched over and alone, I felt sorry for leaving my sisters. They couldn't run away. Poverty shadowed their every move. Poverty lived in their clothes, settling in their school lunch bags and in their holey drawers revealed in play. Wanda, the oldest, was now their protector. Each sister in turn protected the other until it reached my baby brother, Jerome. Being the oldest I escaped their lot by running away and leaving poverty for them to bear without me. I embraced a newfound poverty of aloneness on poorly lit streets and White Castle restaurants, where for a twenty-five-cent cup of coffee I rented a stool to wait for the sun to awaken me before the day shift arrived.

It had gotten colder, and as I reached Vine Street near Liberty I saw the harsh neon light of the Laundromat splash against the night. I stopped and hugged tight to a building a block away before getting any closer. From where I stood I could see there was no one inside. I moved forward slowly, looking all around me to make sure that no one was watching. A whoosh of warm air embraced me the moment I stepped inside. I closed my eyes. It was sweet. I swore I would never run away in cold weather again.

I was getting sleepy. The tables for folding clothes on my left weren't strong enough to support me, and besides, they could be seen from outside. The two plastic chairs wouldn't help. Even if pushed together they were too small, and their curved sides and backs would have made sleep impossible. Looking at the bank of dryers against one wall I knew I'd found a place where I could sleep safely and out of sight. I'd seen the repairman go behind the dryers to fix them in the neighborhood Laundromat before. At the end of the bank of dryers he'd entered a closed-in space behind the machines, just wide enough for his shoulders and tall enough to stand. I went to the end of the dryers and found that both setups were the same. Without worrying about dust, spiders, rats, or even being electrocuted, I pushed my way through tangled wires and clouds of dust and dirt. Crushing spiders along the way, I fell to my rest behind the dryers in the Laundromat on Liberty and Vine.

I used my Laundromat bed for a week before I got evicted. My early-morning visits had gone unnoticed until I slept too late one morning and was nearly suffocated by the heat of working dryers. I sneaked out of my hidden Hilton too quickly, frightening a couple of women with children, and I knew my days were numbered. I walked quickly out of the door trying to keep my face averted. I knew what would happen next, and it did. The women called the police and made a report. As I watched the Laundromat late that night I saw a police car roll slowly by. Ten minutes later a cop walked casually inside, checked behind the dryers, and walked out.

The Laundromat was no longer safe, so I searched for a building that was isolated—ideally near a vacant lot or sitting far enough away from the sidewalk that it wouldn't easily attract attention. Seeing one surrounded on three sides by a vacant lot with the other side facing an alley, I found quarters for the night. Approaching the building I saw it had been condemned for quite a while. It leaned to the right. Fallen bricks were scattered about, and every window and door was missing or ravaged. *Perfect*, I said to myself. *Perfect.*

The bars were closed, and every minute threatened my exposure, increasing my chances of being caught. Entering the naked door frame that tilted sideways across the stoop, I picked my way through the hallway floor debris and started tipping up the rickety stairs. Used to climbing crumbling stairways, I knew how to place each footfall carefully and how much weight to place on each step. Too much pressure and my foot would crash through. I couldn't risk falling. One misstep could be my last.

I carefully reached the gutted third floor. As I crossed the open floor littered with empty White Castle bags, crushed paper cups, and wine bottles, I could barely make out an unkempt form laying partially hidden by a pile of debris. His head of dirty, puffy cotton lay propped against the wall for a pillow. Even at the distance of a few feet, the stench of filth and vomit was so intense that the odor grabbed me by the throat and left me gagging.

Struggling to breathe, I heard the stairs creak behind me and I stepped quickly to the edge of the open staircase and looked down. I saw the staircase between the second and third floors begin to sway, and a moment later watched it crash to the floor below. With the lower end of the steps gone I could sleep undisturbed if it hadn't been for the pile of filth stretched out before me. I tiptoed forward Indianlike, one foot in front of the other, until I was standing over him. Covered with bloated patches of black skin, his face looked like a patched-up bicycle tire gone flat. *Maybe that's where the smell came from*, I thought. He had a grizzled thatch of gray hair that stuck out like bristles on a brush. But the most remarkable thing about him was his hands. They were large, looked strong, and were cleaner than the rest of his body. I didn't want to risk his waking up while I was sleeping, but I had no other choice than to wake him.

I didn't want to touch him so I called out, "Hey man, wake up. Get up. Let's talk." At first he didn't move, and I thought he didn't hear me. But in the next moment he instantly awoke, closed his fingers around my shin like a hydraulic press, and nearly pulled me to the floor. Stunned by the attack I pulled back, sickened by his having touched me and tried to kick myself free. Holding my ankle in his viselike grip, he used my leg to pull himself up. That's when I saw his knife.

"Listen, Youngblood," he hissed. "I'll fuck you up if you don't get out of here. You hear me? I'll fuck you up. Move it."

Standing, he pushed me and backed away, pointing his knife in my direction. It wasn't a switchblade or anything like that. His large, muscular hand gripped a hunting knife with a fist-size handle and a wicked nine-inch blade. It looked like he could skin rats with it or people if he got the chance. I was too jumbled to think, let alone talk. I slowly backed away while keeping my eyes on his knife. Careful not to trip, I turned and ran. Reaching the remaining staircase, I leaped to the hallway floor without breaking my stride. I landed on both feet, still, yet somehow in motion. My brain wouldn't catch up, and I couldn't still my trembling muscles. All I could do was stand in place.

I decided it was time to go home.

———

"We thought you were dead," Daddy said when I walked through the door. "You didn't call. No one had seen you. Why don't you sit down, get something to eat, and go in there and take a bath?"

I hadn't realized how ragged I looked, how dirty and unkempt or how I smelled until then. He looked stern, but I saw genuine concern in his eyes. *Maybe he had been worried*, I thought. Was there a little bit of Sport still left in him? Had I missed it all along?

After I was all cleaned up and changed into some of the clothes I'd left behind, he called me back into the kitchen. My sisters weren't allowed. Just Daddy, Nellie, and me sitting around the table talking about my future.

"I should whip you till tomorrow comes for that crazy shit you pulled. Don't you know what you put your sisters through? They never stop asking, 'What's Junior doing? Where's Junior?' You don't care about anybody but yourself. If you want to stay in my house, some things are going to have to change. Do you understand that? If you keep on doing what you're doing, you're going to wind up in jail. I can see it coming. And when it happens I can't help you. Just remember you brought it on yourself."

"Yes, Sir," I said. He made sense. I realized I could easily end up in jail the way I was going. But I didn't care. I wanted him to feel bad, to feel responsible. He was the one who'd brought me back to the West End.

"When Nellie tells you to do something, stop acting like a fool and do what she says. She won't say anything that I ain't already told her to. Okay?"

"Okay, Daddy," I answered. I wonder if she told him about those times she had me zip up her girdle before she was going out with him. I bet she didn't say anything about that. I sure wasn't going to. I didn't want to get killed.

"It's a good thing you found your way back when you did," said Nellie.

"Why?" I asked. "What's going on?"

Daddy said, "We're getting ready to move."

I said, "Where 'bouts?"

"We don't know yet, but it's somewhere out of the city," said Nellie.

"It should be in a month or so. The construction company's still working on the new expressway, I-71. It will be going up by Madisonville pretty soon, and I can get more hours if we live up that way," Daddy said.

I couldn't imagine where that might be or how it came about. Except for living with the Jacksons in Walnut Hills, we'd lived in the West End for as long as I could remember. Nothing could be worse than the West End, or could it? If I could get out of the West End I might find my way back to a real future. Regardless of what the move meant to him, I was still angry. If I'd never returned to the West End, I'd still be in Walnut Hills. Had we moved earlier I may have escaped its legacy: my juvenile criminal record. Whether it became a platform to build an adult record on or some filth left behind in the mud made little difference to me then. I was too angry to care.

BOOK FOUR

MADEIRA

Madeira, Ohio, looked as if Norman Rockwell had painted it. With our move to Madeira we'd stepped off the West End's police blotter onto the cover of the *Saturday Evening Post*. No two places could have been less alike.

I thought the ride through the city and up Camargo Pike to Madeira would take forever.

"When are when going to get there, Daddy?" I asked.

"We're almost there."

That's when I heard the train whistle to my left. Looking up the embankment I saw a freight train clipping along beside us. In less than five minutes the train had passed.

"It wasn't that loud," said Nellie.

"I told you," Daddy said. "Twice a day. It'll be in back of us. You'll hardly hear it."

We entered Madeira through Euclid Avenue. Euclid ran across town, and every intersecting street had a proper name except First Street. First Street was near the train depot, a geographical identity, not a social one like where I'd come from. We didn't see any streets with numbers for names. Numbers made you a victim instead of a person. Another Rockwell touch, all of the houses had gabled roofs and were two stories or less. As if by rule, none of the buildings in town had flat roofs.

The town sign read, "Madeira Village, The Friendly Town, Population 6,250." Nearly matching the combined population of three of Cincinnati's largest high schools, I wondered how many of the people were black.

Everyday people walked around doing what to them were ordinary things: walking in and out of neighbors' homes, stopping and talking in small shops downtown. Madeira kids were different from West End kids. They didn't seem to be afraid of adults or of each other. They laughed more, even in the cold. From my first impression, it all looked good. I only wished that it would hold. What held most clings to me still. Everyone was clean. Their clothes looked as if they'd just put them on that morning. On Gest Street we sometimes wore the same pants for the entire week. The streets, the yards, the buildings, everywhere I looked I found clean. Maybe the move happened too quickly. I felt something like the startled awe that the blind experience with the sudden intensity of sight. Maybe people normally looked and dressed like them? Maybe the ones I'd grown up with were abnormal? People looked as if they took baths every day and sometimes two. They didn't worry about paying the water bill and didn't bathe in number-ten tubs with hot water brought in from the sink. Even before we got to our new place, I knew I wanted to live that way.

The houses grew farther apart as we crossed the tracks in the center of town and turned left onto Dawson Road toward our new place. The yards were almost as big as Mr. Wright's yard in Eden Park, yards that later would come in handy for cutting grass. Soon houses stopped appearing on the left side of the street. We drove a bit farther till we reached a gravel driveway on the left and turned into it.

The sloping driveway ended at a large farmhouse on our right. A two-story garage stood below a short hill on the left side of the driveway. Sprawled out like a mound of dirty clothes lay a dump yard barely twenty yards beyond the garage. Parked beside the dump yard stood a Cadillac of garbage trucks with its shiny barrel-shaped trash compacter. I could see that our new landlord, Mr. Rosewood, wasn't your average garbageman.

Daddy had heard about Mr. Rosewood from our foster mother, Mrs. Johnson. She and her brother, Mr. Charles Rosewood, had grown up in Madeira on land their grandfather had bought after World War II. Land that far outside of the city had been cheap. He sold much of it to developers who helped expand Madeira. As the only trash hauler in town, he became the sole hauler for private homes and small businesses. The larger businesses contracted firms from Cincinnati.

Mr. Rosewood wasn't home when we arrived. Miss Dorothy, his wife (or Dot as Nellie came to know her), came out to meet us.

"Charlie's finishing up over on Miami," she began. "He wishes he could be here, but he left the key."

I looked around and couldn't see what he'd left the key to. Daddy said, "Thanks," took the key, and started walking down the hill to the garage. We all followed. Nellie, though looking pleased, walked the slowest.

By the time Mr. Rosewood got home and Daddy went over to talk to him, the garage was livable. Daddy had rented the second floor of the garage, which had been converted into three small rooms and a kitchen. The first floor was divided into halves, one for the furnace and the other for a car.

Much of the furnace side was taken up by the coal bin, a five-by-five area edged with wood. Trucks funneled coal through a chute on the side of the garage into a bin to be shoveled later into the furnace. I'd never had to shovel gas into our radiator, and I wasn't eager about shoveling coal into a furnace.

When Mr. Rosewood returned with his sons, Richard and Ralph, they unloaded the salvageable trash. All the real garbage had been taken to the county dump. After he and the boys had cleaned up, Mr. Rosewood invited everyone to his house for dinner.

Everything inside was old but sturdy. Miss Dorothy told Nellie most of it came with the house and had been passed down from Mr. Rosewood's father. With two of its heavy oak leaves placed to expand the table, all twelve of us were seated.

"Hey, Lou. Everything okay? Sorry I missed you," said Mr. Rosewood.

"Everything's okay, Charles. Thanks for all this," said Daddy, nodding at the full table.

"First night. You ain't set up yet. Sit down. Let's eat something," Mr. Rosewood said.

They kept on talking throughout dinner. Nellie and Miss Dorothy, too. Robert excused himself from the table, looked at his father and then at me, and said, "Come on, Junior." I excused myself and followed him. Ralph came along behind.

Robert, just seventeen, resembled his father the most: deep-chested, big arms, and wide face. He didn't smile much, but it was more from his being shy than his attitude. When we became friends, he and I had lots of fun riding his Moped, with him driving and me riding behind.

Both Ralph and I were fifteen. Taller than Robert and me, Ralph always appeared to be falling forward. Lean and sinewy he looked like a stranger's son, as if he and Robert didn't belong in the same family. I never saw Ralph without his wearing a sly smile that seemed to say, "I even cheat at marbles." I took him for a sneak, and that impression never changed.

Robert led Ralph and me outside. The night was soft and dark, and I heard owls hooting. The lights from Dawson Road didn't reach deep enough to touch us. October, outside the city, and nearly surrounded by trees ... even the night felt different in Madeira. It promised a peace and innocence that I hadn't felt in a very long time.

"Hey, man, you from downtown. Right?" said Robert.

"Yeah," I answered.

"Like to dance?"

"What you think?"

"Cool, there's a dance down in Madisonville this weekend. You might want to check it out. You can ride with us," he said, motioning to Ralph.

Remembering what had happened at the Lincoln Court, I needed to get my bearings settled before going to a dance in a strange place. "Thanks, man," I said, "but I won't be going anywhere till we get all moved in. Daddy'll see to that. But what's happening out here?" I asked. "What's going on in town?"

"Nothing really," said Ralph. "We usually go down to Madisonville. Ain't nothing happening out here."

"The kids are cool, but they're lame and the school's a bitch," said Robert. "I don't even go there anymore. I transferred."

"Where to?"

"Withrow High in Madisonville."

"That's a long ride."

"It's worth it. I'll be graduating this year."

"I'm kind of looking forward to the school," I said. "What's with it?"

"They've got all this honors crap. Honors classes, National Honor Society, college prep. Normal classes are at the bottom," said Ralph. "That's what I take. Normal."

I couldn't believe my ears. Madeira High School sounded stricter than Walnut Hills. Had my trail leading outside the city to Madeira given me another exit from the crime and poverty of the West End? Had it been an unintended outcome of Daddy's move, or had he planned it? Either way I jumped at the chance to try it.

MADEIRA HIGH

Spread over what may have been five acres, Madeira High School looked the total opposite of Walnut Hills High. One large single-story building with two wings veering off the main hall, MHS sat quietly in a wooded area, a school bus ride away from where we lived above the garage. It had a circular driveway that held four buses at the same time, plus some parents' cars. A parking lot for teachers and staff lay in back of the main building, and students' cars were parked on the side. It was a modern school with all the conveniences, everything properly kept up and no graffiti on the walls. Total enrollment was only 250, small enough for me to shine and large enough to satisfy my needs.

Looking at the course offerings when I first enrolled, I figured I'd jump out ahead right away. Latin and/or French were required for honors courses. Those classes were limited to students with 4.0 grade point averages. Only fifteen students to each honors class ensured they received the kind of personal attention their special needs warranted. I never made it to the full honors program because of the foreign language requirement. I would never have a 4.0 average with a foreign language as one of my subjects. I made the A/B honors program in my second semester and kept it until we moved back downtown at the end of my junior year. More like college than Walnut Hills, the grading periods at Madeira were arranged in semesters, and our academic standing was posted at the end of each one. Madeira schools had a national ranking, and college prep classes, the least challenging of the honors classes, were taken in place of electives. Normal or standard high school courses were considered, as Ralph said, the lowest rung.

Like a dried seed reconstituted by water I exploded into fullness at Madeira High. In addition to the academics I found Susan and Garth.

A second-string basketball player at Walnut Hills, I easily made first team in the limited talent bank at Madeira. I became well known throughout the small town as the highly visible black player on the basketball team who was an exceptional journalism student. My best friend on the team, Garth Franks, not only played basketball but played the guitar as well. We used to play around singing in the locker room, songs that I was surprised he knew living in Madeira, songs like "Get a Job," "Silhouette on the Shade," and "I'm Not a Juvenile Delinquent." When it was time for the annual talent show, he asked if I'd like to sing for it.

"Man, you must be crazy," I said.

"We've been doing alright in the locker room," he said. "Let's try it."

He convinced me to meet him and two other guys at his house the next day after school, and it all began. I had played basketball in Garth's driveway before and still marveled at his neighborhood. Madeira abutted Indian Hills, Cincinnati's wealthiest suburb, and Garth's family's property ended at the Madeira township line. It sloped backward into shaded, mature woods. Tall trees muffled the sounds, and grass lay carpet-thick close around the house. Rabbits, squirrels, raccoons, and deer regularly passed through. People from my old neighborhood on Gest Street wouldn't have felt comfortable there. It was too quiet and not enough people milling around. But I loved it and relished the peace and the stability it represented.

Rick and Dan were there when I arrived. Both were band members. Rick played trumpet and Dan played drums. All I could do was sing. We all set up in the garage, and Garth passed out some sheet music.

"Here's 'Silhouette on the Shade,'" he said. "It's a piano piece, but we can make it work. Junior, you just stand in front and look cool. We'll make you sound good."

We practiced for about an hour but had to break up when Garth's dad came home. Once Mr. Franks got home, Garth had to get ready for dinner.

Mr. Franks owned the only men's clothing store in town and always finished late. I think he liked talking to his customers as much or more than selling to them. Once he got home, everything stopped, food was put on the table, and the family sat down together to eat—kind of like when Daddy came home from working on construction all day. He'd take a quick wash-up and we'd all stop and sit at the table regardless of what else we may have been doing. No matter who they are or what they do, bread winners are the boss at home.

For the next three weeks we practiced each weekend at Garth's until we had the songs down pat. Next we tried "Get a Job." Then came my favorite, Frankie Lymon's "I'm Not a Juvenile Delinquent." My falsetto would've caused Jim's sisters to swoon. I couldn't wait to perform at the talent show and see how it would do here.

During that same time, things began to take shape at the new place. How Mr. Rosewood managed to make three bedrooms and a kitchen out of the space above the garage would make a drunken architect sober. The rear windows overlooking the berm of trees and shrubs in back that shielded the house from the tracks were its best feature. The berm muffled the sound of the train chugging by every night, and the windows opened an avenue for escape. Together they provided me easy entry and access and shielded me from sight when I learned to sneak out to dances with Robert at night. That very first weekend Robert had invited me to a dance. I didn't go because of my past experience in the Lincoln Court. More comfortable now with my new surroundings, I decided to take a chance.

"We go to the dances down in Madisonville," Robert said when I asked where to find one.

"I know. You said that before. Why, what's wrong with here?"

"Don't act stupid. You know they don't know how to dance. Besides, I don't really know these people."

"But you've been living out here."

"Yeah, but I hang out in Madisonville. I'm more comfortable down there."

"How you going to get there, walk? Ain't no buses running down Camargo Pike. Somebody going to pick you up?"

"No, man. I've got a Moped, and I bought it with my own money. Next time something's happening you can ride down with me. That cool?"

"How?"

"Ain't nothing to it. Just sit down and hang on. I'll show you."

"Alright, I'll try it sometime."

"What you doing after school next week?"

"Basketball practice, then on the weekends practice for the talent show," I said.

"Man, you really into it, ain't you?"

"No big deal. Just getting my feet wet."

"Yeah, well. I hope you know what you're doing."

"What does that mean?"

"Nothing. You don't want to mess things up for yourself."

"Don't you worry about it. I can handle it."

Christmas was just two weeks away when we're due to perform at the annual talent show. Basketball season was in full swing, and I had spent most of my time with Garth and his family. Garth's sister, Susan, a cheerleader and a year ahead of Garth and me, already had her driver's license. Mr. Franks had given her a brand-new Ford Falcon for her six-teenth birthday. She used to ferry us back and forth to basketball prac-tice and often would take me home by herself if Garth had to stay after. In the darkness of winter Daddy never saw who actually dropped me off after practice.

The week before the talent show, our second load of coal had come with a snowstorm predicted to fall that same day. As I helped Daddy shovel the last few lumps of coal down the chute, Ralph walked down the driveway into our yard.

"Hey, Junior," he said.

"What's up, Ralph?"

"You know that white girl who drives you home sometimes?" he said, smiling at me and turning his head toward Daddy. "I just saw her down-town with some other guy. What's happening, brother? Losing your game?"

I stopped shoveling. "Her name is Susan, and the other guy is her brother, Garth. We both are on the basketball team. She gives me a ride home sometimes. So what? She's Garth's sister," I said.

I didn't feel good about Ralph's question. It was meant for Daddy's sake, not mine.

Daddy straightened up. "Does she come all the way to the house?"

"Yes, Sir. She lets me off in the yard. Haven't you seen her?"

"No. How long this been going on?"

"Since basketball season started."

"Well, it just came to an end." Turning to Ralph he said, "Ralph, you can go home now."

Ralph said, "Yes, Sir," looked my way, smiled, and took off.

Daddy said, "After you put the shovels away, Junior, meet me upstairs. We've got to talk."

"Yes, Sir."

Daddy never got over his Down South prejudice and fears. Traumatized by having seen a lynching in his youth, he impressed those fears upon me unconsciously, somehow hoping to protect me. I guess Daddy felt he had to do for me what Pa Joe had done for him. By whipping Daddy and restricting his freedom, Pa Joe felt he was showing his love and keeping him safe. Daddy felt he could keep me safe by doing the same for me. But this was a different time and place. I was not him, and Madeira was not Selma, Alabama. Before I climbed the stairs I knew what he might say. He didn't disappoint me.

"Sit down," he said and touched the table next to him with his palm.

Next he bent face down at the table and placed his face inside both palms. He sat like that for a while and rubbed his face with his hands. Finally, he opened his hands, lifted his head back, looked darkly at me, and said, "Junior, if you ever bring a white girl to this house again, you're going to have to find someplace else to stay."

"Daddy, she's not my girlfriend or anything. She's Garth's sister. She's just giving me a ride home. Nobody cares. Mr. and Mrs. Franks don't mind."

He slammed his fist on the table so hard it sounded like a shot. Nellie and my sisters came running from the back as if there were a fire. "Nellie, get these kids out of here," he commanded. She corralled them out of sight.

"I don't give a damn what the Franks don't mind. I mind, and I don't want that girl around my house," he shouted.

The force of his anger slapped my head back. It didn't make sense. I felt like a pebble being pelted by a tornado in a wind tunnel. I didn't know how to respond.

"You think you know everything, don't you? Don't fool yourself. Just because they like you up at that school don't mean nothing. Start messing with one of them girls and we'll all be in trouble."

"But Daddy," I began.

"Don't 'but Daddy' me," he said and slapped me hard in the face.

His slap took something out of me. "I think I understand, Daddy. I do and I'm sorry. I won't bring her here again. I don't want to cause any trouble for you or for anyone else. Is that what you want?"

"It's for your own good, Junior, you understand? It's for your own good."

I turned, opened the door to the outside, and walked blindly down the stairs. Vaguely aware of touching solid ground, I opened the garage door and walked over to the coal. I sat down in the darkness, leaned back against the coal bin, and cried.

BY THE SKIN OF MY TEETH

"I plan on going to Juilliard," Garth said when we finished our last rehearsal before the talent show. He looked like New York material. Thick black hair, dark eyes, prominent nose, good build—Garth looked like who he was, big man on campus. With my lighter build and light, curly hair, when standing next to him I looked like an intellectual. His mother, a member of the Catholic Interracial Council, said I reminded her of Julian Bond. Yet we made a good team together. His skills were music and math, mine were journalism and art.

Garth could play anything on the piano. Whether he heard it on the radio or heard someone else play it, he could do it. But even more than that, he could improvise and enhance it and jazz it up. That came in handy when we sang "I'm Not a Juvenile Delinquent," because I forgot some of the words. Garth filled it in smoothly, and nobody was the wiser. It made no difference to anyone there that I was a true juvenile delinquent. They didn't know.

After the talent show it was too late to do anything else. Madeira closed up around 10 p.m. Daddy and Nellie didn't come to see the show. Ralph wasn't in it, so the Rosewoods didn't come either. The Franks offered to take me home, and Susan spoke up. "Don't worry, Mom, I can take him. Garth can ride with you, if that's okay?"

"Okay, Susan," Mrs. Franks said. "Bye, Junior."

"Good-bye, Mr. and Mrs. Franks," I said. "See you, Garth," I waved.

Susan was a varsity cheerleader and looked it. She wore bangs with her thick dark hair cascading down to her shoulders. While cheerleading she wore a ponytail. She often wore a pleated wool skirt with a sweater. Tonight they were a matching blue. What enticed me the most about Susan was her wholesomeness. Just looking at her made me feel happy. She had no hidden agenda. Her face told her whole story, and she had the kindest face I'd ever seen. Susan was a totally new experience for me. She was the first girl I'd accepted as a friend separate from any sexual overtones, and I relished that friendship.

"What do you plan on doing when you leave Madeira?" Susan asked as she drove up Dawson Road toward my house.

"Probably go to Ohio State. What about you?"

"I'd like to go to Oberlin. That's Mom's alma mater. Ever thought of going to Harvard? Garth's going to Julliard."

"I know. I'd like to go to Columbia and be in New York," I said.

Just then Daddy's car passed us going the opposite way. He didn't know Susan's car, and I didn't think he saw us. I wondered if he was looking for me.

When we reached my driveway I asked Susan to stop at the top instead of taking me all the way down to the house.

"Okay," she said. "You sure you don't want me to take you the rest of the way?"

"Thanks, Susan," I said and jumped out of the car. She backed up, turned around in the driveway, and stopped next to me.

"Why are you acting so strange? Don't you want to talk? Why are you in such a hurry to go home?"

"Susan, I want to talk. It's just that I can't stay too late. My father's got a problem with it. Don't worry. I'll straighten it out."

"If it's about your getting home late, he can talk to my mom. She'll be glad to help. Okay?"

"Great. I'll let you know." She didn't know that Daddy's talking to Mrs. Franks would only make matters worse. I started walking down the driveway just as she turned down Dawson Road. Before I'd walked twenty feet, Daddy's car pulled up beside me and stopped.

I didn't need to look up. Even in the dark I could recognize the familiar thump of that engine as it stood idling by, stealing my joy. Daddy didn't have to say anything. He just looked through his passenger window at me with eyes that said, "I told you once about that girl, and now it's up to you."

Stepping slowly on the gas he rolled hearselike down the driveway with me trailing even slower behind. I no longer cared what Daddy might do to me. I went upstairs and followed him into the kitchen. He sat down at the table and motioned for me to sit next to him.

"If you're not going to stop seeing her, I'm not going to be responsible," he said. "You're on your own."

"Yes, Sir," I said. "I understand."

That's all I needed to hear. Without his restrictions, Madeira became a place for me to really come alive.

By the time spring break came around, I was a regular visitor at Susan and Garth's. Garth had gotten his driver's license and often borrowed Susan's car. The two of us went from Mariemont to Indian Hills to every party we could find, except for one time at a party in Mariemont.

We walked up to the door past about six guys who were standing on the porch. The party was in the basement, and we could hear the music drifting up the stairs. I was bouncing, ready to jam. Garth walked ahead of me, ignoring the group on the porch. One of the guys wearing a cheap shirt and jeans stepped toward Garth and asked, "Where are you guys going? Who invited you?"

"Mary invited us," said Garth and stepped in closer, pushed his open palm toward me to hold me back, and whispered something in the closest guy's ear. The guy looked at me with widened eyes and let us pass.

"What did you tell him?" I asked Garth after we'd gone farther downstairs.

"I told him you were that lightweight from the Police Athletic League in Cincinnati giving exhibition bouts down at the Y."

I flexed my biceps and moved on farther down the stairs.

CORN SQUEEZINGS

Shortly after we moved to Madeira, Daddy bought two dozen chickens and built a chicken coop in back of the garage as a front for making "corn squeezings." Since it was normal for me to be in the basement, he put me in charge of the cooker. I banked the furnace at night and started the fire before I left for school each morning. We were far down the driveway, and no whiff of alcohol could reach Mr. Rosewood's house. If Ralph found out we'd be arrested, because he'd surely tell someone.

The basement didn't look like a still but worked like the best. Half coal bin and furnace with the rest given to the garage, the basement was larger than it appeared. Daddy usually parked in the gravel driveway in front to make room inside. The wooden barrel with the fermented mash sat near the furnace on the right, next to the metal drum cooker. Connected to the furnace, the cooker had a copper outlet that ran through the laundry sinks. Raw whiskey that I tested for purity every morning dripped through cheesecloth into a large Mason jar. Its purity polluted my growth but expanded my education. I'd strike a match, ignite it, and taste it with the tip of my tongue. If the whiskey burned like turpentine, it meant Daddy could cut it and make more money. Except for detailing the car, my making corn squeezings was the only thing I ever did to Daddy's satisfaction.

You can't make corn squeezings without the corn, and you can't have the corn without chicken feed. You don't need chicken feed if you ain't got chickens.

Daddy had a good business taking quart Mason jars to work. Many of his coworkers were from Down South, both black and white, and they all knew about corn squeezings. Some of the men called it "white lightning," but it was all the same. Daddy's business fell apart when the chickens started eating each other.

Once a week I'd go into the chicken coop to gather eggs and return to take a chicken out for dinner. Too squeamish to wring its neck as I'd seen Mama Liza do, I'd chop its head off with the hatchet. The chicken would run around the yard, blood sprouting from its neck like a fountain. When it fell I'd pick it up, take it inside, dip it in boiling water, and pluck off its feathers. Then Nellie would take it and prepare it for dinner. I was slowly decimating our crop, but disease and cannibalism are what killed off our whiskey business.

I stepped into the coop one afternoon, and one chicken lay on the roost floor, just an empty rib cage and feathers. His blood-soaked feathers were a mute testimony to the murderous appetite of his fellows. I didn't know what to think. Daddy said, "Keep an eye on them. They don't usually act like that unless they're overcrowded."

"Yes, Sir," I said, and kept watch.

The next day I noticed two chickens run down another, and catch and peck it in the same spot until it bled to death. Watching chickens peck one another to death gave me a nasty taste in my mouth when I tried to eat them. In my mind I kept seeing their bloody open wounds made bloodier and deeper as they ran trying to escape. I told Daddy about it.

"It's disease, Junior," he said, "and it's going to spread. We can't eat any more of them, and they'll peck each other to death."

"What do you want me to do?"

"Let 'em do what they want to. We ain't going to spend any more money buying chickens, and I ain't going to buy more corn either. I'm going to stop doing what I'm doing anyway. This is it."

Daddy sold what was left in the whiskey still and I dismantled it. Barely soon enough to escape Ralph's snooping around, I trashed everything as best I could and put it on Mr. Rosewood's trash pile. By the time Ralph found it, most of the smell was gone. After discovering it Ralph asked if I knew anything about it.

"Yeah," I said, "some white girl put it there," and smiled.

RIDING THE RAILS

Picking up garbage and throwing it in the truck is a lot like picking cotton. It looks cleaner than it is, can prick your fingers, and takes more to fill up the canister than it appears. I know, I've done it.

There weren't many ways for me to earn extra money in Madeira, but right at hand Mr. Rosewood's trucks left empty every morning and returned with a load of useful trash. The junk pile below our house kept growing day by day with rags, bike frames, old vacuum cleaners, and anything else that might someday be fixed or sold. It looked as if middle-class folk always had trash that others could use. Navigator Jack would have loved it out here.

One day while we were sitting around back of the berm over the railroad tracks, Robert asked, "You want to make some money, Junior?"

"Sure, man, you know I do."

"Ralph's sick. You want to take his place on the truck?"

"What will he say?"

"I'm the boss. Fuck Ralph."

"I'm in."

"Cool, we start tomorrow at seven."

We heard the train whistle moaning in the distance heading our way.

"Hey, you ever jumped a train?" said Robert.

"No, man, and ain't about to."

"Aww, ain't nothing to it."

"We can get killed."

"Bums do it all the time. You can do it. Come on," he said as the train chugged into view. "We've got to catch it."

It was a freight train, the kind I'd seen a hundred times before. We ran down the hill and up the ditch leading to the tracks. The train was moving fast, its wheels hitting each joint broadcasting its speed, *clink, clink . . . clink, clink, clink, clink.* The noise was deafening. I could barely hear Robert as he ran up the gravel to the tracks and drew even with an open boxcar as it whizzed along.

"Stay even with the car," he shouted as he ran. "Stay even."

I ran as fast I could.

The floor of the boxcar was about as high as my head. I didn't see any way I was going to grab it, hold on, and climb in without falling off. Robert didn't stop running. The car was about even with us. I was about to give up when he shouted, "Grab hold of the ladder," and he grabbed the bottom rung of the ladder going down the side of the car in front of the open boxcar. I quickly did the same with the one at the other end of the opening near the end of the boxcar. With the wind whipping my body, I held on and watched Robert as he held the ladder, stretched his leg till he touched the floor of the boxcar with his foot, leaned over and reached his arm inside the door, then let go of the ladder and fell inside.

I couldn't hold on to the ladder much longer and had no choice other than to try what Robert had done.

"Come on, man," he urged.

With the train thumping and bumping along and the wind pushing my body backward, going forward was a whole lot harder than it looked. Just as I was losing faith in my ability, Robert reached out, grabbed my arm, and almost jerked it off, pulling me inside.

"Thanks, man," I said with relief.

"Don't worry, you'll do better next time."

"How long we going to ride?"

"Not long, just up to Kugler Mill, near Indian Hills. Won't take long. Twenty minutes, and we'll head back."

That was fine with me. Twenty minutes riding the rails. Well, not counting the twenty minutes coming back. Wonder what Navigator Jack would think of that? Had he ever ridden the rails? The train kept on bumping along and rocking side to side. Just as I'd gotten used to the rhythm Robert said, "Get ready, it's almost time to leave."

"Where's the stop?" I asked.

"We ain't stopping," he said. "We're jumping. It's got to slow down some as we approach Indian Hills. When it does, we jump."

He didn't tell me that when we got on. Getting on was bad enough, and he wanted me to jump off. "This really is some crazy shit," I said. "I ain't jumping out of no train."

He laughed. "You can always walk back, but your daddy's going to miss you. I know you don't want that.

"Listen, man, this is how you do it," he said. "Get back on the ladder, climb down to the last rung, and step down running with the train while keeping hold of the ladder. Run as fast as you can till your speed matches the train, then let go and keep on running. When you start slowing down, do a forward roll and that will keep you from falling on your face."

That all sounded good, but gym wasn't my strongest suit and one wrong move might put me under the train. It didn't do much good to worry about it because I didn't have a choice.

As we reached Kugler Mill and the train began to slow, I felt the cars jump as if hesitating to move forward. At that moment Robert said, "Go." He reached out of the open car, got back on the ladder, and did as he instructed me. The train kept rolling. I quickly reached out, got on my ladder, and climbed down to the last rung. Then I stepped down to the ground. My toe hit the gravel, pulled my hands off the ladder, and rolled me end over end till I slammed up against a tree in a ditch filled with gravel. After a quick once-over, I determined my wounds were few. A scraped elbow, pants ripped at the knee, and scuffed shoes. Then it hit me, a pain throbbing so hard you could almost hear it. My thumb had instantly exploded to twice its size with a pain to match. I must've fallen on it and turned it backward. It had tried to go the wrong way and didn't make it. I wouldn't be jumping the train back home, that was clear.

About three minutes later Robert caught up with me. It didn't take long for him to see the shape I was in. "I've got some money," he said. "You can't make it home like that. We'll ride a cab."

We made it home without Daddy seeing me. I said I was too sick to eat dinner when he came home from work, and he didn't get a chance to see my hand. The next day I was on the garbage truck with Robert and didn't get back till late. When Daddy finally saw it, I told him I hurt it picking up a can that was heavier than I thought.

GOOD GARBAGE

I never thought I'd like being a garbageman. Good garbage depends on a lot of things: where you're picking it up, who you're picking it up from, what you call garbage, and how you're picking it up. I was doing alright in all four categories.

Picking up garbage in Madeira wasn't like picking it up downtown, for instance. The streets in Madeira were clean, but downtown you needed a street cleaner before you could get the garbage truck to come through. The garbage cans weren't kept in front of the houses to ugly up the streets. They were put out in alleys between the houses to keep the streets neat. And who were we picking up the garbage from in Madeira?

Both private homes and small businesses kept their cans in the back, which made garbage picking easy. We stocked half our house with things picked from the Rosewoods' trash pile. Private homes treated you like any other service person in Madeira. At Christmastime they handed you an envelope with "Thank You" cash inside, and at other times they gave you a used sweater or an old overcoat. I worked part-time on Mr. Rosewood's garbage truck where many of the people knew me from the high school. I never tried to hide my being poor, and it never affected their respect for me. I always got top grades and wasn't afraid to work.

The best thing about being a garbageman in Madeira, and Navigator Jack would've agreed, is that what folk called garbage in Madeira was still useful to folk elsewhere—both big stuff and small, like the couches and easy chairs I'd helped load. In Madeira they were thrown away. At Goodwill or the Salvation Army they'd bring a nice price—small things like lawn chairs, scuffed-up desks, and too many blankets and curtains to count. The people in Madeira weren't rich, just well off. They lived next door to people in Indian Hills who were very rich, and we picked up stuff sometimes over there. Surprisingly they didn't throw many useful things away.

The last category is as important as the first three: how the garbage is picked up. You could pick up the garbage in a truck that looks like garbage and sounds like garbage. With a truck with paint peeling, a nasty garbage bay open and awash with a terrible smell, and brakes squealing at every stop, what have you got? The epitome of the dirty, stinking garbage pickup with the dirty, stinking garbageman. Compare that with how we did it at Mr. Rosewood's.

First, he gave each of us a gray uniform with his name, Rosewood, across the back. We weren't permitted to curse or smoke while on duty. At threat of immediate dismissal, we had to handle each customer's can as if it were our own. (He owned a Buick Riviera that he bought cash the first year it was produced and told us he didn't get it running a sloppy business.) Next there was the truck.

Mr. Rosewood's truck would put most cars to shame. It had a barrel-shaped body with an opening in the middle where the hydraulic arm pushed the trash back. I never saw it full. On his first run for garbage he took it to the north Cincinnati dump in Mariemont when it was half full. When he returned he made a trash run. The trash run is where he made his extra money. Small businesses throwing away generation-old business machines called Mr. Rosewood for removal. Private homes with gently used goods called him to their homes, and he was always ready to help. His contacts in Madisonville and Milford relied on him for used goods, and Mr. Rosewood never failed. I made a good bit of extra money working for Mr. Rosewood, and I'd be a garbageman for him anytime. He's got the cleanest garbage you'll ever find. By the time we left Madeira and moved back to the West End, we had a new dinette set for the kitchen and a nice leather couch for the living room. I had five new sweaters and two winter jackets. What couldn't be seen was the $375 I had stashed in a tin box wrapped in plastic under the berm in back of our house. I wasn't going back to the West End broke.

IT STARTED WITH A FUNERAL

Uncle Eb died of a heart attack, and Daddy had to go home. Everybody related to him directly—sons, daughters, cousins, nephews, and indirectly through marriage—had to be there. Not given permission by your employer was the only acceptable excuse for missing a relative's funeral in Daddy's family. Even then, some considered your absence disloyal.

Daddy hadn't taken Nellie to Selma, and Uncle Eb's death gave him a reason. Uncle Eb was Mama Liza's only brother, and Daddy had to go home. Aunt Lil found him on the bathroom floor after he'd taken a break from their cooking together. She said that before he went into the bathroom, Uncle Eb said, "Don't let them sweet potatoes stay in that water too long, Lil. They get too soft."

"That's the last thing he ever said to me," she said, crying, shaking her head, and smiling at the same time. "Something about food. That sure was Eb."

Daddy packed five of us kids and Nellie into the car and left for Selma on March 2, the day after Uncle Eb's death. Wanda rode with Uncle Ted who followed later that same morning. Daddy's new car was the same year as the Chevy he'd driven earlier, but this time it was an Olds. He'd detailed it till it looked as good as it could, bought some used whitewalls, and off we went. We left at 5:30 a.m. and pulled into Mama Liza's front yard a little after 4:30 p.m.

After Mama's funeral I never wanted to attend another one for as long as I lived. After seeing her lying there with that wig and her face made up so unnatural, it frightened and sickened me beyond understanding. They had mutilated Mama, raped her beauty for some artificial show, and stolen my last memories of her with her long brown hair. I came to Selma because I had to and Mama Liza was there. I had no intentions of attending Uncle Eb's funeral.

Daddy said, "I didn't bring you all the way down here to act no fool, Junior. Put your suit on and go outside and get in the car. Don't make me have to hurt you."

There were too many other people around for him to make good on his threat, and I didn't think Mama Liza would let him whip me in front of everyone.

"I just can't go, Daddy. I'll be sick. Look what happened at Mama's funeral. Don't make me go. If I go it'll make me sick."

Just then Mama Liza stepped into the room, "Sport, the boy is still sick after Cassie's death. He still misses his mama. Don't make him go if he don't want to."

Turning to me she said, "Junior, don't be telling your daddy what you ain't gonna do, or I'll whip you myself. Understand?"

"Yes, ma'am."

"Okay, Butch, now go on, get outta here, baby."

After the funeral I met everyone over at the Elks Lodge. Uncle Eb was an Elk. The members' wives and the sisters from the Usher Board at Ebenezer First Baptist Church, where Uncle Eb attended, prepared an after-service meal called the repass. It actually may have been called the we-pass, the we-passed, or the repass, I'm not sure, but it had lots of collards, corn, okra, cornbread, and macaroni and cheese. In addition to chicken—fried, baked, and barbecued—they had tea, coffee, and soft drinks. For people like me who wanted finger food, they had barbecued pork ribs that fell off the bone. If you still had room after all those courses, you could eat your way through the best sweet potato pies, pound cakes, and triple-layer chocolate cakes a fork has ever known. I don't know how his funeral went, but Uncle Eb's repass was a hit.

The next day the people who lived the farthest started heading back. Uncle Eb's daughter, Mary, lived in San Francisco, and she left for the airport in Montgomery before breakfast. James, Uncle Eb's wife's cousin, lived in Detroit, and he left for the airport with Mary. The other four, who in addition to the eight of us lived close enough to drive, stayed around to cook and clean house for Mama Liza for about a week. On the morning we left, Mama Liza gave Nellie some hoe cakes, told Daddy to drive carefully, kissed us kids goodbye, and stood waving until we could no longer see her.

The next time I saw Mama Liza I was no longer a little boy and the struggle for civil rights had finally reached Selma. Walking through the middle of town was like walking on hot lava where your next step might burn you alive. Black anger smoldered like smoke around the lava and filled the air with resentment. The main street of downtown Selma ran directly into and over the Edmund Pettus Bridge, the same route chosen for a Sunday demonstration.

Tee brought me up to date on the events. "Dr. King will be speaking at Brown Chapel tomorrow night at seven. Everybody will be there. We been staying away from downtown for weeks. White folks look at you like they gonna kill you if you say something. Joe Burks and Gee got beat and put in jail last week for nothing, just for being by the show. And they work up there. It's a bad time."

What time you want to go?" I asked.

"We ain't going. Mama Liza would kill us."

"Man, you must be nuts. We gotta go. This is about us. About freedom," I begged.

"Don't tell Mama Liza that. She say all this freedom stuff ain't gonna do nothing but make everything worse, and she better not find any of us in that mess. You know what that means. I ain't about to go against Mama Liza."

I hunched my shoulders, didn't say anything, and moved on.

Just before dinner the next day, I cornered Joseph and asked him whether he was going to hear Dr. King speak at Brown Chapel. Joseph, who was shorter than Tee and a year younger, would fight the Grand Wizard blindfolded. He said, "Mama Liza say don't go. She always say something like that 'cause she don't want to mess up her thing with them people downtown. She don't like white people like some people do. She just scared of not getting paid. I don't work for 'em, and I'm going."

The church was already full when Joseph and I arrived around 6 p.m. and people were still coming. The pews were filled with people stuffed together like kernels of corn on a cob. Others stood four-deep against the walls, and the ones in back were constantly being pushed aside to let more in. The stairs leading to the balcony where the forty-person gold-robed choir sang were a fire marshal's nightmare. People sat on the stairs atop each other and leaned against railings, blocking any escape route for those above. With people standing like cattails and their heads bobbing above stemlike bodies, the choir stand above them was just a pool of heads.

Some activity at the side door leading to the pulpit moved every eye in that direction as Reverend Abernathy, Dr. King's right hand, entered. He stepped up and shook the pastor's hand and turned around as Dr. King, unhurried, strode proud but humbly to the pulpit. After shaking the pastor's hand in both of his, bending, and whispering something in Dr. Abernathy's ear, he turned to the pulpit and said a prayer.

Standing behind the oak pulpit in a dark suit, white shirt, dark tie, and short haircut, Dr. King could have been a businessman or politician. He looked the part. When he started speaking, after quietly laying out his points and punctuating them with scripture, his voice began to rise. His cadence unlocked the voice of safety that was locked deep within me through the voice of Elder Sanders. As his voice grew stronger, almost like a trumpet, I became his tuning fork and my whole body trembled. His words reached out from the pulpit, opened my heart, and massaged it with his vision. I don't remember the words, but I remember the feeling. I remember the man.

Dr. King wasn't a man *of the people* like most popular leaders. He was a man *with the people*. He wasn't popular with all blacks and didn't try to be. Folks like Mama Liza thought he threatened their livelihood. When he was there in Brown Chapel, he was there with us to help guide us, to share our pains and carry us through. He didn't come there to be liked by black or white. He came there because he had a mission, a responsibility that he had to fulfill. I saw it in his eyes, the unyielding strength of his faith in people and in his God. When I came to Brown Chapel I knew about the movement and I thought I knew why it was important. I didn't know why I believed. Right there in Brown Chapel, seeing and listening to Dr. King, seeing a man who actually believed that all people deserved to be free, made my nose run and filled my eyes with tears. I didn't know what to believe before I went to Brown Chapel, but when I left I had something to believe in. I believed in him.

Mama Liza didn't learn that Joseph and I heard Dr. King speak Wednesday night. Nor had she heard about the planned demonstration to march across the Edmund Pettus Bridge in two weeks. Dr. King was going back to Atlanta and would return next Saturday. In the meantime, Joseph said we had to get ready.

"Student Nonviolent Coordinating Committee has a house over in the projects where they're training people about the march," he said. "You wanna go tonight?"

"How do you know? Where is it? Can anybody come?"

"Over by Shirley's," he said, "in the Carver Homes. Shirley told me to come. Let's go. We'll get in."

It took fifteen minutes to walk to Shirley's apartment in the George Washington Carver Homes. Shirley was Joseph's sister from one of

Daddy's outside relationships before the war. He stayed there sometimes when he found day work uptown because it was closer. We knocked, and Shirley let us in. She was taller than the boys, slender with high cheekbones, almond-shaped eyes, and chestnut-colored skin. I couldn't compare her to anyone I'd seen. She was unbelievable. She was her own self.

"Hey, Shirley, you remember Junior?" Joseph said. "He wants to get some training for the march."

"They're doing the training upstairs on the third floor right now. Stokely isn't there," she said. "John Lewis might be. Get on up there. I told them you might be coming."

"Glad to see you, Junior," she said, smiling at me. "Come by later so we can talk. See you, Joseph," she said, and closed the door.

It was like getting into a speakeasy. We knocked, and someone opened the door no further than the chain and asked what we wanted. "I'm Joseph, this is Junior. We're Shirley's brothers. She told you we were coming."

The door closed and opened again, this time with a different face. "Who told you to come?"

"Shirley, our sister, lives downstairs," said Joseph.

"Okay, let 'em in," said a voice coming from deeper in the room.

There were only four rooms: kitchen, two bedrooms, and a front room. The training was being held in the front room.

Dressed in farmer's overalls like Joseph, one of the brothers from SNCC was standing in front of an easel with a marking pen. A map of Selma's main street leading to the Edmund Pettus Bridge and of Highway 80 leading away from it was on the easel. Aside from the two of us, six others had come that night for training. The brother with the marking pen began.

"Glad to see you brothers out tonight. We're here to help you protect yourself next Sunday. We don't know what might happen out there, but we want you to be ready for whatever it is. The white folks know we are here but just don't know where. Let's keep it that way.

"We'll gather here," he said, pointing to a place four blocks away from the bridge's approach. "Dr. King and the others will be at the head of the group, and we'll have brothers stationed throughout to help keep things moving."

"What do you expect to happen?" a boy younger than I said. "What am I supposed to do if things get rough?"

"If anything is going to happen, it won't happen till we get on the bridge. Jim Clark has already said he's not going to let anyone cross the Alabama River without going through him, so be looking for something to happen. Just be prepared for it."

The brother doing the training spoke like a veteran of many demonstrations. He told us to expect the worst but to never forget why we're here. "You are the winners here," he said. "Dr. King says we can defeat prejudice and injustice by showcasing its ugliness. Maintain your dignity. And always protect yourselves."

With his usual spirit Joseph said, "I know how to protect myself and it ain't by nonviolence."

"Alright, what about the women and the others who can't fight like you? What's going to happen to them while you're getting your ass kicked by Jim Clark's thugs? Who's going to look out for them? Will your fight help us reach our goal? You better rethink why you're here, brother. If you're not thinking about using your head, you need to go home," said the trainer.

Joseph sat down.

I still hadn't gotten what I'd come there to learn: how to protect myself during the march. After Joseph sat down I stood up. "Bull Connor used water hoses in Birmingham, but Jim Clark has horses. What if one of those horses comes running at me? Those deputies will mow us like grass with their cattle prods if they ride us down with their horses."

"Yes, if the horse hasn't the space to get around you he might step on you. His natural urge is to leap over or go around you to avoid stepping on you just as if you were a log or a rock in his path. The safest thing to do and the most difficult for most people is to lie down in the horse's path as he comes toward you. He will leap over you so quickly you won't know he's gone. Believe me. I've seen it happen."

"Thanks, brother," I said. I looked over at Joseph. He rolled his eyes. I sat back down and settled back to listen.

"It's simple, really," he began. "If they're calling you names, spitting on you, anything except touching you, you're fairly safe. Keep your cool and remember that name calling is just their own fears and ignorance being expressed out loud. You've all heard it before. It's nothing."

"What about being spit on?" Joseph said. "I've handled being called 'nigger' my whole life. That ain't nothing new. I don't know if I can deal with being spit on."

"What is spit but saliva?" said the trainer. "It's soft, comes from inside, and except when it's infected it's clean. Spit is nothing. Now, rocks are something else. If rocks are being thrown, you are at risk."

"Yeah," one of the guys sitting behind me said. "Rocks are serious."

The guy from SNCC said, "Rocks can escalate into a physical attack. It's time to get out of there. Don't stand still. Keep on marching. Pick up the pace and get past the rock throwers. There won't be any people on the bridge. Jim Clark's men will be lining each side of the highway when we come down on the other side. Won't be any room for anybody else. Clark's men are the threat, and they won't be any throwing rocks.

"This is what we want you to do," he said. "Bend your head forward and clasp your hands over your neck and hold your arms close to your chest. That gives some protection to your neck, head, and sides of your face. If you get knocked down, curl up in a fetal position. It won't protect your backs, but men, it can protect your genitals. Women should hold their arms across their breasts and curl into the tightest ball they can. Hopefully, this will also save you from getting kicked in the stomach, but once you are on the ground, anything can happen."

"This sounds like some war shit," someone said.

"It is a war, brother," the trainer said, "a war between justice and injustice. With all of us pulling together it's a war that we're going to win."

"How can it be a war if only one side's doing all the shooting?" said the guy who'd asked the question. "Sounds like slaughter to me."

"Let's face it, brother. I don't want you to go into this blindfolded. We've been getting slaughtered for centuries, and what has it gotten us?" said the trainer. "We didn't come down here to play. This is business. Hard business. Some of us won't make it through, and we accept that. But what we are doing will get us through even if some of us don't make it. We believe in our struggle and have accepted that. Dr. King has accepted it. I can't tell you if anything is going to happen to you on the march or not. Just be prepared. It's Jim Clark. We can expect anything."

After an hour had passed, Joseph and I felt comfortable enough to commit ourselves to the march. We realized that no training could make us safe from Jim Clark's troops. With SNCC's help, we were at least prepared to face them. The training gave me greater confidence in the imminent success of our actions. It helped me believe I could find the strength to rise above the expected confrontation.

The day the march took place I was completely unprepared.

INSIDE CHAOS / THE EDMUND PETTUS BRIDGE

The Student Nonviolent Coordinating Committee didn't wait for Dr. King's return and started the assault on the bridge a week ahead of schedule. Unwilling to risk losing the offensive, the Southern Christian Leadership Conference went along. Not wanting to deal with Mama Liza's fears, I moved in with Shirley.

As one of the families boarding out-of-town guests, Shirley hosted a priest during my stay. I couldn't tell whether he was Catholic or Episcopalian. He arrived the day before the march, and we shared the same bed. Used to sharing a bed in a crowded house, it made little difference to me. What did bother me was when his arm accidently fell across my crotch while he was turning over half-asleep. I abruptly pulled back, and it supposedly woke him up.

"What's with you, man? I don't play that shit." I said as sharply as I could without awakening Shirley. "Get out. You got to go, man."

Clean shaven with thin hair parted on the side and an undefined jaw-line, he would've gone unnoticed in a lineup. Medium height, not flabby but not firm, and a regular desk-job-type body. He didn't look queer or talk funny. Just a regular guy in a priest's collar.

"Nothing's going on," he said. "What happened?"

"Don't give me that. You know what happened. Listen, you came down here to help us fight injustice. I get that. That's beautiful, but this other...."

"That's the only reason I'm here," he said, interrupting me.

"If I'm wrong, I'm wrong," I said. "I'm sleeping downstairs the rest of the night. Take everything with you when you leave for the march tomorrow because you won't be coming back."

He didn't argue. He lay still and looked at me guardedly as I left the room. I had mixed feelings as I headed downstairs. He'd come from Chicago to Selma at his own risk because he believed in our cause. Maybe he really had touched me by accident. Maybe I was too sensitive. No, he knew what he wanted. And he knew that I knew. I stopped second-guessing myself, grabbed a blanket out of the closet, and fell asleep on Shirley's sofa.

Dr. King wasn't supposed to return until the following Saturday, but SNCC leaders decided to start the march without him. Many out-of-town visitors had come from up north. SNCC felt it too dangerous to try and keep them over another week. More than twelve hundred people gathered together at the staging area like ants spilling over from an ant-hill. Older people walked arm in arm with kids my age. SNCC volunteers scurried up and down the perimeter like cowboys herding cattle trying to maintain order. When the lead line started to move, the rest of the crowd followed. Men dressed in overalls like farmers seeded themselves throughout the throng. Their presence aimed to keep us rooted to our goal.

People whom I hadn't seen before, those I'd seen only once or twice, and people who I knew from around town were there, but no Joseph. There were just too many people, too much movement, and too much going on. I hadn't realized just how many people were there from out of town: ministers, civil rights workers, committed people representing other states, and others—all just regular people committed to righting a great wrong. Many of them were people like myself and Joseph, who weren't there because of anything special. We hadn't sacrificed or given our lives to the struggle as many of the others there had done. Because the struggle had culminated in Selma and we lived there when it happened, it swept us up. Would I have traveled hundreds of miles to be there for the cause, like others in the crowd had done? I doubt it. I felt others were more fit for that kind of commitment than I. As I looked around, I saw lots of people who didn't appear any braver or more committed than I. Like me, their lives had intersected with something greater than themselves without their having planned it. That intersection nudged each of them to stand up and be counted. Unlike the visitors, Selma's natives shared an intimate relationship with the Edmund Pettus Bridge.

Almost within walking distance of the bridge and spread out over miles along Highway 80, Craig Air Force Base percolated as the economic artery of the town. Money flowed into Selma through government paychecks of every form. Servicemen and servicewomen training as Air Force pilots and support forces buoyed Selma's nightlife all weekend long, and locals working as domestics, cafeteria employees, and flight line personnel kept the working class afloat. The Edmund Pettus Bridge served as the conduit, providing the milk and honey of the town's survival. It was the perfect symbol of its freedom.

When I placed my foot on the bridge that I'd crossed many times before I felt a sense of purpose I hadn't expected. It must have been carried over from the time at Brown Chapel. I felt I belonged to something larger than myself and greater than I'd imagined. Wanting to appear worldly, I tried not to show what I felt inside but couldn't resist smiling at everyone around me and calling them "sister" and "brother."

Swept along in the updraft of freedom's song, it didn't take long for us to reach the middle of the bridge. There, against an invisible wall, everything stopped. I'd never been in combat before, but I'd heard veterans talk about the tense silence that preceded it. I spied Joseph across a sea of faces as he seemed to move in slow motion, picking his way through motionless mannequins toward me. From my position near the rear I could see the heads of men whom I assumed were leaders of the march standing firm and talking to someone—men I'd only heard of, like SNCC's Hosea Williams and James Bevel. I couldn't tell if Stokely was there but knew of two locals standing near the front, Miss Amelia Boynton of the Dallas County Voters League and the Reverend Frederick D. Reese from Brown Chapel.

Somebody in back of me said, "I hear Sheriff Jim Clark's up ahead and Commander Cloud's with him. Ain't no time for no bullshit now." And that was it. Sound, noise, and color exploded together in one terrible moment. When time attempted to start up again, it felt like I stood on a boat going down river and everyone on the banks looked to be moving forward as I was moving backward, when in fact I was standing still. Nothing that SNCC training had said made any difference to me then, because in that moment SNCC didn't exist in my consciousness. When movement started again, horrific screams erupted in concert with my slightest twitch and I instantaneously collapsed. My only impulse, my sole existence, my only purpose was to flee. From my eyes to my brain to my feet, one command shattered all others: *Run*, it said, *run*. And I ran.

In that state of mind, nothing could stop me. I avoided every obstacle and leaped over those I couldn't. My whole being was in full, unforgiving flight. Nothing could slow me down. Nothing. Not even a trooper with his gun drawn and finger on the trigger.

Racing back down the bridge, through the side streets, and keeping as far away from downtown as I could, I reached the George Washington Carver Homes and Shirley's apartment while the march was still being televised.

I slammed on the door like a policeman. "Shirley, let me in. It's Junior. Let me in," I cried. She quickly opened the door.

"Junior, where's Joseph? What are you doing here?" she said. "Are you alright?"

"I don't know. I saw him on the bridge," I said. "He'll be by soon. I'm good."

She pointed at the TV. Tear gas was clouding up the screen. Bodies were knocked down by troopers with clubs. One woman who looked familiar was lying bloody and senseless on the ground. "Looks like Miss Boynton!" Shirley screamed. We learned later she was right. Miss Amelia Boynton had been billy clubbed to the ground for the whole nation to see. And not only that, John Lewis, one of the SNCC leaders, had been beaten just as badly.

"What happened?" Shirley asked.

"I don't really know," I said. "One minute we're singing 'We Shall Overcome,' and the next moment Jim Clark stops us. Everything fell apart after that."

"I know," she said. "I've been watching it on TV. He had troopers armed with tear gas just waiting to start something. I hope Mama Liza didn't see any of that. She'll be worried to death about you and Joseph. 'Specially you 'cause you don't live down here."

"I know," I said. "I'm more worried about her getting me than Jim Clark. She told me and Joseph not to come."

"Don't pay no attention to Mama Liza," Shirley said. "Mama Liza's old. Old folks is scared of what's going down. She'll be alright when it's over."

I had done it. I had marched for my freedom, nearly gotten teargassed and beaten, but didn't feel anything heroic or special. While visiting my grandmother I'd snuck over to hear Dr. King speak at Brown Chapel. Now that was heroic. That was special. To hear Dr. King and to defy Mama Liza at the same time. Yeah. That truly counted for something.

I wanted to feel special for participating in what the newscasters would later call "Bloody Sunday." But to be perfectly honest, it started off as a joyride. Almost all of the younger black folk in Selma were involved in some form of resistance when I visited that summer. In Cincinnati we called Alabama boys "country" when they came up north. When Joseph and Tee visited us in Cincinnati as adults, they may have dressed "country" by our standards but lived by stronger work ethics. They both found jobs quickly, and after finding them, except for stints in the military, kept them for life. Not many native Cincinnatians could boast about that.

Selma was bubbling with civil rights thunder underground. At Selma University, a teachers' college attended mostly by blacks, leaders of the Southern Christian Leadership Conference were well known and revered by the entire student body. Students there had participated in other civil rights and civil liberties activities throughout the South. The ministers in town stood as bulwarks of freedom for the black community, and their churches served as places of refuge and of inspiration. Because our southern relatives seemed to always talk about the Bible, they were too pious for us streetwise folk in Cincinnati. But it wasn't as we thought. The Bible spoke to them of revolution and hope. Brown Chapel sat in the center of the George Washington Carver Homes, where a majority of the poor people lived. My sister Shirley and her friends seldom missed a service there. Unlike Elder Sanders at Independent Missionary Baptist Church where I grew up, Reverend Reese held voter registration drives in the church basement and left saving souls up to the Lord. Three thousand people were arrested in local and regional protests in the year that I marched in Selma. In one way or another most of those locals touched base with Brown Chapel.

SURVIVAL BEFORE THE MARCH

I stayed over in Selma and learned what it meant to stand up and fight. Back home in downtown Cincinnati, everyone valued being "cool" and "hip." In Selma, men and women and guys and girls my age were up against issues of life and death. Sure, life in the ghetto wasn't anybody's cakewalk, but I'd never known anyone who'd gotten lynched or tarred and feathered in my neighborhood. My father and my friends' fathers had gone to prison and some had died there. But nobody on Gest or Thirteenth Street worried about the Ku Klux Klan or being enslaved on a chain gang.

Mama Liza had learned how to survive when all around her was against her. She kept Sport whole and alive by inserting him into safe havens that she created while working as a domestic. One boss after another unwittingly sheltered Daddy by giving him jobs that Mama Liza had secured for him by working a system she knew well. By the time he was a teenager almost every white businessman knew Sport from his having worked on their car at some point. Sport was Mama Liza's boy. Mayor Joseph Smitherman and the other rich white families who ruled Selma each knew and respected Mama Liza and trusted her as much as they could trust any colored woman. She returned their trust by working hard and long and trying to do whatever they asked—within reason. It was the "within reason" part that made them respect her. She would not work on Sundays and would not do anything for anyone whom she personally disliked. They returned her trustworthiness with fair to middling wages and letting her set own work schedules. It was a feudal system, but it worked for her. Dr. King, the SCLC, and SNCC were waging a full-scale war against the system she'd learned to negotiate so well. She continued using it to her advantage even as the civil rights struggle grew stronger. Two years after that first march on Montgomery, I visited Mama Liza for the summer and asked if she had any work for me to do.

She said, "Butch, are you asking me for work? Well, I'll be. Walk with me after breakfast tomorrow and I'll show you something."

After breakfast the next day Mama Liza took me down to Ray's Cotton Gin. "What we going to do down here?" I asked.

"I want to speak to Mr. Tim Ray. His daddy built this gin. It used to be one of the biggest businesses around. Sport used to do work for him," she said. "He'll do something for you or know somebody who can."

The cotton gin was a two-story building with the gin itself sitting like a big comb on the first floor. Loose cotton was thrown into its hopper and the seeds combed out of the cotton balls. Soft, puffy balls rolled out the other end onto a belt to be washed, dried, and wrapped into bales. The bales were stacked and shipped to factories up north. Watching the men go through the process with cotton still in their hair from the last time they'd washed, I imagined things there hadn't changed much from the days before the Civil War. It wasn't exactly the kind of place I had in mind when I'd asked Mama Liza for some work.

Coming from up north (as everybody called Cincinnati), I felt a bit put off about working in a cotton gin, but I couldn't tell Mama Liza that. This was her way of helping me and an important link in her lifestyle. This privileged key to open doors that otherwise would be closed to her was being used as a gift for me. I learned to value that gift.

Everybody who worked there was black, at least on the floor where the cotton was handled. The men totaling up poundage and directing the gin were white, all except one. That reminded me of some kind of *Gone with the Wind* setup, using a black overseer to push the field hands. Jim and the guys back on Gest Street would never let me live that down.

While I was figuring out a way to politely wiggle out of a cotton gin offer, Mr. Tim called us into his office. We walked up five steps to a balcony that surrounded the entire first floor like a courtyard and entered an open door to his office. His small office with two large, cloudy windows facing inside the factory along the wall was loaded with loose-leafed canvas-backed notebooks. They looked unused due to the thin layer of dirty cotton dust on their covers.

Sitting behind his desk cluttered with tufts of cotton, Mr. Tim looked like any other businessman, not at all like anyone I expected to see. He had a sport coat draped over the back of his chair, a white dress shirt kept open at the neck, no tie, and gray slacks. He was a short man with a full head of hair; solid, not thick; carrying a belly like Jim Clark; and with quick, intelligent eyes. Unlike what I'd expected from a southern white man, he stood up and reached out his hand when Mama Liza entered the room.

"Morning, Miss Liza," said Mr. Tim as he shook her hand and sat back down.

"Morning, Mr. Tim," said Mama Liza.

"What you need, Liza? How can I help?" he said.

"Mr. Tim, sir. This is my son Sport's boy, Butch. He's down here for the summer and wants to work while he's here," she said. "Is there anything he can do for you while he's here? I'd really appreciate it, and Sport would, too."

Mr. Tim looked around his office for a second or two and peered out his office windows down at the ginning floor below.

"Tell the truth, Miss Liza, this year's crop is about finished and ain't too much work for the boy to do. But this is Sport's boy," he said enthusiastically as he turned to me. "What's your name, son? Butch?" he asked.

"Yes, Sir," I answered.

"I remember your daddy. He kept my daddy's cars running and helped me a lot around the gin before leaving for the war. How's Sport getting along?" he said.

"He's doing fine, Mr. Tim."

"Well, tell him I said 'Hey' when you see him, alright?" he said.

I said, "Yes, Sir."

Standing up from behind his desk he said, "What kind of work you been doing, Butch?"

"Mostly restaurant and some warehouse," I said.

"This ain't like no restaurant, but your warehouse experience might work 'round here," he said.

Turning back to Mama Liza he said, "Liza, I truly don't have anything worthwhile for Butch to do, but since he's Sport's son, here's what I'll do. My cleanup man, Jesse, has been asking for a week off to visit his mama in Atlanta. I thought about having one of my ginners stay late to clean up while he is away. You think maybe Butch could fill in that spot for me and keep me from having to use Bill for that? What do you think?"

"That'll work just fine, Mr. Tim. I can't tell you how much we appreciate it," she said.

"I'm sure that I could do a good cleanup for you," I said. "Thanks, Mr. Tim. I can't wait to start," I lied.

"Okay. I'm glad you're going to help us out," he said. "Show up tomorrow at 6:30 on the dot, and I'll introduce you to Jack, the foreman, and he'll get you started."

I walked out the door in a stupor and followed Mama Liza down the steps and out of the gin.

I had gotten a job in the cotton gin, one of the town's chief employers, simply because I was Mama Liza's grandson. I didn't have any experience and couldn't have gotten the job on my own. Mama Liza and others of her generation suffered unintended consequences of integration and the civil rights struggle. It threatened to destroy her tenuous relationship across society's racial divide with people like Mr. Tim. That relationship let her live with a degree of influence and control in her segregated society under the paternalistic eye of a caring power broker. When I had participated in the march at Selma, some of the relationships that she had spent so many years developing were severed by the activities and not necessarily its results. It was a time of confusion for us all. I came through it still searching for meaning.

HAIR RAISING / STRAIGHTENING COMB

It seems that girls had a harder time being black than boys. Before it was hip to wear a natural or an Afro, my sisters had their hair pressed with a straightening comb. It reminded me of the old branding iron used to brand cattle. Used with a curling iron that heated until it almost glowed and then gripped the hair between its prongs, burning the life out of it until it was straight or curled, the straightening comb was torture. Getting your hair done with the straightening comb really meant getting it "done."

When "Black Is Beautiful" swept the country, lots of women found a new freedom: freedom from the straightening comb. No more sitting in Miss Addie's back room waiting to be a supplicant to the comb. No more having your scalp roasted as the hot prongs raked those naps into submission, filling the air with the odor of singed hair and burning oil. And no more having to inch your neck away from the molten liquid running down the nape of your neck trying to reach your "kitchen," those tightly curled hairs too small to be touched by the hot comb.

Yes, black was beautiful, but it never became beautiful enough for some sisters to give up their straightening combs. Performers, academics, and revolutionaries like Angela Davis wore Afros. They didn't need straightening combs. Straightening combs became political and generational. Younger people, like myself, and those who wanted to appear radical commonly wore Afros.

The vast majority of black folk were like my sister Debra. She said, "Afros might be beautiful on other people, but they still look like nappy hair needing to be put in its place. I can't stand those half-assed Afro-wearing sistahs needing their hair pressed, and I sure ain't going to look like one."

My sisters grew up in foster homes with foster parents who took them to church three times a week. They were infused with a moral certitude that spewed absolute truths regarding many social restrictions, especially those of dress and behavior. Going to church on Sunday without first undergoing the torturous ritual of the straightening comb was close to blasphemy. The offender would be pitied, laughed at, or reviled, and then sent straight to hell.

Today the natural is making a last stand with mostly holdouts from the sixties and young fashionistas or sophisticates. A new player has entered the game to fill the space once filled by the natural: the hair relaxer. Relaxed hair is at the opposite end of the spectrum from the Afro. It is almost undetectable from naturally straight hair and looks more like white folks' hair than any of the other treatment methods. It's in essence a chemical straightening comb.

The problem with relaxer is that it is used best on long hair. It's hard to toss back naps that have had the growth scorched out of them. How relaxed can a three-inch stalk of dry hair get? Thus the beginning of the epitaph for the straightening comb.

On my last visit to my sister's house, the beauty parlor on the corner had become Jolie's Wig and Fashion Center. Wigs were the thing now. Even Debra had one—two actually: one for during the week and the other one for church on Sunday.

Straightening combs will soon go the way of Mother Rose's Skin Lightening Creme. Small groups of women will still use it to lighten their skin but will do it without broadcasting it. Few stores carry it, and no one wants to be seen with it in the checkout line. Skin lightening has gone upscale, and folks now go to spas or get facials. Facials are more socially acceptable. It's okay to buy facial scrubs and other face cremes. Facial scrubs cleanse and smooth the skin, and if they happen to make it lighter also, so be it.

But the straightening comb hasn't given up. Not yet. If you look hard enough, maybe you'll still find a sister with nappy hairs at the nape of her neck. Wait till Saturday night and follow her down the street for two blocks, 'round the corner and up the stairs at the first building you reach. Wait till she disappears and just stand there.

At first you'll hear the faint sound of women talking, and as you move closer you'll start getting a taste in the back of your throat like a dry paper bag slowly burning. Your nose hairs will begin to itch. You'll know just where to go. As you reach the door at the end of the hall, the lingering smell of smoke, the furnace of an open gas burner heating a hot iron comb, and the acrid smell of singed hair will jerk you to a stop.

And then it'll hit you. The straightening comb was never in any danger of extinction. It wasn't ever going the way of Mother Rose's Skin Lightening Creme. Beneath the wigs and in between the hair relaxing, there will still be nappy hair needing to be straightened. And not only that, the straightening comb is so intertwined in our culture that it has become part of who we are. When we are ready to give up collards and cornbread, fried chicken, snap peas, bread pudding, and real sweet potato pie, only then will we be able to give up Miss Addie's Straightening Comb.

GOOD HAIR

Women weren't the only ones whose grooming was affected by the changing focus to blackness. To someone like myself with "good hair," things were about to change.

What is good hair? Good hair looks good and feels good. Good hair is as close to white hair as a black person can get. It is as far away from nappy as Africa is from America.

When Huey Newton came in, good hair went out. I never saw a Black Panther with good hair. Good hair didn't make a good Afro. It didn't puff out from under a black beret and stand up and say, "I'm black and I'm proud." Good hair just lay there, smooth, soft, and submissive—too easily controlled by a beret. Nappy hair puffed out from under Huey Newton's beret: black, nappy, and proud.

Before Huey made it hip, nappy hair was something to be hidden under headscarves, pomaded or slicked into submission, chemically transformed into a "process" with a pompadour, hidden under a wig, or completely shaved off your head. Girls couldn't run their fingers through nappy hair, but nappy hair made one hell of an Afro.

During the Black Liberation Movement, my good hair signified my compromised ancestry. It meant white blood in my woodshed. I tried tamping my hair down with Royal Crown Hairdressing, but that just made it worse. The curls fell into deep shiny waves, making me look more like Smokey Robinson or a weekend pimp. Good hair didn't make a good Afro.

Prior to "Black Is Beautiful," my good hair had been good to me. Good hair meant having good sex—and that's just one benefit. It meant letting my best friend's sister touch my hair to feel how soft it was, and my getting to touch her to feel how soft she was—and that was only the beginning. Good hair was my calling card to social heaven. It meant being let in the front of the line by girls at school and being invited to their parties on the weekends.

Good hair looks good wet or dry. With good hair you can shower or swim without worrying about your hair going back to the naps. My sisters don't have good hair and are deathly afraid of getting their hair wet. Their hair curls up tightly like wire around a telephone cord at just the mention of water. My sister Debra would rather drown than swim.

To keep the naps at bay and to look like they had good hair, some of the guys I knew kept their hair processed. Processed hair was chemically straightened and glistened with hair dressing to keep its pressed waves or high pompadours in place. It looked good but didn't feel soft.

A costly process would be ruined if you ran your fingers through it like good hair. Most black entertainers wore processes in the late fifties and early sixties. At night the wearer wore a do-rag to keep his process in place. Many guys in my neighborhood wore stocking caps as their do-rags.

But just like good hair, the process fell victim to the Black Liberation Movement. Even James Brown stopped wearing a process when Huey Newton accused men wearing them of being Uncle Toms trying to imitate their slave masters. It didn't stop Sammy Davis Jr. from wearing one, though.

To some of the older people in my neighborhood, especially those from Down South, good hair meant you had some white folk in you, and that was a good thing. Good hair and light skin were as close to white as you could get without being white yourself. I guess it made me a good catch for their daughters. Any accidental grandchild I produced might have good hair.

Mama had said that my phantom father, whom I never met, had light skin and good hair. Light skin and good hair generally go together, kind of like red hair and freckles. I've got Big Red's good hair, but I'm not light-skinned. Huey Newton was light-skinned and had nappy hair. I wonder who'd been in his woodshed?

BOOK FIVE

GOOD RIDDANCE/BAD TIMES

After three years we moved back downtown from Madeira. They no longer needed Daddy's help on I-71, and we couldn't afford living there without the extra pay. Once we moved back downtown I left home. I didn't run away. I simply left. The dangling thread holding us together had snapped even before leaving Madeira. It became increasingly harder for Daddy and me to get along, especially where women were involved. He kept inserting himself into my relationships with girls.

It all came to a head when I dated a girl from Madisonville. Because no buses ran between Madeira and Madisonville I had to pick Velma up and send her home by cab. To make matters easier she'd sometimes pay the cab fare up and I'd pay for the return. We made it work, but we both saw that it couldn't go on like that unless something changed. Daddy learned of our situation and graciously offered to take Velma home.

"Junior, don't worry about getting Velma home. If I'm not doing anything, I don't mind taking her back. That way all you'll have to worry about is paying her cab fare up here. Think that'll work?"

I was shocked. Daddy hadn't offered to help with anything else that involved girls, like my going to dances. I wasn't sure of his motive but decided to wait and see.

"Thanks, Daddy, that will help a lot." Velma just smiled and dropped her head.

Things worked that way for about three visits before Velma stopped coming.

"I just can't come out there anymore." she said over the phone. "Why don't you come down here. You okay with that?"

"Sure, I'm good with that. How about this weekend?"

She said yes, and I said I'd see her at seven on Saturday. As I hung up the phone, something didn't feel right. What made her stop wanting to visit me in Madeira? She'd invited me to visit her at home, so she still liked me. I stopped worrying about it and figured I'd find out when we met.

Velma's family lived in the second-floor apartment of a single-family house. I approached her apartment from the covered staircase on the side of the house. She opened the door before I could knock.

"Hi, Junior," she said and hugged me. "Come on in."

Of everything I'd gotten from Robert by going to Madisonville, Velma was the best.

"Hi, Velma," I said. "Is your mama home? Can we talk?"

"Mama's home. She knows you were coming. Why don't you say hi?"

She took me by the hand and led me to the living room where her mama was watching TV.

"Hi, Mrs. Washington."

"Hi, Junior. Good to see you, boy. What you two doing tonight?"

"Probably walk down to the park and back," said Velma.

"Yes, ma'am, ain't too hot tonight."

"Better enjoy it then. Don't stay too long."

"Alright, Mama," said Velma, and off we went.

It was a bit hotter than we thought, and when I saw the dry grass of the park with little shade around I said, "Why don't we go someplace where it's cool and we can sit down and talk?"

"Hot Fries is close. It's cool and has fries if you want," Velma said.

"I don't care as long as it's cool."

Two blocks past the park on a street corner sat a storefront. Under the streetlight I saw a hand-painted sign in a long window that read, "Hot Fries." I could see people moving around inside and could tell it wasn't jam-packed. From the looks of it I might be able to get cooled off and still have privacy enough to talk.

We got inside, I bought a bag of greasy fries for twenty-five cents, and we sat down at a booth in back. It was somewhat private. Another couple's booth backed up against ours. It was as far from the Coke machine as we could get, and that helped. I brought a Coke over for Velma, and we started to eat. Before the bag was emptied, hot, saucy fries had incinerated my tongue. Hot Fries would never be accused of false advertising. When I could finally talk without croaking we got down to business. Sitting next to me in the booth, Velma rested her hand on my thigh under the table. She felt warm and comfortable. No matter what her mama may have thought, Velma was no child.

I remember when we first met. I saw her at a dance at the center in Madisonville. Being from Madeira, Robert and I were hot picks for the girls but competition for the guys. We made our peace by establishing a relationship with Jerome. I wasn't interested in Jerome or what he felt or thought about our coming to a dance in his neighborhood. He didn't look or talk like any of the guys downtown. He was just a guy living in Madisonville far away from downtown pretending to be tough. He and Robert knew each other from school. They both attended Withrow High in the heart of Madisonville.

"I've dealt with him at school. He's okay. Just wants to feel important. Give him some slack, Junior. We'll be alright," said Robert.

Unlike with Big Otis in the Lincoln Court, I could choose whoever I wanted to dance with in Jerome's neighborhood. I noticed Velma right away.

She wore a yellow dress that belted at her waist. Her tiny waist made the skirt stretch out above the middle of her thighs when she moved on the dance floor. Whether dancing with her or not, if you were a man you looked at her. You had no choice. Too short and dark to be Miss America and too thin to model for the Ebony Fashion Fair, her pixie smile and fairy figure put them both to shame. I got to her just in time for the last dance, a slow one. Having her close to me made me want to pick her up and carry her away. I felt that same way again tonight.

"Now tell me," I said. "What's going on? Why can't you come out to Madeira anymore?"

She leaned her head against my shoulder and looked straight ahead, away from me. "It's really no big deal. It's too much trouble with the cab and all. Takes up too much time."

"Yeah," I said. "If you didn't want to tell me, why am I here? You brought me all the way to Madisonville just to say that? Come on, tell me what's really going on."

"Okay, this is it," she said. I didn't know if she was mad or crying. "The last time he brought me home, your daddy tried to make me go to bed with him."

I couldn't talk. My hands were balled into fists so tight blood couldn't pass through. I could see his face, partially smiling as he looked at her trying to pull her in. I opened my mouth, the words barely able to roll over my tongue.

"What do you mean he tried to make you go to bed?"

"He asked how much would it take for him to 'get some of that.'"

"Did you tell your mama?"

"No, she'd want to call the police. I didn't want to get your family in trouble."

"Has he done this before?"

"Yes," she said, "the week before last. I didn't want to tell you. I thought if I ignored him it wouldn't happen again. And I didn't want you to get in any trouble with your daddy."

I could see why she didn't want to tell me. The sonofabitch. I was already in trouble because the moment I spoke to him it would be over. He'd already knocked me down the stairs on Gest Street for zipping up

Nellie's girdle, and it was her fault. She'd asked me to do it. My sister Wanda had seen us and told Daddy when he came home from work. He went berserk, punched me in the face, and knocked me down the steps. If I approached him about Velma it definitely would result in something physical. I knew I couldn't beat him, and I didn't want it to come to that.

"Listen, I'm so sorry you had to deal with this," I said. "I can understand why you didn't want to say anything, but it's too late for that now. I've got to see him."

"What do you mean?" she said.

"I don't know. I've just got to talk to him, to find out what the hell he's doing."

"He's your daddy, Junior. He can mess you up. I just won't come out there anymore. We can still see each other like this. It'll be better this way anyway."

"No, it ain't alright. Don't worry about me. I ain't going to do anything stupid."

"Promise me, Junior," she said. "Promise me. I mean it."

———

After my talk with Velma I could barely stand to be in Daddy's company. Whenever he came home I tried to be out. I needed more money to add to what I'd saved from working on Mr. Rosewood's garbage truck. That extra money would help me make my escape. I held my tongue while my anger smoldered. Whenever I wanted to see Velma, I'd go to Madisonville. I didn't mention it to Daddy. It wasn't the right time for a fight.

I found a job at the Red Barn on lower Vine Street. Worse than a Kentucky Fried Chicken without the colonel, a cheap Chicken Shack without wings, the food tasted as bad as it looked. Without any experience, I was hired as a cashier. I advised my friends to eat there only if they were hungry. I saw the food being prepared.

My pay equaled my experience. Someone like me with no experience and not even a high school diploma couldn't expect to earn very much.

Red Barn didn't check my employment application because I lied about having a high school education. I guess they figured they could pay me less knowing that I lied and couldn't risk being checked out. They were right. They hadn't counted on my voracious appetite. I could eat more than they were paying me and would have, had they not established a policy that limited when and how much we could eat. It made no difference, though, because we were at war. The Red Barn tried to pay as little as they could, and I tried to eat as much as I could. In the end I lost. I gained twelve pounds and lost my job. The Red Barn kept on clucking.

Never a whiz at math, I managed to check out orders fairly well. Besides, the machine did most of the work. My speed did me in. Daddy used to say, "Junior, you were born slow and went downhill ever since." My top speed faded when two customers stepped in line. Once that threshold shattered, things began to crawl. Give me three customers and my legs turned to stone. Little Leaguers were the worst. A gang of Little Leaguers paralyzed me. I hate the YMCA.

Saturday after dinner most folk are home. Evening rush started about seven and lasted till around nine. Customers came in drips and drabs until eleven and I checked out. That's how it should have gone, except for the Blue Horde.

There must have been a Little League game nearby that Saturday, because a horde of boys wearing blue YMCA baseball uniforms stampeded the Red Barn around 6:30. They rushed into the lobby like a hurricane of locusts. Everyone moving, shouting, crushing stillness with their energy. Their entrance alone could've given me a seizure. I tried to take charge.

"Alright, if you want to get waited on, make a line. I'll take one order at a time," I said.

It was like telling a busted lip not to bleed. The group became its own organ. Once the team discipline was gone, nothing could hold it back. To my good fortune, one of their teammates stepped up to take charge.

He had a smooth, angelic face with steely, unwavering eyes. He looked shorter than the others but appeared unshakable. A little general. He stood as if he couldn't be moved.

"Alright, guys," he said, "are we the Kings or what? Tighten up. Let's get this line together."

To my surprise everyone fell right into line. No wonder they were the Kings, with this take-charge master on the team. I wondered if he knew how to operate a cash register. One by one their orders came pouring in. "Two chicken sandwiches, fries, and a Pepsi," said one.

"Two-twenty-five," I answered.

"All I've got is a five," he said, and my downfall began.

Nobody ever carries two dollars and twenty-five cents conveniently separated in their pockets. Little Leaguers have pockets, not purses, and don't carry change. Their mamas give them singles or fives, and maybe a ten if they're hurried. The ones with all change caused another problem: waiting while they dug it out. I started getting the hang of it and foolishly thought the horde might be slowing down, when I suddenly remembered the seven o'clock rush.

Panic is only a third cousin to the chaos I felt. Cash register bells tinkled nonstop in my head. The Blue Horde of the YMCA Kings shrank to a platoon of stamping feet as the doors opened and closed faster than my fingers could punch the cash register. As I looked over the heads of the last of the Blue Horde, I could see adults shaking with impatience waiting for me to toss the horde aside. I had nearly crossed the finish line when it happened. With the very last "One chicken, fry, and a Pepsi" order taken and the previous one delivered, my angel morphed into the devil.

The woman behind the last of the horde shoved him away from the counter before I'd given him his change.

"Move out of the way," she said. "I've been waiting here long enough. Now go on."

It wasn't that hard, but the boy fell from the force of her shove and laid there a moment before getting up. Before my manager or I could say anything, one of the Kings rushed to pick up his teammate. It was the little general, the same one who'd helped get everyone quiet and lined up ready to order. He helped his friend up, walked him and the remaining team members out of the restaurant, and returned. I thought he had forgotten something, and before I could ask he walked over to the pusher, pulled her down by the collar, and shotgunned his fist into her jaw.

"Don't mess with one of the Kings, bitch," he said, and walked out while the rest of us stood there in shock.

"Call the police," someone shouted.

She might as well have yelled, "Fire!" Customers jumped up from the tables, and others rushed forward to look. People in line rushed to comfort the one who'd been punched. Her jaw already swelling and blood trickling from her nose, she looked like the loser in a boxing match. Miss Jones, the manager, came from out back where she'd been smoking Virginia Slims and eased the woman into a chair.

"Call the police," someone called again.

I turned to go to the phone on the wall by the grill.

"Don't touch that phone, Junior," yelled Miss Jones. "We ain't having no police in here."

"Somebody better call the police," said the woman who'd been punched, "or I'll have this place closed down. I didn't come in here to get attacked."

No one had thought about the Blue Horde until she'd mentioned the attack. I looked out the window into the parking lot and the horde had vanished. If they ran around the bases as fast as they ran away from the Red Barn, they must've won every game. I stepped outside and imagined them halfway to the Y with the general whipping them along.

No one from inside called the police, not even the victim, and yet they came. I don't think we ever found out who called. The police came inside and got a statement from the woman who'd been punched and asked if she wanted to come downtown to file a report. She said yes and left in her car. They questioned Miss Jones and me about it, and I told them everything as it happened. Miss Jones looked at me with blood in her eyes. I didn't like the way she looked at me. It made my shoulders bunch. I'd seen a guy with eyes like that stab a guy shooting craps in the alley by Jim's house. He didn't say a word while the dice were rolling. He just looked at him through angry, bloodshot eyes. When the dice stopped rolling, he casually stepped up and stabbed the shooter in the neck. That's how I felt Miss Jones's eyes were on me while I gave my statement.

"Didn't I tell you not to call the police?" she said. "Didn't I say that I didn't want no police up in here?"

"I don't know who called the police. It wasn't me."

"Don't lie to me. I know it was you. You think I don't know you ain't got no high school diploma and trying to talk all proper. Who do you think you are anyway? I only hired you 'cause we needed someone right away. You can take your apron off and get your ass out of here now, today."

"But Miss Jones, I'll work extra shifts for the same pay. Just let me stay on for two more weeks."

"Two more weeks. Slow as you are and as much as you eat I'll be in the hole if I kept you one more day, let alone two more weeks. Naw. Gimme your apron and get your ass out of here."

Being fired from the Red Barn I no longer had to live with Daddy. With the little money from working at the Red Barn added to my nest egg from working on the garbage truck, it was time to go. I waited until I'd picked up the check for my last nine days at the Red Barn before conducting my showdown with Daddy. Hiding it from Nellie, I'd collected my clothes and given them to my oldest sister, Wanda. I asked her to put them in shopping bags and give them to me when I called. I waited until Friday to catch Daddy in his best mood before confronting him about Velma. I caught him at the kitchen table drinking coffee after Nellie had left the room.

"Hi, Daddy."

"Hi, Junior. What's going on?"

"Can I talk to you about something for a minute?"

"Yeah, what is it?"

"It's about something that Velma said."

I saw the crease in his brow begin to form.

"Umm, what did she say?"

"She said that you tried to hit on her."

His lids lifted, and he turned toward me, half smiling as his left temple started to throb.

"What do you mean, I tried to hit on her?"

"She said you tried to pay her to go to bed with you."

The creases in his brow grew deeper. His eyelids lifted to reveal black fires burning inside. The vein in his right temple started throbbing.

"What is this about, Junior? Don't come in here questioning me about something some girl said."

"Daddy, I just wanted to find out if she was telling the truth. That's all."

His burning fires became molten pools. He could barely see. His hands were sledges on the table.

"You just want to find out. To find out what? You come in *my* house to question *me*, question me about something some little hot-ass girl said. Boy, you better watch yourself."

I knew he was lying. I felt his anger, his fear of being found out. I didn't give a damn about his anger. The worst he could do was hit me. I was too smart for that. Like a jungle animal with his back against the wall, I knew his next response might be to attack. I backed up.

"Okay, Daddy. I'm through with it. Okay?"

"Oh, so now you're through with it. *You're through with it.*" And his fist slammed the table. "I'm so grateful you're through with it. Nigger, I don't know who you think you are, but ain't but one man living in this house. I ain't having no grown-ass nigger living under my roof. I pay the rent here, understand? It's time for you to get your own house, Mr. Man, and get the hell out of mine. Since you so grown, go take care of yourself."

I got up without a word and gratefully walked away. I rushed to my room, dug out my hidden money stash, got my jacket, stuffed a change of clothes and underwear in a garbage bag, and headed for the door. Passing Wanda on the way I said, "I'm good, just take care of my stuff and wait for my call," and stepped through the door. I leaped down the stairs with one thought on my mind: *I'm free.*

Seeking a job and a place to stay, I hitchhiked my way with bag in hand to the top of the Vine Street hill, looking for a job at the Frisch's on Calhoun Street. It didn't take long before a used Ford sedan with four people pulled up to a stop at the curb next to me. Looking at them you could tell they were college kids about my age. Two girls in back and boy and girl in front. With my eyes closed I could tell they had a party going on.

"Hey, man," the driver said. "Where you going?"

"Up on Calhoun," I said.

"Jump in back."

I jumped in. The girls scooted over and put me in the middle. I don't see how the driver managed. I was floating and had just gotten in. It was like riding a giant joint with tires on it.

"You want a joint?" said the girl to my right as she rolled another one.

"Yeah," I said. "What the hell is this?"

"It's Lebanese Blonde," said the other girl as I pulled on it. She took it from me and inhaled.

"We got more where that came from," said the driver. "Where you headed?"

"Wherever you're going." Off we went, and the four of us were together for the next three months.

I had been up on Calhoun before. Calhoun Street was Cincinnati's version of the Haight-Ashbury district in San Francisco. It wasn't as large and didn't have as many buildings but fostered the same community. I had smoked reefer at parties in Madisonville, though nothing as strong as what they had. Their smoke was the bomb for real.

Calhoun interested me for more than its smoke. Nobody downtown offered strangers a joint and seldom offered anyone a joint for free. No one trusted strangers. Here I had jumped into a stranger's car, been offered a joint, and not asked for any money. Most of the guys I'd grown up with lived by the maxim that nothing that could be sold should be given away. This group seemed generous and trusting, even to strangers. It was worth checking out.

Pete, Bettie, and JoAnn lived on the first floor of a shabby three-story apartment building on Calhoun Street hemmed in by others like it. I don't know where they were coming from when we met, but they invited me to eat.

"Hey man, get something to eat," said Bettie, the one who'd first given me a joint.

"Yeah, dig in," said Pete.

They had lots of vegetables and fruit, some packed in containers and some in boxes. I looked in the plastic garbage can in the corner and saw some Frisch's wrappers. Their sight alone satisfied my soul. I couldn't stand living without meat, no matter how generous my roommates or how powerful their smoke.

JoAnn gave us the peace sign and headed for the bedroom. In a moment I smelled the fresh aroma of pot drifting our way.

Noticing my bag Bettie asked, "Where you staying, Junior?"

"I'm working on it."

"We got room. You can crash here if you want."

"Sounds good to me."

Every night somebody had a jam, and good and better smoke came through. Some folk had hash, some even had LSD. Hallucinogens drove folk crazy, and I stayed away from them. Most of the people that I knew had marijuana or hash. Where the money came from remained a mystery—though we all knew and no one voiced it. Somebody was selling big time. Working people stopped in to buy reefer, and we'd say they'd gotten the wrong information and send them elsewhere.

I kept my own schedule. I spent much of the time rambling around the University of Cincinnati trying to slip into seminars or public lectures for free. I found people everywhere, even during summer session. The guys in my neighborhood called the "students up on the hill" squares because of the way they dressed. They put Levi's and khakis in a category for kids. Teenagers wore tailor-made slacks or wool or sharkskins. I got infected with the square disease when I determined the clothes I'd brought with me didn't fit in with my new self. With a little help from Bettie I sold anything of mine worthwhile to a used clothing store and bought a few things for myself.

Bettie didn't have a large wardrobe. With her looks and spirit, she didn't need one. She could wear the same thing every day, and all you'd ever notice was her person. She had short black hair, dark smoky eyes, a swimsuit body, and stood about five-feet-six. She reminded me of Annette Funicello. People in the house who didn't know her called her the "Mouseketeer." We smoked lots of reefer, had fantastic sex, and slept together like rolled-up puppies on the floor.

Bettie made my life on Calhoun worthwhile. She and I hung out on campus and attended any open seminar we could when a writer was speaking. I loved to write, and Bettie enjoyed writing as much as I did. Though drugs and sex held the house together, our shared love for writing was the glue that joined us.

The house reminded me a lot of living on Thirteenth Street. Like on Thirteenth, it was a community of itself: an old tenement building with two apartments on each floor of a three-story building filled with people who knew and looked out for one another. We didn't always know one another's names, but we knew each other. Jerry, the guy on the third floor with the Lennon glasses, would eat anything, so keep your food away from him. Louise, on the second floor, was gay, and everybody in the building loved her. On the other hand, her partner was a bitch. It continued like that throughout the building. We got along. I never thought about our harmony until it was gone.

After living up on Calhoun for a short time, I stopped by Daddy's apartment prepared to square things up and to get something to eat. I knocked. No answer. Knocked again and still no sound. Much bigger than when he boosted me through the transom on Thirteenth Street, I looked around to make sure no one saw me, lifted my arms high against the door, and pushed against the bottom of the transom window. It moved slightly backward at my touch. Using the top of the door for support, I lifted myself up as if doing a pull-up. In a hurry to get inside and to keep from being mistakenly seen as a burglar, I placed my left foot on the door handle, lifted myself, and pushed the transom completely open. I held onto the door sill and twisted my body until I forced one knee into the room and held onto the door until I squeezed the other knee through, pulling my calf after it. Then, with both legs inside and still hanging onto the transom sill, I let go of the sill and landed with a whisper on the kitchen floor. Daddy would be proud of me. With an entry that smooth, maybe I should have been a burglar.

I quietly walked around the kitchen and decided to check Daddy's bedroom before raiding the refrigerator. Quietly peeking into the room, I saw him lying on his side with his left hand dangling over the side of the bed. A burned-out Pall Mall held limply between his fingers barely brushed against the carpet just inches away. Daddy lay sprawled and formless, like a deflated balloon—a shrunken, Thanksgivinglike balloon of Mama Liza's Sport, a man unable to live outside of Selma. He lay there too sad to awaken and too beaten to care. I felt bad for him, but not bad enough to cry.

I cried with him the day he brought home the news that Mama had died. He had been such a strong man, but all strength deserted his body like water swirling down a drain. His head fell upon the table with such searing agony that it forged our pain into one. That day I cried for his loss and for mine. But when I saw him passed out dead drunk on his bed, I thought, *It's his shit. Let him deal with it.* I went back to his refrigerator and took out some cold chicken, cornbread, and greens. I heated everything in the oven, ate, and left. I thought about leaving him some money, but I had already shut the door behind me. Later that summer, after breakfast one day up on Calhoun, Pete tapped me on the shoulder with a newspaper and said, "Thought you might want to see this. Your dad's dead."

In the lower right-hand corner of the inside third page where they usually reported small crimes and accidents, the headline read "West End Man Dies in Fire." The reporter wrote that Daddy died overcome by the smoke. Neither the reporter nor the firemen knew the cause of the fire, but I imagine it to be 20 Grand Ale and Pall Malls. I wondered what my sisters felt. He was their loving daddy who protected and supported them when he could. I'm sure they felt his loss very dearly. I didn't cry, but I mourned.

I mourned for the loss of the good times we had before Thirteenth Street, when he worked at the slaughterhouse on Colerain Avenue. We lived in O'Bryonville and played catch together at the Horace Mann School with the genuine Reds leather glove he'd bought me, even though it wasn't Christmas. Sometimes we'd walk through the woods over by Mayor Berry's house. Mama said Mr. Ted Berry was Cincinnati's first black mayor and that I should see him. We never did see him out in his yard or anything, but it felt good, just the three of us walking together. Daddy bought a brand-new Kaiser when we lived in O'Bryonville before my sisters were born. When he died I couldn't cry. We both had lost too much.

———

Things started to change when school started in the fall and party time had to cut back. Parents who funded their kids' educations made demands that didn't include Calhoun Street.

I hadn't seen Bettie all day. Her mother had called the day before, and Bettie agreed to meet at a coffee shop near campus. When she returned she looked both shaky and anxious.

"School's about to start," she said.

"Yeah, I'm hip."

"Mama says they won't pay my tuition this year if I don't get my shit together."

We both knew this was coming, and the real deal was school. Our relationship was great, but it was all part of our being together on Calhoun for a summer.

"Hey, you know what to do. I'm with you. Take care of business, Bettie. I'll miss you."

We hung out together for another day, smoked, made love through the night, and her mother stopped by and picked her up the next morning.

Life with Bettie had made my living on Calhoun an adventure. Sitting around talking about abstract freedoms versus concrete laws felt invigorating under a haze of marijuana. It became stale after being there for a while. Bettie emerged as the one thing interesting enough to make it livable. After she left, it was like cotton in my mouth and difficult to swallow without being high.

As earlier residents left to be replaced by others, the make-believe security we had created for ourselves began to crack. The new, unfamiliar community turned our naïve existence into an arrogant prescription for our own demise. We knew that someone among us was buying and selling large amounts of drugs. It only followed that someone was making huge sums of money. The dealers lived like us, people whom we knew. It wasn't our business to know how they made their money. After all, the rest of us benefited. How else could we rent an entire apartment building when no one among us had a real job? Some of us had brought a little money with us and occasionally added to it with day work. I once worked with a janitorial crew cleaning office buildings downtown. It amazed me how spacious and luxurious some of them were. Hardwood doors and marble floors, sinks with gilt faucets, toilets with seats that automatically came back down. Those bathrooms looked better than most of the apartments I'd grown up in. But I paid my fair share of the keep, and that's what mattered to me. As in any jungle, unguarded self-sufficiency is a predator's clarion call.

Everyone in town said that "the hippies up on Calhoun are making a killing." But we were smart, or so we thought. We figured that because we didn't look well off, no one would be the wiser. Many of the residents, especially the girls who'd come from poorer parts of the city, felt doubly stigmatized by living in the house. When asked, "Why don't you leave?" one girl answered, "I don't know where else to go." The house became noted for harboring more lost souls and refugees than it was able to support.

Because there were lots of college girls who always appeared to be high, tricks stopped by looking for sex. Once in a while they'd strike it rich, but most times they'd strike out. Campus regulars stopped by chasing drugs like dogs chasing rabbits. Sex chased those who bought the drugs.

Older guys, street hustlers who weren't college students, started stopping by on a pretense of "looking for smoke." Looking like Jim and I had just a few years earlier, they easily stood out in their big hats, highly shined shoes, and sharply creased pants. I had morphed into Jimi Hendrix, wearing a bandanna around my forehead, a cloth belt, bell bottoms, and Cuban heels. We lived in different worlds now. If we offered them something for free, they wanted more. They sucked on our goodwill like parasites. Others soon followed who wanted to "meet the main man" because they wanted to buy some weight. This scenario happened time and again with the same result. One day I saw one of them whom I knew. He had entered through the alley onto the first floor.

"Hey," I said when I saw him. "What's happening, brother?"

He looked at me without showing any recognition.

"Hey, brother. You live here?"

"Yeah, man. Who you looking for?"

"I ain't really looking for anybody. Just trying to find out about some weed. You know anybody?"

"No, man. I'm just here. I don't know anybody. What other people do is their business, not mine."

"Well, why don't you make it yours, motherfucker?" he said and grabbed me by the collar.

By that time Pete had heard the noise and, seeing what happened, came to back me up. I pulled away from the guy's hand and said, "What the fuck? You better raise up out of here, man. We don't play that shit."

He backed out and said, "Yeah, your little white boys can't protect you. I'll be back. The next time I won't be buying. I'll just take your shit."

The drug dealers on Calhoun fell just like sitting ducks to the jackals from downtown. Someone would meet them pretending to buy, pistol whip them, and take their drugs and money. The open society that had welcomed newcomers like me with drugs and sex no longer existed. In its place arose a society of secrecy, violence, and distrust that was a direct result of the change in drug usage. Marijuana was a soft drug that didn't bring the kind of money that heroin produced. Heroin brought hardened criminals into a world of neophytes. It brought drug addicts with cookers and needles into the socially addicted world of marijuana. Many students who could use reefer and still produce in college couldn't do the same on heroin. Heroin usage could lead to overdose and death. With heroin, there was no pretense of innocence, no redemption. As one addict put it, "It was a shit hole with no bottom."

"Jeff was beaten with a pipe behind the house," Albert told me when I returned from buying tickets for a Stones concert.

"*What?*"

"Yeah, and he's in General Hospital almost dead."

"For what? What is this all about?"

"JoAnn saw it."

"Where is she? What did she say?"

"She's gone, scared the fuck out of her."

"What did she see?"

"Two guys, black guys, one who's been here before, you probably know him. They kept asking Jeff to give up his money and his stash, like they thought he was Lance or something. Lance is the one with the money. Jeff just looks like him. Damn shame."

"JoAnn saw them beat him?"

"Yeah, they beat the hell out of him with a pipe and then stabbed him. If it wasn't for that garbage truck, he could be dead."

In an attempt to take Lance's stash and bankroll, supposedly two heroin dealers had tried to rob Jeff in the alley behind our house. They couldn't take his money because he didn't have any. He couldn't give up his stash because he didn't have one. They beat him with a pipe, stabbed him, and left him in the alley to die. He probably would have died if the truck hadn't stopped to empty the dumpster that day.

Jeff's attack spotlighted the cancer that poisoned Calhoun Street. So close to the University of Cincinnati that you could smell education, the wealth surrounding the university cursed Calhoun. Like pulling predators to a water hole, drugs pulled dealers and addicts to Calhoun, producing a maelstrom of money. Its proximity to UC protected it somewhat because most of its customers were students. Students had money and weren't street criminals. That distinction became one of the reasons I stayed for the whole Calhoun experience. I wanted to be part of that group—a group I'd seen as separate from us on Gest Street, a group that could commit crimes like smoking reefer without regard to their penalties, or so I thought. They could get away with things that would send the people on Gest Street to jail. It gave me a sense of freedom without responsibility, a kind of freedom I wanted to explore.

When the police came to investigate the assault, they couldn't get any information from anyone living there. Noting drug paraphernalia around, the cops called for backup. It looked like twenty cars rolled up with red and blue lights flashing. They screeched up on the sidewalk and fanned out like a hand of cards. Looking through the window I saw people gathered in the streets, some looking upstairs, others toward the alley, and all in joyous anticipation of someone running from the house being chased down and roped like a rodeo pony gone wild. "Those damn hippies," I heard someone say. "Get rid of them. Damn smokeheads."

Like roaches stampeding over one other trying to escape a can of Raid, everyone tried to get away but only stumbled into more cops. Addicts and smokeheads were all rounded up and taken in a blue wagon downtown. I thought for sure my time was up and stood next to the back door, waiting for the best time to run, when somebody rushed by and grabbed me by the arm.

"You want to go to jail, man?" he shouted.

It was Pete, the same guy who'd given me a ride when I first hitch-hiked up the hill.

"No," I shouted back as he kept going.

"Stop fucking around and follow me."

We ducked and ran through the door under the stairs that led to the cellar, one of those doors where the topside of the door is cut the same slope as the staircase. It didn't have a handle, and if you didn't see it you could easily miss it. The cellar ran the full length of the house and, like in the movies, was filled with concrete arches for supports. It was pitch-black and musty, with the odor of dead rats, rotten and rusted furniture, and maybe a corpse or two, for all I could tell. We squeezed ourselves into the darkest, smelliest corner we could find and tried to shrink our bodies into the horrors we couldn't see.

"If they find us in all this shit, we need to go to jail," said Pete.

I said nothing, tried not to inhale, and waited. After about thirty minutes or more we didn't hear any noises coming from above. We unfolded ourselves and moved forward on cramped muscles to listen at the foot of the stairs.

We thought the house was empty when we pushed the door open into the first floor and were surprised by two cops still there. One was seated on the couch counting a stack of bills that must have belonged to Lance. The other was standing guard, making sure no one else was watching. The moment I saw him, I got the fuck out of there. The same cop who'd arrested me and Jim on Gest Street for hauling window weights caught Pete first.

"You and your buddy over here dealing, ain't you? Well, we got you now," he said as he threw Pete against the wall and cuffed him. "Where's your buddy?"

I had almost made it to the front door before his partner grabbed me by the neck of my dashiki. I tried to slide out of it, but my arms got tied up.

The big blue wagon was gone, so Pete and I had the luxury of riding in the back of one of the cop's limos. Not exactly a limo, but with the screen separating the passengers from the driver, we could pretend the cop was our chauffeur. I felt like asking Pete for some Grey Poupon, but our driver wasn't in a humorous mood. I kept my mouth shut.

We found many of our housemates in holding cells at the county jail. Some looked afraid, some were angry, and a few like me were more curious than anything else. I had been before a judge as a juvenile and didn't fear appearing before one again. Unlike my juvenile appearance, I now had to speak with a court-appointed attorney before being tried.

"Is this your first offense?"

"Yes, Sir."

"We can probably get you probation. Where do you live?"

"Right now I'm on my own."

"That doesn't look good. Got any place to stay? Any relatives you can live with?"

"No, just my sisters, and they stay in a foster home."

"Well, the sentence for living in a house where drugs are present is from three to six months in the Workhouse. This is easy. You'll just plead guilty to the misdemeanor, and I'll ask for the minimum. You'll be out in forty-five days."

The confiscated drugs made it downtown as evidence, but I doubt if all of the money did. Pete and I beat the drug-dealing charge because we weren't dealing and there was no proof that anyone had made any buys. It couldn't be denied that we "resided in an area with drugs on the premises." We both pled guilty as we'd been instructed and were sentenced to ninety days in the Cincinnati Workhouse.

It felt anticlimactic riding to the Workhouse with about thirty others in the long yellow bus with "Cincinnati Workhouse" painted on the side. Like the guys who'd grown up in the Lincoln Courts and Laurel Homes, I wasn't alarmed by what I was about to face. Although I had seen a different life in Walnut Hills and Madeira, I never let my street guard down. It protected me on Gest Street, and the Workhouse couldn't be any worse. I just hunkered down and kept my cool.

Before we arrived I overheard one of the guys from Calhoun say, "Man, we're really going to the Workhouse?"

"Yeah," said the guy beside him.

"This kind of shit don't happen to me. What am I doing here? I ain't no fucking criminal."

I said, "What do you think smoking weed is, some kind of law school exercise? It's against the law. You smoked it. You got caught. That's why you're here."

Three or four seats ahead of me, a thin, hard-eyed guy chimed in, "How many times you broke the law and ain't got caught?"

No reply from the Calhoun innocent.

"Yeah, I thought so. Well, this is payback for all that other shit. Indians call it karma. This is yours. Roll with it, bitch, and stop crying."

A quiet guy in back said, "Wake up, my man, this shit is real."

By the time the big yellow bus rolled through the brick archway of the Workhouse gate, the noise and jokes stopped. Last-minute memories crowded our minds before being snuffed out by the minutiae of incarceration. The bus stopped in front of a short building surrounded by barbed wire. We filed out toward an open door that revealed open showers waiting for new arrivals. All the welcoming team wore Workhouse blues. No guards were present. (If I didn't know people like Navigator Jack on Thirteenth Street, I wouldn't know how valuable those hard-worn men are.)

The welcoming team was made up of older, used-up men who had lost years of their lives in installments at the Workhouse and had grown comfortable there. Trusted men, well known to the staff. Outside, thrown away, useless, and unseen. Inside, you couldn't find a more faithful friend and staunch ally

I stepped off the bus onto the gravel of the bathhouse drive. A grandfatherly looking man threw me an outfit of Workhouse blues on my way to the shower inside.

"These look a little too big," I said.

"Beats being too small."

I guess he did me a favor. Too big, I looked like a regular. Too tight, and I'd look like a bitch.

WORKOUT AT THE WORKHOUSE

From outside, the Cincinnati Workhouse didn't look as I'd expected. The central building of red stone blocks with two wings and three outbuildings looked larger than most prisons I'd seen on TV. When I jumped off the yellow bus to serve a ninety-day sentence, all that TV shit blew apart like a watermelon dropped from a ten-story building.

I'd heard guys in the neighborhood who'd been there say, "Aside from the smell, it ain't all that bad." But you couldn't get "aside from the smell." A permanent toxic haze settled over every inch of the Workhouse—one that crept up your pants leg, mixed with the sweat and urine in your shorts, and scratched its way upward out of your shirt where it settled in your nose. You wore it and bore it through every waking and sleeping moment of your sentence. Some of us believed that alone could've been sentence enough. Even if we had the technology, no law would allow that smell on TV. I never have forgotten it and probably never will. The rest of my time showed me where my road could end and how easily I could end it there.

Built as a prison between 1867 and 1869 to hold 360 male and 240 female prisoners, the Workhouse still held both sexes, our orientation guard said. I felt better after that. Maybe I'd get a chance to meet some women.

Reading my mind, the guard said, "You don't want to have anything to do with these women. They are all dope addicts, or here for disorderly conduct, child neglect, and everything else. If caught trying to contact one of them, you'll go straight to the hole. Up to you to make it easy on yourself."

I celled in a two-bed cell with another young guy like me. Caught driving without a license, he got thirty days. I asked him, "What's the deal? What's the routine? Who's the main man?"

"I've only been here a minute," said Top Cat. "On this side Barley's got everything sewed up. I hear he's even fucking one of those girls from the other side. Meets one in the laundry room when that skinny guard's on at night. You'll meet him. He's cool."

I'd heard about Barley but figured the talk about his fucking that girl was a joke. If true, and he relied on people like Top Cat to stay cool about it, he was already busted. Dominating the center of the main house, the central block divided into two sections, with four stories of twenty two-man cells on each range. Each cell stank of lies resting on stalks of truth. It wasn't the best atmosphere for growth. We lived in Cell Block A, fourth range, Cell 5. Each range left in turn from the first to the fourth for chow. If you missed stepping out when your cell opened, you missed eating. I never missed a meal.

I'd been there for about a week trying to chew up time before I got an unexpected visit. In the wide spaces between the cell blocks and the tall metal-framed glass windows that looked like a Gothic cathedral, wooden picnic or game tables were spaced along the floor. Games kept us busy and out of the guards' hair. I played dominoes, whist, and sometimes checkers. In rise and fly I could only keep a hand as long as I won. In whist I had to rely on a partner. So I spent more time playing dominoes than anything else. I had a streak going since breakfast, and it was an hour before lunch when I heard my number called. "16713 to the Visiting Room, 16713."

When I reached the visiting room, the guard handed me a pass and went through the door into the room where the visitors waited. It was packed with people, black and white. Crying babies. Pregnant girls and women. Girlfriends and wives. Little boys trying to relate to fathers who were in jail once again. There for me stood Bettie, bringing light and something solid from my past. We were directed to a small aluminum table with connecting seats. I reached out to hug and bring her to me. "No touching," the guard quickly reminded me. It made no difference to me. Just having her there touched me deeper than anything physical could do.

"Well, I see you're still looking good," I said.

"Yeah, I'm doing alright. What about you?"

"Not bad. How did you know I was here?"

"JoAnn told me. She came to see Pete."

I didn't know if I wanted her to see me here or not. She looked so different in these surroundings. Even though we'd laid around on Calhoun and smoked together, she represented another part of me. I'd found someone who loved writing as I did, someone I'd sneaked into lectures with up at UC. I couldn't see myself doing any of those things with anyone else in this visiting room.

"You know we only get fifteen minutes?" I said.

"I know. I just wanted to come and see you. Just to say hi."

My little Mouseketeer looked so cute and so sexy. She didn't fit in these surroundings. Neither would I if I stayed in the world we'd shared together. Some folk claimed I was getting too white, with my hanging around on Calhoun and talking all proper. I said fuck 'em. I'm just becoming more human.

She said she majored in poli-sci and found each day better than the last. "I love it. You'd love it, too. Before I go I want to leave my phone number."

"Cool. Where are you staying?"

"In a place off campus. Sharing with two other girls. Come by when you get out. We can get together. Hey, do you need anything? Like money or anything?"

"No, I'm cool."

"JoAnn said I could leave you some money. I brought twenty-five dollars. Will that help?"

"Seriously, I'm good. But yeah, that would help a lot. Thanks, Bettie."

"Anything I can do, you know I will. Just take care of yourself."

I didn't know if she really meant it or just wanted to be kind. Her coming to see me in such a place may have closed a chapter in order for her to move on. Whatever the reason, I enjoyed seeing her again and would look her up when I got out.

"Will you call?" she said, smiling.

"Do cherry blossoms bloom in spring? You know I will." We both stood up, touched each other lightly on the hand, and she left.

I loped into the cell block feeling woozy from the high of Bettie's visit. I rode it over to the game table and sat down rocking. Someone else, someone I'd seen but didn't know, said, "I saw you with that snow in the visiting room, man. How'd you get something like that? She's the bomb. You hitting that?"

I didn't want to blow up and try beating him to death and end any possibility of getting early release, so I said, "She ain't some 'snow' I picked up on the street. She's my woman. Keep my business out of your mouth, motherfucker, or I'll fuck you up."

He studied me for a moment, making the same calculation I'd made just the moment before. "Ease up, motherfucker. I just made a comment. I'll leave your crazy ass alone."

It's always the same thing with black guys and white women. Other black guys either like it or hate it. It's magnified, though, when you're locked up. I had to constantly deal with, "You got that white girl, man. She can bring you lots of bucks. Nigger knows how to hustle." And others on the down side said, "Yeah, nigger think you better than us. Got you that white bitch. Yeah, and even hung out with them honkies up on Calhoun. Yeah, you ain't shit. Get in my way, I'll fuck you up."

Having gone to school at Walnut Hills and lived in Madeira, I'd already felt some of the envy and hatred the guys in the Workhouse expressed. None of the guys on Gest Street or anywhere in the West End wanted to believe in a relationship like mine and Bettie's. Mixed pimp and prostitute relationships were fine, but noting legitimate like ours. Nothing square.

Not everyone had a gripe about me and Bettie. Back in the cell after lockup a week after Bettie's visit, Top Cat said, "If you want to hook up with one of those bitches from the other side tomorrow, Barleycorn's gonna be down at the whist table. Go check him out." I didn't want to meet any of the girls on the other side, but I did want to meet Barley.

When I got there the next day, Barley and his partner had just won a game of bid whist. A group of guys stood behind his chair waiting for him. Barley played another game, slapped the winning card on the table, stood up, and said, "That'll do you. Don't feel bad, son. You just lost to the best."

Barley looked like he could have been handsome but had something missing, maybe time. No taller than James Cagney, he had Cagney's swagger. Altogether he looked like a Cadillac in today's modern Cadillac world. His once dark and wavy good hair was thinning and not so dark now. He wore a thin mustache, Clark Gable style. No one disliked Barley. His disarming smile and easy patter could put a trembling psycho at ease. *P. T. Barnum with a dash of Daddy Grace* should be his epitaph.

As he stepped away from the table, Top Cat edged his way in front of the group waiting around his chair and said, "Hey Barley, here's my cellie, Junior. He wants to talk about something. You know?"

Someone else piped up, "Yeah, better be careful, Barley. It's the young dude with that white girl."

"So?" said Barley. "What does that mean? Sounds like it means he's got a girl and you don't. Come over here, blood. What's happening?"

From that day on I knew Barley as the real deal, and I wanted to know more about him.

———

Nobody in the Workhouse really worked. The chief pastime was gambling, and Barleycorn was the expert. He kept a cigar box full of tokens under the bunk in his cell. Some guys borrowed from him at his two-for-one rates. At night he ran the poker game on the range, though it didn't profit him as much as his bullpen crap game. But he made a living. He'd been there for six months when I met him and could have been released in three more with good time. But he wasn't in a hurry. He made a good living and paid the guard on third shift to bring him smoke every week.

I knew about Barley from his reputation on the streets. For most of my life he'd been in and out of prison for crimes like forgery and narcotics abuse. He lived in prison. He always looked healthier when he got paroled, like he'd been on another "vacation," as he called it. He didn't know me, but he knew Eddie-B and the other guys on Gest Street. Staking his rep on knowing "everyone in the streets," he said he knew about me through Eddie-B.

"Yeah, Eddie-B's cool with me. You'll be alright. This ain't nothing," he informed me. "Need anything let me know."

"No, I'm good right now. Thanks, man," I said. "But I heard about something that might help in the long run."

"What is it, blood?" he asked.

"You know anything about that GED program they're supposed to have for first-timers?" I said.

"Yeah," he said. "It's for first-timers with thirty days or more. You looking at it?"

"Thinking about it," I said.

"Well, you better get on it," he said. "There's a sign-up after breakfast next Monday. Thirty days after that you'll get a practice session before the final."

"Cool," I said. "Do I owe you anything, Barley?"

"Don't worry 'bout it, blood," he said. "I'll let you know."

He never did ask me to square up.

Luckily, if you could call it that, my ninety-day sentence gave me enough time to sign up and get in the thirty-day refresher course with time to spare. With my head free of reefer haze, I quickly got down to work and passed the GED with ease. The only other thing of consequence that happened during my stint in the Workhouse was my daily work assignment.

Most people were assigned to work in maintenance, the kitchen, boiler room, or janitorial services. Veterans like Barleycorn always got the cleanest jobs. He worked in the laundry, wore clothes that fit, and changed them every day. The rest of us wore the same ill-fitting clothes for a week. The best jobs were those that took you outside the Workhouse each day. Later, as a short-timer, I got one of those outside jobs: washing cars at the police station on Lincoln Park Drive. I changed clothes every day I worked. The other job, picking up trash from state highways, wasn't my cup of tea. Before I could get one of those easier jobs, I first had to pull sump duty, the filthiest job of all.

Originally a Civil War prison, the Workhouse didn't have flush toilets. Everyone kept a bucket filled with disinfectant under his bunk.

The buckets were emptied each morning into a huge bowl-shaped open sewer called a sump. With water constantly shooting down the revolving insides of the sump, the buckets' contents whirled down through a large hole in the center. As sump man I was given a long metal pole with the responsibility to break apart any clumps that might stop the study flow of urine and shit.

After each bucket was emptied, a new line would form on my right, where my partner deposited two gallons of a mixture of disinfectant and water into each man's fresh bucket. No one was exempt from this routine. Every man's bucket had to be emptied and filled before any of the day's business could begin. My job was critical. A stopped-up sump would give everybody a bad day. It was the first thing done before break-fast and enabled the cells to be clean for the rest of the day. Otherwise the entire cell block smelled like a giant stopped-up toilet. Everything smelled better after the morning's sump dump. I rinsed the sump, took my privileged daily shower, and rushed off to breakfast with the last range. Even now I start scratching myself when I remember the sump.

CATCHING MY BREATH

Every waking moment of every day I thought of my release. Whether you'd just arrived or had been there for weeks, if someone asked, "How much time you doing, man? When's your out date?" you could tell them without a thought. It was seared into your brain like a branding iron onto a steer. I accepted my ninety-day sentence as a given, the forty-five days' good time just a carrot for behavior. When called to the captain's office two weeks before my forty-fifth anniversary and told my time would be up in two weeks, I just shook my head and said, "Thanks."

He said, "Do you have a ride?" I wasn't sure. "Well, you've got two weeks to get one. Good luck."

I didn't have anyone to pick me up or any place to go. I went straight to my resource for anything extra and told him. "Barley, I'll be hitting the streets in a minute and don't have anywhere to go. I need somebody to pick me up."

"What about that girl who came to visit you? Can't she pick you up?"

"Probably, but I don't want to hit on her. She's got too much to do. Know what I mean?"

"Let me check on it, blood. I'll see what I can do."

"Thanks, Barley. I really need this."

"Don't worry. I'll straighten you out."

My not having a ride was no big deal. I could catch the bus if I had to.

My leaving and not having anyone outside waiting for me, that hurt. All I could do was shrug and face it. As protection, I had tried to keep myself from having any close connections. As payback, no one felt connected enough to take me home. In forty-five days I couldn't have learned how prisoners being released felt after their years of imprisonment. Yet in my shared moments with them, I often peeled back their bravado.

Barley told me it went something like this. While imprisoned they lived in a communal delusion they'd purposely designed for their own survival, a deception that allowed them to embrace their imprisonment as a temporary inconvenience. After so long, it became a game—a game of trying to balance the time spent locked up against the time spent outside. When the scale weighed the heaviest on the locked-up side, the game was over and you'd lost. As Barley used to say to those who tried to complain to him about their time, "You play, you got to pay. It's all in the game."

Barley would never admit it to anyone else, but he'd lost the game years ago. He'd spent more time inside than out. When released, he felt disoriented and unnerved. Confronted by barren landscapes of lost relationships and missed opportunities, he'd turned back to crime. Locked up, the familiar connections and controlled lifestyle of prison put Barley in the driver's seat. He became a big fish in a small pond. I heard a guy with no upper teeth brag, "I drove a money-green Coupe de Ville and had so much money I couldn't give it away. Ask anyone downtown if you don't believe me." Guys like Snaggletooth could claim of being anything while locked up. He opened his cache of unrealized dreams and convinced himself they were true.

A week later Barley had me meet him in his cell during recreation time where he often held poker games. I stood lookout during games to alert him if a guard mounted the stairs. "Loons" issued by the commissary for money in your account were used as chips. Barley carried a bag full of loons around with him every day. Besides loaning cigarettes, he also loaned loons, but at a higher rate.

"I think I've got something, blood. Check it out. You hip to Model Cities?"

"Yeah, the government's throwing money away trying to clean up the ghetto."

"That's it, but the best thing about it is they're using people from the ghetto to do it. My cousin works there, and she's raking it in. I bet she can help you."

"Whoa. That would be right on time. What's her name, Barley?"

"Connie. You know her?"

"No, but I've heard of her. She's all about business. She don't mess around. That's your cousin?"

"Yeah, my mama's sister's only child, and she'll do anything for me. I told her me and you were cool and asked her to pick you up as a favor to me. And also if you could lay for a minute if you need to."

It all sounded good to me. As part of President Johnson's War on Poverty, the Model Cities Program had taken off all over the country. Certain poverty-stricken areas, primarily urban, were targeted for renewal. I had first heard about it from Chuck, one of the guys on Calhoun who was a sociology major. He said the Model Cities was an urban development program that might succeed if the right people ran it.

"The program was supposed to hire local people to help find solutions to the problems of each area. It provided government funding to help develop programs and where to invest the funds. And who would know better to do that than the people who live there?"

My cell opened early the day I left. Those of us being released ate an early breakfast. We then went through the process of settling our accounts, getting the money due to us from our work assignments and any remaining from our cash accounts. We signed for the money and later for the belongings we'd worn and carried when we arrived at the Workhouse. Finally, we were set free to walk into the area where the buses dropped off the visitors. There stood the cars waiting for the men lucky enough to have a ride home. Barley told me to look for Connie's green and white Olds Cutlass and for me to stand on the corner away from the bus. "How will I recognize her when I see her?"

"Blood, you'll recognize her. There's only one of her. When God made Connie, he broke the mold."

I saw Connie's Cutlass before I saw her. Barley was right. Connie moved like a Cadillac in a Chevrolet world. I knew many women— black, white, middle-class, poor—and she didn't look like any of them. Connie was almost an albino, with rare violet eyes. I stood stuck like a nail in place when I saw her. She didn't smile at first and looked awfully sure of herself. I winced with uncertainty when she spied me. When her lips formed a smile that covered half of her face, I knew definitely that she was Barley's cousin. She'd borrowed his smile.

She raised her hand and waved for me to come over.

"I'm Connie. You must be Junior? Barley said for me to pick you up. You ready?"

"I'm Junior, Connie. I've been ready. I can't tell you how much this means to me. I'd really be stuck if it wasn't for Barley."

"Barley's like that. You're cool with him, you're cool with me. Except, and we can get this straight now, I don't want any crazy shit going on in my house. You mess around, you'll be out on the streets in a minute. I don't care how cool you and Barley are."

"I got you. You don't have to worry about anything like that with me."

"Good. Let's go to the house. Get you straight."

———

Connie lived in Avondale about a twenty-minute drive from the Work-house in a small apartment on Ridgeway. Once a larger house, it had been divided into apartments when its owner moved out. I had come full circle since my roll-away bed on Thirteenth Street. This time I would sleep on a roll-away in the living room instead of the kitchen. Only three rooms: a bedroom, kitchen, and living room. It could have been a dollhouse. Every piece of furniture complimented the next. You could tell no children lived there, and certainly no careless male roommate like me. We sat down on a brown leather couch in the living room with lamp tables on each side. She got straight down to business.

"What do you intend to do with yourself, Junior? You can't hang out here all day. What's on your mind?"

"Barley said you work in Model Cities and maybe you could help me find something."

"What did he tell you I do at Model Cities?"

"He didn't really say, just that you help people from the West End get paid to do things for the West End."

"Yeah, that might be part of it, but it ain't that easy. Everybody wants to make a dollar but not everybody wants to earn it. I know Barley thinks I give money away and I do, but it's not as he thinks. What kind of education do you have?"

While she waited for my answer, Connie picked up a pack of Virginia Slims off the lamp table, shook one out, and lit it. She turned and offered me the pack. "You want one?"

"Yeah," I laughed, "but since I don't smoke any of that crazy shit anymore, I've given it all up for a while."

"It makes sense, I guess."

Seeing Connie smoking seemed out of character. She was so well put together, so neat and in control. Cigarettes were outside of that control box. As flimsy and weak as the smoke they produced, cigarettes didn't fit the box I'd put her in.

"I didn't know you smoked." I said.

"No big deal. I just do it at home every now and then. It relaxes me. What kind of education did you say you have again?"

"I got a GED at the Workhouse, but it doesn't mean anything. What counts is I attended Walnut Hills and Madeira High School, the best schools in Cincinnati, if not the state. I got the GED just to put a cap on it."

"That'll help. You have any work experience? We might be able to put something together with that."

"I don't have much other than my intern experience where I worked for the magazine *Your Space*. Oh, and some small things for a community newspaper where I wrote the obituaries. Just about everything I've done and the things I've excelled at involve writing. If you could find me anything like that, I'd do whatever you need."

The next day we rode to the Model Cities program headquarters on Colerain Avenue. It sat within walking distance of downtown and upper Vine Street where people who needed its services could reach it, situated in a three-story brown brick building with the third floor reserved for training classes, while the other two floors handled research, recruitment, and assignments. My future looked great with Connie as assignment supervisor. The black chairman and primarily black staff worked like dogs on a leash. White government overseers held the leashes to "observe and assist." Except for Connie, Model Cities struck me as a ship without a captain and too many officers trying to plot its course.

I had a sense of being on a reefer high. The people around me seemed to move like figures in a silent movie. Everyone jerked and walked fast in a silent world. I stood on the edge of those movements totally disconnected. Leaving the Workhouse and emerging through Connie's portal into freedom had depleted all my batteries. I needed to find someplace to live, someplace that I controlled, someplace I had the responsibility to maintain. The Workhouse had little to do with work. It took everything from me. My only responsibility while there was waking up and going to bed, and even that had to be done on schedule. More than a city prison, the Workhouse became a mortuary. Men and women who'd fallen off society's carousel came to live at the Workhouse. Like a mortician draining blood from his charges, the Workhouse drained self-respect, ambition, and trust before pushing us aside. Why did so many return? I damn sure wouldn't be one of them.

I followed Connie to her cubicle and sat down opposite her desk. "You don't really have anything for me to challenge you with, if what you say is true. But it might help us both decide what's best if you get some training before I try to give you an assignment."

It didn't matter what she wanted me to do. I'd find a way. Whatever it took, I would master it. "If training will help me get situated into a paying job, training is what I want."

"You can get paid while in training, Junior. I'll see to that. The question is, what would we be training you for? What do we have available that will help you get there?"

Model Cities didn't have the time or money to train me for what I wanted to do because I wasn't sure of what I wanted. Still, I wanted to earn Connie's respect. I fell back on what I knew best. "How can you use my writing skills to do what you need? Whatever you need done, if it's writing I can do it."

"I've got something in mind but don't know if you're ready. Get upstairs with Lolli for a couple of weeks, and we'll have a better idea of what's happening. I won't have you going into anything blind and fronting me off. Before I send you out, you've got to be ready. You can bet on it."

Turning my head while getting up from the chair in her office, something passed by quickly on my right. Nearly out of sight by the time I saw her, a girl in a blue skirt moving toward the stairway turned and quickly looked away. I lost many things in the Workhouse. My appreciation for a good-looking woman wasn't one of them. I called out to her and asked, "Hold up a minute. Can I ask you something?"

She stopped and turned, facing me. "Sure, what's up?"

She looked like my sister Wanda, and that could be good or bad. Wanda was cute and reminded me of Mama. I didn't think I'd want to hit on a woman who reminded me of Mama. Too much going on. Kissing might be a problem, and doing anything else wouldn't work. But just coming home from the Workhouse I needed to be with a woman other than Connie. I didn't really know her yet, but I put Connie on another level. Like a stabilizer on the back of a race car, Connie kept me from swerving during sharp turns. She provided grounding for me to counter strong winds. The more I thought about it, Connie may have been the Mama problem.

"What's your name? I'm Junior. You been here long?"

"Joyce. I've been in training for three weeks. Office skills. What about you?"

My glimpse of Joyce was like a sneak peek of an award-winning movie. It only hinted at the pleasure to come. She had a special sort of beauty, the kind that Mama Liza spoke of when she said, "Beauty is what beauty does."

"I just started today and not really sure what I'll be doing. What do you think about what's going on here?"

"It's cool, I guess. They give us some training and a little cash while we're getting it. I can't complain."

"Sounds okay. What's happening at lunchtime? Is there someplace close by or what?"

She looked around as if trying to locate someone else who might be going out also.

"Depends on what you want. Some eat down the street at Frisch's, others bring their lunch."

"What do you do?" I asked.

"I go home to eat. I live close enough."

"Maybe next time we could go out to lunch together. I'll buy."

She hesitated for a moment and said, "Well, you could come up to my place. It's just a minute up the street. That sound okay?"

Joyce lived on Milton Street near the top of the hill close to Reading Road. It was a bit farther than a minute. Milton Street was in the Over-the-Rhine section of the city east of the West End. The once robust three-storied German-village buildings with their small courtyards stood out like worn memories of better years across the shoulders of the hill. Joyce's family rented the house, and the backyard had crabgrass growing around the sides of the brick pathways. The stairwells were dark, and odors of good food trapped for years in the walls greeted me in the hall. Joyce opened the door to the first-floor kitchen, which faced the courtyard in the back. "Nobody's home this time of day," she said. "Mama's at work, and my little brothers are at school. We can eat whatever we want in peace."

She went to the refrigerator and took out some real food, none of that fast-food junk. Slices of meatloaf, a cup of cold gravy, Brussel sprouts, and corn to round it out.

"I'll just throw this in the oven and it'll be warm in no time."

Something about these women at Model Cities affected their eating habits. Before Mama died, I ate lots of fatback, collards, rice, and cornbread. Joyce ate meals like the family on *Father Knows Best.* Connie served the same kind of meals with lots of vegetables. They fed me mostly carbs at the Workhouse. I would eat Brussel sprouts as Joyce's guest but could never buy them on my own. Despite the Brussel sprouts, the meal put the hungries at bay and tasted good. Joyce said her father had died three years ago, and she and her two brothers lived there with their mother.

"I'm taking office skills down at Model Cities so that I can get a good job and help Mama and my brothers stay in this house. The rent is killing her."

"What kind of job you looking to get?"

"Something in one of the businesses downtown. In the back office maybe, doing invoices. They said one of their graduates works doing that at Shillito's. They'll write me a recommendation and send me on my first interview after I graduate."

Maybe I had become jaded. I liked Joyce, but something sounded a bit off kilter to me. Instead of the boost she expected, maybe Model Cities' training wouldn't prepare her for the real world. I'd seen Workhouse

office staff use IBM electric typewriters instead of the standard Rem-
ington models used by trainers here. Even secretaries at Madeira High
appeared to have better office equipment. I didn't want to tell Joyce
any of that. Her expectations generated some doubts about the Model
Cities' training. Training unqualified folk on outdated tools for nonexis-
tent positions only sabotaged their success. Were these people conning
the government or conning the people they were supposed to serve?
I wished Barleycorn were here. He'd know. He bred cons like this for
chump change.

Despite any unrealistic expectations I had about being alone with
Joyce, I still felt kind of let down when she said, "We better start getting
back if I want to get to class on time."

"Yeah, I know what you mean. I haven't talked with Lolli yet, so I still
have time to look around."

"Take your time. Once your training starts it just swallows you up. I
enjoy it."

The following day I found Lolli upstairs in an office similar to Connie's. Actually it was a corner cubicle that let in some light. I was surprised to find that Lolli was a man and not a woman. Short for Lollipop,
he didn't flounce around or mince when he spoke. He looked like one of
those European aristocrats you've seen in paintings hanging from castle
walls. Tall and slender, as strong as a spider web made of steel. I knew
immediately he was in charge.

———

Ever since I'd gone to church I'd met people like Lolli. Many of them
were choir leaders. They were good at their jobs, and the church loved
them, especially the women. No one ever mentioned they were homo-
sexuals, or that homosexuality existed inside the church. They were generally described as "funny" by most of us. Many families that I knew had
a funny relative. Their names were always mentioned with an explana-
tion. "Uncle Bob is funny but he's alright." My respect for Connie grew

stronger when she told me to go see Lolli without volunteering anything judgmental.

Like Connie, Lolli was no-nonsense when it came to work. I learned a lot from him in our two weeks together. Teaching illiterates who didn't even know how to fill out a form to fill out a work application meant success. He helped others to prepare a resume by extracting assets from their experiences and tailoring them for a specific job. Since few of his students had work experiences beyond fast food and no high school education, he became a magician. Most of his students would never see the kinds of jobs that required a resume. They couldn't capitalize on what they learned from Lolli without other help. Model Cities answered that problem with job skills training. How to dress, speak properly, walk, shake hands, and above all, arrive on time were rungs on the ladders of success. Lolli helped three classes every thirty days try to achieve those goals.

After reading my intake file as I sat on the other side of his desk, Lolli looked at me as if sizing me up. "Connie says here that you went to two great high schools and have some real writing experience. Is that so?"

I didn't know how to handle the situation. Should I say, "Yes sir," and keep things formal, or should I make things casual? After all, this was supposed to be people from the neighborhood helping other people from the neighborhood. Lolli looked like he could take it either way, so I decided to keep it comfortable.

"Yeah, Walnut Hills and Madeira. College prep all the way. I feel comfortable doing anything that requires writing. I've lived and worked with white, college-educated people and people in my neighborhood. I can work with anyone in any setting."

"Alright, you've told me what you can do. What can you do that you haven't done?"

"What do you mean?"

"How good at you at tackling something you've never done before and have no skills for?"

I didn't know what he was getting at but felt from what I'd seen so far there wasn't anything at Model Cities I couldn't do. "I'd love to try something I haven't done before. Anything. What are you thinking about?"

"I evaluate each program based on the number of students it serves, its number of graduates, their age, and the area of the city in which they live. Do you think you could handle separating out that kind of information from each program and putting it together in a report for me? It involves writing but calls for your being able to synthesize data, interpret it, and create information that will come together as a complete report for me to use. Can you see what I have in mind?"

It sounded like a little bit more than what I had in mind. "I'd like to try it," I said.

"Good. Why don't you go out to lunch, and when you come back we can look at some things together?"

I took the steps downstairs looking for Connie. When I reached her office, I saw someone in the chair by her desk. She waved for me to come in when she saw me. "This is Junior," she said to the guy sitting in the chair.

"Hey," he said. "I'm Milt. Connie's told me you're staying with her."

I didn't know anything about any Milt. Connie hadn't said anything about him to me. What appeared to be six-feet-four of Milt seemed to fill her office even as he sat. I wondered what he did. He didn't look like any of the Model Cities clients I'd seen.

"Junior," said Connie, "you going anywhere? Why don't you join me and Milt for lunch?"

"Thanks, I'm good. Nice to meet you, Milt. I'll see you later, Connie. We'll talk then."

"Alright. See you after lunch."

I didn't want to interrupt their time together. Besides, I wanted to find Joyce and have lunch with her. I would feel more comfortable with Joyce than eating with Milt and Connie. I didn't know what their relationship meant and how he might feel about my rooming at Connie's. Early on I'd asked, "What would your boyfriend think about my staying here?"

"I don't have a boyfriend. I go out with a man I've been seeing for a while. But it doesn't make any difference what he thinks. This is my house, and I pay the rent here."

I breathed a little easier after that. I'd seen too many guys in the Workhouse serving time for breaking down the door of their girlfriend's apartment trying to catch another man inside. After meeting Milt, I had to figure whether to count him as a door buster before letting myself get too comfortable around him.

I ran into Joyce just as she came up from the first floor and stepped into the hallway. We saw each other at about the same time and met like old friends. "You got time for lunch now?" I asked.

"Yeah, why not? We've got time."

We talked all the way up the hill to Joyce's house, and just like before, she fixed a great meal. Just like before, we enjoyed being together, and just like before, we left. I don't know what I expected to happen, as we'd only been alone twice. I had to face it. Spoiled by my life on Calhoun I expected sex to be as casual, comfortable, and regular as breathing. Not in the real world. In the real world, relationships had to come first. I knew that all along. I just wanted to fool myself for a moment, and it didn't work.

I didn't see Connie again until that night. I caught the bus home, and she had already cooked dinner. She didn't waste time. "What did you think of Milt? I wish you had joined us for lunch. Where did you go?"

"I had lunch with Joyce, a girl in the office skills program."

"Oh, I know her. She'll be graduating soon."

"Yeah, that's her."

"Junior, we're all grown-ups in this house."

"What do you mean?"

"Come on. Something's going on with you. Is it Milt?"

"Not really. I just want to know where he's coming from. I got some negative vibes from him, and I don't think he likes me staying here with you."

Connie laughed. "Honey, you're a lot younger than you look if that's what's bothering you. I've known Milt for years. We went to high school together. He has his associate degree and is working on becoming an RN at General Hospital. We often go out to lunch together, and he wondered why you didn't join us. He told me about a bachelor's program at the University of Cincinnati that I might be interested in. There could be something you might qualify for at UC. You ever thought about it?"

I'd gone to college-prep high schools and socialized with kids whose parents were college graduates and kids who expected to go to college themselves. I'd hung out for a summer on Calhoun with college kids and some who were throwing it away. Having the opportunity to attend college had driven my passion for learning all my life. In spite of all that, the idea of my actually being a college student seemed unreal, almost a fantasy, something unattainable. It became a goal for me to chase and never obtain, like a greyhound chases a lure around the track. The chase becomes his life's purpose. Overtaking and catching the lure would put an end to that purpose.

"Yes, I've thought about it but never expected it to be real."

"If you want it, you can make it real here, and I'll help you."

———

After two weeks of my working with Lolli, Connie called me into her office. Lolli was seated in the chair opposite her desk. I felt like a kid being called into the principal's office with his homeroom teacher present. I'd enjoyed working with Lolli. He taught me how to analyze program data and make a comprehensive report. My reports had helped him determine which programs were failing and why. I thought I already had a good idea of why they were failing. They weren't designed to succeed. Lolli wasn't surprised by my observation. "That's what you believe? Then validate it. Find some facts to support it and make your case. Otherwise, it's just bullshit." From then on, I consumed each program's data like a locust consuming crops.

Analyzing information to help determine its value enhanced my writing. I wrote with more precision and clarity than ever before. It felt as if I'd been an apprentice up till then. Without any fanfare I'd reached a new level. I'd become a professional. Unemployed and unheralded at the moment, but a true professional. Information based on my analysis could affect the livelihoods of many. It validated me to a degree that I hadn't imagined. I felt as if I'd become the insider I'd watched eating steak as I looked on from outside. I had succeeded at something that the outsiders of my world would never imagine ourselves doing.

Connie waved for me to come closer. I stepped between the two of them. She looked at Lolli and back at me. "Junior, Lolli says you've become a real asset. He hates to see you leave." I didn't know where she might go with that and hoped it wouldn't lead to an offer to work at the center. I liked working with Lolli but didn't want to work at the center. I wanted to get away, go out into the city, and step out on my own.

"Lolli let me do some real work. I can do things now that I had no idea about two weeks ago." I turned to Lolli and said, "Thanks to you, man."

Then I turned to face Connie.

"Connie, I'm not ready for what I really want. I need a job that will help me get a place of my own. I don't think two weeks of training can get me a job like that. What can Model Cities do to help me get that kind of job?"

"I know you haven't saved enough money to find a place yet," Connie said. "I ain't hurting and won't mind you staying a bit longer with me. Besides, you know me. You'll have to pay a little something after a while. What I'm saying is I've worked out an assignment with Lolli for you. It can help you out in the short run, or for as long as you like. Up to you."

I still needed a place to stay and couldn't have imagined someone like Connie coming into my life. Sure, she was Barleycorn's cousin, and were it not for Barleycorn I'd have had to walk away from the Workhouse. Once again, someone with no real tie to me had reached out and helped me when I needed it most. Maybe the best thing might be to leave things as they were and just strike out on my own.

"Um, what's it about?"

She turned to Lolli and said, "Lolli?"

"We've got six centers throughout the city: East Walnut Hills, Clifton Heights, Evanston, University Heights, Mount Auburn, and Avondale. I need to keep a hand on each one's needs, monitor its progress, review its programs, and other things. I can't do all of that from here," he said, looking at me.

"We've been analyzing the data sent to us by the centers. Hasn't that helped enough?" I said.

"Yeah, for pickup basketball games. The money each program gets is based on needs, and I feel that data isn't giving us a real picture of what's needed to accomplish anything. We can't do anything real with the money we've been asking for. You can't even run a neighborhood recreation center with the budget request I've just gotten from Evanston. The staff would have to operate everything without any supplies or equipment. And that's just one little program. I don't know what the money is spent on and if it's making any real difference."

"See where we're going, Junior?" said Connie.

"Not really." I didn't want to do anything for Model Cities. Just the two weeks while working with Lolli I learned a bit about it. As part of Lyndon Johnson's War on Poverty, Cincinnati's poorest neighborhoods were targeted for new antipoverty programs. Lolli said the program couldn't work as it was being run.

Lolli kept talking, his voice hard, stripping each word down to its harsh, dry facts.

"These programs are supposed to be for the people who live here. They know the area, know the people, what's working, and what's not. What they don't know is what it takes to fix it. They're supposed to run things, but they can't. It looks like a setup to me. They don't have the skills. These government folk come in and pick out a reverend or two, make him the chairman of his district, and tell him to choose his committee. That's where it begins to fall apart. The government watchdogs 'advise' the committee out of the decision process. They decide where the problems are and where the money should go. Consequently, the programs that get funded are based on their needs and not ours."

I'd never heard Lolli talk about Model Cities in that way. He sounded as if revitalizing our city was a mission. He wasn't just getting a paycheck from the Model Cities program. He was seriously trying to help make Cincinnati a city for the rest of the country to model. I was glad that I had learned how to view the system through him.

Lolli tried to establish needs for each program based on the data we received. He felt that current data didn't provide the information he desired to define each program's needs. That's what he wanted my help for. This sounded like my working at the center. In two weeks I'd done a lot with data but hadn't learned anything about who generated it and how. It sounded pretty boring to me. I felt more afraid than anything else, afraid that this would be too much for my limited experience.

"Okay, Junior," said Lolli. "If you want to make some real money, you can work with me."

"I don't know, Lolli. You know how much we enjoy working together. I don't know. Are you talking about me working here, in this place, with you?"

"I don't need anybody hanging around me all day. I need somebody who can verify the data I've been receiving and who can get down in the dirt with the street people. These white folk ain't going to get anything together in those neighborhoods because they don't know the people.

Everybody resents them anyway when they come in wearing their loose khakis and button-down shirts. You're from the West End, ain't you?"

"Yeah, Gest Street."

"Well, that's what I'm talking about. You know most of the people down there?"

"Mostly from the projects, down Lincoln Park almost to Crosley Field and back up past Freeman Avenue to Music Hall on Colerain. Then Gest Street over to Carr Street, past that to the border of Price Hill where the white guys live. Yeah, I know most of that."

"Alright, just what I thought. What if I said I wanted you to be my field evaluator?"

This was beginning to sound like a real job, a position. If the money matched the responsibilities, it might take me where I wanted.

"Let's talk particulars, Lolli. I'd like to do something with that."

BOOK SIX

COLONEL LATEEF, KADEEM, AND MWANZA

"Sometimes I feel if it wasn't for bad luck I wouldn't have no luck at all," goes the blues lyric that once described me. The Model Cities program I'd worked for after leaving the Workhouse didn't get its proposed ten-year funding, and I didn't get to be Lolli's field evaluator. I chose not to stay with Connie any longer and accept her supporting me "in between jobs." In the end, Lolli found me a way to get something together.

"Junior, we are all devastated by this blow. You felt it coming and didn't even know what I knew. But it's too late for all that. I'm sorry you got caught up in it just when you were getting on your feet." I believed in Lolli. He had given me so much to move forward with, so much to feel proud of. There was no reason for him to feel sorry.

"Listen, man. You're the best. You've done more than enough. Believe me. I can handle this."

"I know and believe you can make it. That's why I'm sending you to one of the smartest men I know, a man I grew up with in Clifton and is a lifelong friend. He will be coming home today from Lexington. I want you two to meet."

"I hear you, Lolli, but I just came from the Workhouse. Coming here was supposed to get me back on my feet. Now you're sending me to meet someone coming from the joint? What is that about?"

Lolli took a half-step forward and stared hard into my eyes. "Not every man who goes to prison is guilty. I know Frank. He's not the old Frank. He's a new man with a plan, a program, and connections. If you two can hook up together, something good can happen that's bigger than you both."

I didn't know what to think. I hadn't thought about Lolli as anyone other than a strong, smart, and astute manager. Did his relationship with Frank show the other side of him? How did he know so much about Frank's plans? Were they writing to one another? I hadn't seen any display of his personal relationships before. To be Lolli's friend, this Frank guy had to be the bomb.

"Hey, if he's all that to you, he's worthwhile to me. Where do I meet him?"

"Down at the Greyhound Bus station, Monday after Easter, 11:30 in the morning."

"Thanks, Lolli, I'm already there."

The day I met Lolli's friend Frank became a turning point in my life. When we met that day at the bus station, he'd already become Colonel Suli Lateef. Frank Harris no longer existed, and the Colonel had arisen like a phoenix from his death. Lolli had been right about one thing, though. Even though I didn't know it yet, the Colonel was probably the smartest man I'd ever know. Lolli didn't tell me how to identify him. He didn't need to. From the way he paused at the head of the stairs before descending into the bus station, I knew. The Colonel had arrived.

I once saw a picture of Marcus Garvey alongside Malcolm X, Stokely Carmichael, and Elijah Muhammad, in a barbershop near the projects. If I didn't know that he had died, I would have sworn that Marcus Garvey had stepped off the bus. The Colonel stood about five-feet-eight with a thick, barrel-shaped body. Coupled with his dark skin, fat cheeks, and receding hairline, the Colonel could have easily gotten arrested as Marcus Garvey. He might have just as easily been carried on the shoulders of a crowd of Black Nationalists. Only the absence of a mustache and his third eye (a mole) in the center of his forehead set the two apart.

I spent three glorious years with the Colonel. With him as my guide, I left Junior behind and became Major Kadeem.

———

Suli Lateef, or the Colonel as we all came to know him, was the only man I've met who fully believes he descends from the kings he teaches about. When I asked him about the mole in the center of his forehead, he said, "That mole is my third eye. It allows me to see into a person's heart and know who he really is."

I believed him. He could quote obscure passages and dates from history as if they were printed on a screen in his head. Wherever he sat, he became the head of any table, regardless of who else was there. Visitors to the Blackman's Development Center, where he taught Black History, called his gift "eidetic memory." Those of us who knew him called it genius. He gave substance and form to the great kings and conquerors who weren't even phantoms to me before. All I'd learned in high school was Booker T. Washington and George Washington Carver. The Colonel told me about empires and rulers that didn't even exist in the history books I'd known. He drew marvelous portraits of the kingdoms of Mali, Songhai, and Ghana. He gave me new heroes, like Mansa Musa, Memnon, Hannibal, and Sheba. Under the Colonel's wing, the study of Egypt became a veritable oasis of black life and a source of pride.

Colonel Suli Lateef reattached Egypt to the rest of Africa geographically and racially. I learned that many of the pharaohs weren't white like Yul Brynner but had wide noses and wooly hair like Senefru, Khufu, Imhotep, and my friend Jim. The Blackman's Development Center with its Black History and Culture Group became my passion. I enthusiastically welcomed Colonel Suli Lateef as my mentor.

An owlish-looking intellectual who claimed to be a Blackamoor, Colonel Lateef earned the title of El, or teacher, after studying the teachings of Noble Drew Ali in the Moorish Science Temple. He wasn't "Colonel" to me then. He was simply my teacher. I've met many Els since then, but Suli is the only one I've accepted as authentic.

The Colonel took a liking to me because I wrote well, had marched in Selma, and listened attentively to his lectures. As a reward for my passion and to tie me to the group, he made me the group's executive secretary.

"Along with my teachings, the executive secretary's role is very critical at this point. Your major responsibility will be to establish a nationwide correspondence network with black activists and historians. Are you up for it?" he asked.

It looked like my training at Walnut Hills, Madeira, and *Your Space* was about to pay off.

"I've been preparing for this for years, Colonel. I can do it."

"I knew you could. Go to it."

I quickly established a correspondence that stretched from New York University to California's Marin County Jail. I wrote to Angela Davis while she was imprisoned. She wrote a stirring letter of support back to our group. Professor Addison Gayle Jr. flew down from New York to attend one of Colonel Suli El's lectures. He was so impressed by the Colonel's historical knowledge that he donated three hundred dollars toward the establishment of our new library. With the Colonel's spell-binding oratory and my wide-ranging correspondence, the Black Culture and History Group exploded on the scene.

During the next two years, the Colonel relied more and more on my skills to enhance the group. I had been involved with the Student Non-violent Coordinating Committee and Bloody Sunday. My credentials as a civil rights fighter opened doors for me that may have been locked to others. I established correspondence that first year with most of the civil rights leaders and frontline fighters throughout the country, but what impressed him most was my second year's accomplishments. Colonel Suli Lateef was a teacher of the first rank. No university would hire him because of the years of research he'd spent teaching himself in the federal penitentiary at Lexington, Kentucky. As we became friends, I realized that his greatest regret was not being allowed to teach at a university. It was partially that regret that drove his almost rabid search for more knowledge.

After returning from a speaking engagement at Ohio State University with the Colonel, I began contacting Black History departments throughout Ohio and inviting them down to hear the Colonel speak. I sent tapes of his addresses and copies of letters we'd received from Angela Davis, Eldridge Cleaver, Imiri Baraka, and others that established the group as a legitimate academic resource. The director of Black Studies from Ohio State, Dr. Charles Ross—"Mwanza"—was one of our first guests. We later had guests from Central State University, the University of Dayton, and Ohio University. To the Colonel's utmost delight each of those universities invited him to come to campus to speak.

We were just as popular with community action agencies as we were on the college campuses. It was a good time to be black, and the Colonel, whose hero was Marcus Garvey, the flamboyant force behind the United Negro Improvement Association, looked and acted like Garvey reborn. During his lectures he demanded total involvement not only by his delivery but by his dress. He came to each lecture dressed like a Mwalimu (professor) from historic Timbuktu. Wearing a fez or tarbush on his head and a flowing dashiki over his shoulders he was the picture of a black liberator.

According to the Colonel we were emissaries of freedom and we arrived that way, whether on campus or at a community affair. We rode in a Blackman's Development Center van, painted in red, black, and green: liberation colors. The community demanded more lectures at BDC than we could schedule. Since we represented freedom from the "man," we focused on freedom for self, which also meant freedom from drugs. It was hard to dispute the image we projected of proud black men. It naturally followed that we were invited to address drug use in the community.

Methadone clinics and drug counseling therapy were too well known for most BDC brothers. Many had been recruits from the streets whose lives were saved by the group. Having been to prison himself the Colonel had established BDC and himself as a stopgap for drugs, someone who drug dealers could not frighten or con. The Colonel instilled a style of vigilante justice that met dealers on their own turf. We met them in alleys, bars, and community centers, and dictated rules to a new game: No drug sales in the immediate community. If the Colonel sent a dealer a personal invitation for a meeting, somebody's business was about to end. In recognition of the Colonel and BDC's impact, one dealer stopped his sales in the community surrounding BDC before meeting with the Colonel. He still maintained his businesses in other parts of the city. Big dealers could afford to live by the Colonel's new rules. Only the small ones were really hurt. Still, the Colonel made our presence in the community known. I'd like to think we made a difference.

After a dramatic decrease of drug usage in the BDC community, the Colonel announced to the staff that we were opening a drug rehabilitation center in Avondale. Other than downtown, Avondale was the city's most drug-ridden area. "As strong, black men," he said, "it is our job to help addicts kick their habits, provide counseling, and educate them about who they are. We've got to make them feel proud again so that they can stand up as men."

"How can we afford to do all of that and teach Black History and Culture, too?" asked a tall guy with a full beard.

Never at a loss for handling the situation, Colonel Lateef said, "Through a federal grant we are working with the Hamilton County prosecutor's office to screen the brothers in jail who are ready for treatment and bring them to the center if they are eligible."

"Who determines their eligibility, Colonel?" I asked.

"We do," he said, with that owlish intellectual smile of his.

Drug dealers who'd escaped being arrested now had the Colonel to fear. He could have them beaten up and their immediate stashes destroyed or turned in, but that would only delay the inevitable. If the dealer wouldn't respond to physical force, the Colonel could pinpoint him for the drug squad and schedule a raid when a pickup or delivery was to be made. Being called a snitch by one of the guys in the group meant nothing to the Colonel. First, it better not be uttered out loud. Second, if brought to his attention the Colonel addressed it in front of us all.

"You all know I've been to the joint," he said, "so you know that I know what a snitch is. A snitch is someone who gives up information to harm another for his personal gain. He wants to harm them out of jealousy or fear. Snitches live in darkness. They won't step into the light and be seen like me and you. And why? Because a snitch is a coward."

The Colonel spat his words out.

"There is nothing for me to gain, nothing for the Blackman's Development Center to gain. Nothing, but the opportunity to clean up our neighborhood. You all know that I confront these cowards face-to-face," he said, "and will continue to. These punks are destroying our families and sending our best young brothers to prison. If you want to call that snitching, then I'm a snitch. And I'm going to keep on snitching."

He stood tall, rubbed the third eye on his forehead, and looked directly at the guy with the beard. When he got no response he went on about business.

"Major Kadeem has designed a questionnaire that we will use to screen the men we see in the county jail who may be approved for treatment at BDC," said the Colonel.

By that time, I had become Major Kadeem. The Colonel felt I needed both a title and an Arabic name to add weight to the scope of our Black History Center In a very solemn and dramatic ceremony he christened me Major Kadeem. Kadeem had many definitions in Swahili, but because of my value to him and the group, the Colonel christened me as "Kadeem the Servant." He said that my leadership was a service to others that made them and myself strong.

In a ceremony much like the Holy Ghost affirmation in Elder Sanders's church, the Colonel touched my forehead with his forefinger that had been dipped in olive oil. He next placed a red, black, and green tarbush on my head and named me.

Ever since I had been in Hoffman Elementary School, my writing had opened doors for me. The GED I'd earned in the Workhouse had little relevance to my skills. It served as a credential. To the Colonel it meant nothing. He considered me "young, gifted, and black," like the lyrics of the song.

I liked working with the men in the county jail. Most times they were on their way to prison, and BDC was their last hope. If we could get them involved in the BDC drug rehab program, they could get "treatment in lieu of incarceration." It wasn't as easy as it sounded. The Colonel was serious and made eight of us get a certificate in reality therapy, paid for by the feds.

Out of necessity, the center moved to a larger, three-story Avondale mansion. Like many mansions formerly owned by Jews in that part of Cincinnati, it had been chopped up into apartments. The four-room apartments on the second and third floors gave us room for eight men for the rehab program. The competition for those eight spaces was fierce. Counting the kitchen and the dayroom, where group therapy was held, and the space for the Colonel's private office and bedroom on the first floor, it was a ten-room house. I helped with some of the interviews, although my main function was to further the educational aspect of the group. One day as I was doing county jail interviews I came across someone from Gest Street.

My days on Gest Street had made me streetwise, and I figured that eventually I would see someone I knew. My experiences on Calhoun Street and at the Workhouse had immersed me into the world of drugs. I knew tricks, petty thieves, pimps, whores and just about any other hustler in the streets. I didn't know what my reaction would be to someone who knew me in that other world. Would I be unable to fulfill my current role? Or would I fall into my former habits and let him ease by? This was the test I'd waited for, to see if I'd really left my past behind.

I walked down the range at the Franklin county jail with my clipboard in my hand and stopped at the newly occupied cell. I still remember it: three cells from the end, D-Range, number 17. He held onto his cell bars and called out to me. I recognized his gravelly voice before I saw him. "Hey, man. Help a brother out," he said. It had been years since I'd heard it, but Eddie-B still sounded the same. He looked like the past I had forgotten. But there he stood still at large, unsettling everything around him. He looked right at me but didn't see me. He only saw someone who had something he wanted.

"Brother, I'll send someone up to do an intake," I said. "If you've got a jones, we can get you some temporary help. Then we can talk about some treatment. How's that, my man?"

"Yeah," he said, "just get me some medicine."

After two more years as executive secretary of BDC and manager of our drug rehab program, I asked the Colonel for help in attending college. He chose Ohio State University since we had established our strongest relationship with its Black Studies director, Dr. Charles Ross.

Due to the national correspondence and statewide stature we'd established with other academic Black Studies programs, my GED qualified me to take the college boards. I initially hoped to qualify for an associate of arts degree, but that quickly changed once I actually got on campus.

I arrived on campus in January after the long Christmas break. The Black Studies Center welcomed me as if I were a returning POW. I felt

I'd cheated Mwanza and the students because I hadn't seen the Selma march through, but they felt otherwise. Bloody Sunday wasn't technically successful because it didn't get past the Edmund Pettus Bridge. However, it brought the nation's attention to Selma and contributed to the success of the following march. Just the fact that I was there made me a living talisman, someone who carried the Selma mystique. It gave me a unique insight on how survivors of other historic events must live. The college found frontline community warfare against drugs admirable, and my work through the Black Culture and History Group made my contribution to OSU's Black Studies program vital. As Major Kadeem of the Blackman's Development Center, my connection with Maulana Ron Karenga at California State University introduced the first celebration of Kwanzaa to Ohio. Though my given name was on all official documents, I was Major Kadeem to some and Kadeem to most.

Instead of having to take exams to pass my Black Studies classes, the instructors called upon me as a guest lecturer on racism and civil rights, and on my experience through BDC with drugs in relation to the criminal justice system. My special exposure to Black History was often used as a backdrop to an instructor's present topic. I got As in all my Black Studies courses, not because I was such a devoted student, but primarily because of what I'd learned with the Black Culture and History Group. History, political science, journalism, and English were my other loves. I got As and Bs in all of them. But Black Studies carried me body and soul into the life of the university.

OSU / POLITICS / EXPLOSION

Being a student at Ohio State with forty thousand others brought about many challenges. Financial challenges were the most difficult. I had lived at the center sparingly for more than two years. Funds from a federal grant supported our rehab program, and the Hamilton County prosecutor's office supported our "treatment in lieu of prison" program. My going to college changed some things. Since we couldn't use any of those funds to pay for my education, I applied for and received two grants: the Ohio Instructional Grant and the federal Pell Grant. With my tuition and books covered, all I needed was some place to live.

The Colonel solved my problem by letting me stay at BDC in return for my managing the correspondence network. It wasn't a sinecure because most of the contacts were mine. If the Colonel wanted to start anything new, I would follow up after he initiated it. Ten of us staff members lived in the reconstituted basement of the center in a barracks-style situation. The Colonel stayed in cell-like quarters in an area we'd built off the dayroom. He wasn't interested in frills and didn't encourage that interest in us.

My mentor at Ohio State was the director of Black Studies, known by those close to him as Mwanza. Mwanza—or the "Wise Protector"— originally entered my life as a guest speaker to the Black Culture and History Group. Originally from Georgia, he came north on a basketball scholarship to the University of Chicago where he met his wife, Ayanna. In Swahili, her name means "beautiful flower." By the time I met him, he and Ayanna had been married for fifteen years and had three daughters.

Mwanza spoke in a Baptist preacher's fiery cadence and was uncompromisingly black. You couldn't find anyone neutral about him. People either hated or loved him. Everyone loved Ayanna.

She was the smallest explosive force I've ever met. Standing about five-feet-two and at ninety-seven pounds, Ayanna was all heart and sinew. She was the backbone to Mwanza's extremism. Her graceful strength under pressure enabled him to alienate powerful foes without fearing their response. When I first met her, she was a teacher. When I left OSU three years later, she had earned her law degree. Without Ayanna behind him, Mwanza may have never been more than a disgruntled social worker. With her, he became the spiritual leader of the city's poor and disenchanted blacks. Two years after Ayanna became a lawyer he even ran for mayor.

Mwanza and I developed a very warm and active friendship during the times he'd visited the center to hear the Colonel speak and the times he'd invited the Colonel to speak on campus. He leased a former rectory from the Catholic Church and started a black alternative school for kids from ages four to twelve. The Colonel and I helped design the curriculum and taught classes on a semiregular schedule. I particularly enjoyed working with those kids because they were poor, and everything around them was at war with their self-image.

My favorite targets were the little guys who came to class with their heads lowered, afraid to speak, and hanging back, not wanting to be noticed. I used to love to watch them respond like flowers to a refreshing rain when being soaked with a bucket of black pride. I remember one little guy, no more than six or seven, who wanted to know how I got the name Major Kadeem.

"That ain't no regular name," he said.

"You're right," I said. "It's a special name. A name I gave myself by earning it."

"You can't name yourself," he said. "Only your mama can do that."

"No. Do you remember when I taught you the Nguzu Saba?" I asked.

"I remember," said his friend.

"What is it?" I asked.

"It's the Seven Principles of Blackness," he answered.

"And remember 'Kujichagulia,' the fourth principle?" I responded, turning around to face him.

"I remember now," he said. "It means to name ourselves, define ourselves, speak for ourselves, instead of being defined, named, and spoken for by others."

"Good," I said. "Now maybe you can name yourself when you've done something very special. Something that you can be proud of. Now you know why I don't have a regular name. Your name can be anything you want. Just make sure it's what you want it to be, and it's something you and your mama will be proud of."

"What does Kadeem mean?" he asked.

"In Swahili it means 'servant,'" I said.

"Servant," he said, "like somebody who cleans up for others?"

"Kind of," I said. "A good leader is also a good servant. Being of service to my brothers and sisters makes them stronger and makes me a better leader. My mother couldn't have known that when I was born. Just like your mother couldn't have known what kind of man you're becoming. I know one thing, though."

"What's that?"

"She's going to be very proud."

We named the school Harambee Uhuru, Swahili for "Freedom Now." I've done lots of things since, but giving those kids a reason to feel good about themselves gave me the first real freedom to be myself. Freedom Now wasn't just a name for our school. It was a mantra for all of us who worked there.

As a sophomore, while still a resident of BDC, I often stopped by Mwanza's office just to talk. After school Mwanza was the state chairman of the African Liberation Support Committee and in charge of the annual African Liberation Day Rally held on April 12. After working with SNCC in Selma, I thought I was politicized about civil liberties, but I was wrong. I hadn't known anything about Nelson Mandela and his imprisonment, nor had I paid any attention to the turbulence going on all over the African continent since African nationalism and European colonialism collided.

Much like with the Colonel, I became a close friend and aide to Mwanza. I soon knew every African Liberation support committee chair throughout Ohio by name and was easily recognized by most of them. Near the end of my sophomore year, I went to Mwanza's office and was surprised by the man I saw there.

"Come in, Kadeem, sit down," said Mwanza. "You know our brother here, don't you?"

I had seen him on TV and was quite surprised to see him there.

"Yeah, Harambee Brother. Thanks for coming. We're glad you're here. It's great to have you."

Then Jesse Jackson turned to me and said, "Good to meet you, Brother Kadeem," and gave me a Black Power handshake.

I had been unable to get Jesse and his organization to come to BDC as I had others. Though Chicago was far from Cincinnati, it wasn't as far away as New York. I wasn't sure what his presence meant.

He was handsome in a rough kind of way because his face was marred. Girls liked him because of his good hair and light skin. His upper lip, though not a harelip, had a small cut or split on the right side as I remember. When he smiled it gave him a swashbuckling air. He stood a bit taller than five-feet-six, but he looked bigger with that smile. I believe that's how he got so many people to follow him, especially women. Guys followed him because he was smart.

He turned back to Mwanza.

"We would love to support your African Liberation Day, Mwanza," he said, "but as head of an organization I have to get a donation if I'm to speak at the rally. We all are fighting the same fight. Fighting outside the university requires greater finances. Right now it's all about how we bring the fight. My best fight is being conducted through my organization. Brother, you know where I'm coming from."

"I understand," said Mwanza, "but this isn't university sponsored. This is us, and we might be able to afford airfare, and Ayanna and I will put you up for a night. But that's it. You are doing some good work up there in Chicago, brother," he continued, "but all I'm asking for is ninety minutes for you to give a talk at the rally. We can't afford to send you a check right now."

"I'm stuck, Mwanza. I just can't do it right now. I can do something for you early next year when we're in better shape, but I'm stuck."

I understood what Mwanza meant when next he said, "Don't let it bother you, brother. We'll get by. I'm glad you were able to come down so we could get together. When I come home I'll stop by and we can talk." He meant, "We'll make it without you, and I don't know when I'll see you again." Mwanza hadn't been home in fifteen years. Jesse Jackson had changed from the man who'd marched with Dr. King in Selma and all over the South with the Southern Christian Leadership Conference. After returning to Chicago and forming his own civil rights organization, some people said he'd become more of a businessman. Others said his energies as head of an organization demanded that he focus his resources on one target at a time. Who knows? We were certainly disappointed at his refusal to serve as speaker at our African Liberation Day rally.

Primarily in Columbus to visit the Urban League, he told Mwanza, "The movement don't stop because of one person. Be good, brother," and left for his meeting.

"What was that about?" I said. "He ain't going to speak at the rally?"

"You heard what he said. He couldn't do it right now," Mwanza said. "Don't worry. We'll get somebody."

And he did.

Huey P. Newton, cofounder of the Black Panther Party, spoke at the rally. He didn't ask for any donation either.

Huey Newton was one of my heroes, someone I never thought I'd meet in person. He had light skin and nappy hair under his black beret. He had a smooth complexion and dark brown eyes. Without being tall or muscular, he impressed me as being solid as a rock. He wore a black leather jacket and looked like he might have been someone I'd known in my old neighborhood. I liked him instantly.

He became the in-fighter and community organizer the Oakland black community needed. As long as he walked around Oakland in his leather jacket and black beret with a shotgun in his hand, the Black Panthers' school breakfast program survived. Others found it hard to reconcile that Huey with the Huey Newton, PhD, he became before being assassinated by a rival gang in Oakland.

The rally was held in the center of the campus on the Oval. The crowd was about four times larger than expected. An expert at reading a crowd, Huey spoke to the crackling anger pulsating through the crowd like a high-tension wire.

"Brothers and sisters," he began, "I do not expect the white media to create positive black male images. Black Power is giving power to people who have not had power to determine their destiny. You have to take back the power that they refuse to give. Whether on campus, in the community, or across the globe, the power is yours to take.

"Mandela and our brothers and sisters in Africa are fighting the same fight. Don't let anyone fool you. Don't let them try to separate you. Laws should be made to serve the people and not the other way around. We have two evils to fight: capitalism and racism. We must destroy both capitalism and racism."

He went on in that vein for over an hour. The African Liberation Support Committee paid his airfare, and he stayed overnight with Mwanza and Ayanna. The next day they talked strategy about the coming fall. After he left, that strategy was useless.

Ever since my first meeting with Mwanza he talked about how campus politics kept his Center of Black Studies from becoming a stand-alone department. He had made enemies of the Math and English department chairs in the College of Arts and Sciences. Those two bulwarks of the college didn't view Black Studies as serious scholarship and Mwanza as a serious scholar. They surely didn't want any Department of African American Studies on an equal footing with theirs.

Independent student groups gathered all over campus during the week following our meeting. Mwanza pulled some of them together, and in his best Baptist preacher tone he began.

"You can't get anywhere all spread out," he said. "Unity is what you want. Unity is your key to open doors. Unity will keep you strong. Unity will keep you safe. Before making any moves, know what you want. Then you'll know how to get it. What do you want?" he asked.

"Freedom," they answered with one voice.

"When do you want it?" he asked.

"Now!" they shouted.

"That's the unity I'm talking about," he said and stepped away. The students gave him the Black Power salute and a rousing cheer.

A week after the African Liberation Support Committee's rally, Mwanza asked me to join him, two of his instructors, and two Women's Studies instructors to write a paper outlining the issues we wanted the administration to address. Kwesi, his instructor for international economics, a Nigerian who never shied from confrontation, said, "So what? What's going to happen when they say, 'Fuck you,' and throw our demands in the trash? What do we do then, Mwanza? What do we do then?"

"There'll be hundreds of brothers out there, Kwesi," said Mwanza. "They've got to give us an answer."

Remembering Selma, I said, "Don't bet on it."

The pot started to bubble when, on April 15, two thousand members of the national antiwar movement marched down High Street to the Ohio statehouse. They protested the war and other issues related to Vietnam, the draft, the university's support of the ROTC program, and racism. It got lots of attention but no response.

With an eye on the future, Mwanza had helped bring about the union between the women's movement and black student groups and said, "You don't want to jump up and be anyone's spokesman, Kadeem. You know what I'm talking about?"

I knew what he was trying to say. I had no intention of putting myself in any danger. Besides, look at what I'd done in Selma.

"Brother, you know I have to give my support," I said, "but I ain't about to jump in front of any cameras."

Black students weren't the only ones making plans. Members of the Students for a Democratic Society (SDS) held antiwar and women's liberation demonstrations throughout campus. People described the atmosphere that existed on campus at that time as electrifying, but the word was too tame. At my every step, my nerves crackled like bubble wrap. It took all my strength to hold my body in check—to stop, be still, and listen. Even the slightest breeze might telegraph the tsunami that was sure to come.

THE TSUNAMI ARRIVES

The Oval was at the center of Ohio State's campus. Everyone either passed or walked through it at some time during the week. I'd once walked across it with a girl in my political science class who was from Chagrin Falls, Ohio. We stopped, sat down on the grass, and talked about women's rights for about twenty minutes. She left for her next class, and I went on to the library. A black student who only knew me though the Black Studies program as Kadeem stopped me before I reached the library.

"Jambo, Brother Kadeem," she said.

"Si Jambo," I answered back.

"It ain't none of my business," she said, "but how can you claim to represent strong black men when you're laid up on the Oval with a white girl?"

"You sure got one thing right," I said. "It ain't none of your business," and kept on walking.

Following me she said, "You're just like the rest of them brothers. You can't fool me. You all want your little Mary Jane. Get you some of that white girl. You ain't foolin' nobody."

I stopped and turned around. "Sister," I said, "sounds like you've got a problem. Why don't you go somewhere and play with yourself? I don't represent anyone but me. I ain't trying to be anybody's idea of what a black man is. Just because you know a few Swahili words and your skin is black, you think you can tell *me* how a black man should act? I'm here to help bring people together to fight injustice, not just against blacks, but injustice everywhere. Why don't you get your head into that, instead of this juvenile boy-and-girl shit? Grow up. Until you're ready to act like an adult, the next time we meet I'll be both blind and deaf to you."

She later followed my advice and joined forces with the girl from Chagrin Falls to face our common foe. As members of the Ad Hoc Committee for Student Rights, they marched with hundreds of other students to the Administration Building and called a student strike. We demanded the addition of Black Studies and Women's Studies to regular university courses before the strike would end. Our long-range goal was to give department status to the Black Studies Center, promote its director to a chair, and do the same for Women's Studies.

I'd helped Mwanza's committee and the Women's Studies committee write those demands. Remembering Selma, I chose not to fade away at the crucial moment despite Mwanza's warning. It wasn't easy to stay in the background once I'd positioned myself near the front of the crowd. Like the surf at Big Sur, the wave of students grew in size and strength with each step forward. Like a roller coaster moving slowly as it climbs, stopping at its apex as if taking a breath, and dropping before slowing to a stop, the crowd carried me to the front of the Administration building.

I didn't know what to do. Eight or nine of us were bunched together on the top steps. Someone produced and read the demands. No one came out to accept them. Without my knowledge, all of this was being filmed to show later on the evening news. Neither Mwanza nor the Colonel would be happy to see that. I never saw it but was told later by someone at the Blackman's Development Center and the Black Studies Department they had a clear full-face shot of me while giving the Black Power salute. I made my movie debut that morning and even got reruns in the following days.

As the crowd eased back toward the Oval and I was given room to breathe, things became unruly. Students not part of the Ad Hoc Committee and motivated simply by a need to be destructive filled our ranks. It reminded me of a river rushing down from the mountains and overflowing its banks. That loud, destructive crowd flooded the Oval and spread onto High Street.

I decided it was time to get out of there. It was easier said than done. A gray haze started to rise, and I heard tear gas being shot near the College Gate. I also saw the revolving blue and red lights of the Highway Patrol cars. When patrol cars showed up, I definitely didn't want to be around. No telling how many patrolmen would be surrounding the campus. I ran away from High Street and found out later what a good move that had been. I escaped the danger by heading straight for the Black Studies Center, off the center of campus and away from the action. But even there I found stragglers, those outside the main protestors trying to sneak into the building and out of the action.

Mwanza had left. Like most faculty even he didn't want to face an uncontrollable mob. Besides, the administration wouldn't be happy to have him on campus during a protest with his interests at stake. It would have been professionally difficult for him to remain.

I stayed in the center because the university was closed off from the rest of the city. No one was supposed to be in a campus building after it was closed, but I took that chance. The Highway Patrol had closed all roads near campus. Watching TV in the study hall on the first floor of the center, I saw why. High Street looked like a Hollywood set with facades of buildings propped up by poles behind a wall of flames. Storefronts were on fire, windows were broken, and Molotov cocktails whizzed through the air. Students were gassed, clubbed, and fired upon. It lasted for hours but felt like it lasted all night. I phoned the Colonel at BDC and told him where I was. He told me to stay there and to call Mwanza to let him know. I did as I was told. Mwanza told me to stay at the center until he called.

There was no real kitchen in the center. Luckily I found something in their snack kitchen the next day that didn't need to be cooked. I watched TV all day in horror. It felt more and more like I was in another land.

Violence erupted again when Nixon's secret war with Cambodia became news on that same day, April 30. By some estimates four thousand students hit the streets. Governor James Rhodes called in the National Guard. Armored personnel carriers and tanks rumbled down High Street. It looked like a bad movie being directed by an idiot. Before it ended, four hundred people were arrested and more than one hundred injured. Seven of them had been shot.

Keeping informed by TV, I called Mwanza. "Mwanza," I said, "you been keeping up with what's happening?"

"Yes, Kadeem," he said. "Are you finding any food?"

"Nothing worth eating," I said.

"I wanted to come get you yesterday," he said, "but there was too much going on. I couldn't get through. I'll see what's happening today."

"You've got faculty ID and you can't get through?" I said.

I knew I was in real trouble if Mwanza couldn't get through with his faculty ID. It was like barring doctors from the hospital.

"They're not letting anybody in," he said. "It might be easier for you to get out. The demonstrations seem to have ended. Security has doubled. Armed checkpoints everywhere. Armed troops. Tanks and armored personnel carriers. Ain't nobody coming in, Kadeem. The best way to get around all of this is to come out. What do you think?"

"Hey, why not?" I said. "Makes sense to me. But what about that shot of me on the news? Think they'd want to hold onto me for something?"

"You haven't done anything, not really, and there's so much that's happened since then," he said. "They don't have your picture in their pocket with words on it saying, 'Watch out for this brother. He'll get you.'"

"Okay," I said. "If I get locked up with a million-dollar bail, you're going to have to pay it."

"Put it on my bill," he said, laughing. Then he said, "But seriously, give me a call the moment you get past the checkpoint so that I can be there to pick you up."

It didn't help my situation any that Governor Rhodes had sent the National Guard into Kent State the day before and students had gotten shot and killed there. That explained some of the reason for the extra-tight security around Ohio State and cordoning off our campus from the rest of the city. I was nervous and pleasantly surprised when I approached a checkpoint at Fifteenth Street and the guardsman asked me to stop. He couldn't have been much older than I. He did not look like a demon who hated protestors. He looked like a guy caught up by circumstances who was just doing his job. I didn't hold anything against him, and he didn't act like he held anything against me.

"You a student here?" he said.

"Yes, I am," I said.

"Where are you headed?" he said.

"Trying to get home," I said. "I've been stuck up here during the strike." I didn't want to say riots. That would put us both on the defensive.

"Let me see your ID," he said.

I showed him my OSU student identification.

"Take this," he said, and handed me something that looked like a ticket. "If someone else stops you, show them this pass and they'll know you've already been stopped."

"Thanks," I said, took the pass, and started past him.

"Go home, man," he said. "Just go home."

IT TAKES GUTS

My ticket was punched at the age of fourteen when Eddie-B welcomed me into his circle with a bottle of wine. There, in the back of Sonny's store, I jumped onto a train that rushed headlong down the tracks to prison. Jumping from the moving train in Madeira was far easier than jumping from Eddie-B's express. Becoming Major Kadeem gave me the confidence I needed to make that jump. Major Kadeem helped set my compass in the direction to escape Gest Street's claws. But more importantly, he gave me the strength to follow the road I'd discovered through Walnut Hills and Madeira.

"I was the first in my family to graduate from college" sounded so cliché when I heard others say it. After having accomplished it, I realized it wasn't the graduation itself that meant so much. It was what the graduation had established: a new reference point in our family's history. Every other educational achievement would start from that point forward, a starting line that I had developed. Sure, being the first in my family was important. Maybe my nieces and nephews would someday follow Uncle Junior's example, but not because they could earn more money. A college degree represented a higher standard of living. My degree was also important because of what it meant to my other family, if anything, in the West End.

Miss Louise would've said I was a credit to my race. I felt lucky just to have been a credit to myself. I had simply wanted to go to college.

Graduation didn't enter into it until later. If I represented anyone other than myself, it was Gest Street.

Nobody in my group had thought about going to college. Our parents didn't go. Jim and I didn't think beyond getting another big hat. If our parents were lucky enough to find work, it involved labor. Daddy didn't actively push me away from college, he just didn't push me toward it. All he wanted was for me to get a good-paying job, one that would let me support a wife and children. He believed that he'd managed to do it without having an education, yet we needed help from the county when he was between jobs. Construction crews were laid off in the winter, and if he couldn't find work as a mechanic, we still had to eat and pay rent.

When loans from the pawn shop and pickup mechanic work weren't enough to provide any security, Daddy applied for rent assistance from the county. They also gave us food, which kept our stomachs from bellowing. Sometimes the county even supplied our clothes, which I hated more than anything.

Most of the men who worked construction were laid off in the winter, and nearly all of them with families had to get county help. None of the guys my age wanted to admit it because we were too cool. Anyone could suspect it, but no one would know for sure. Once the clothes appeared, all doubt vanished. Everyone knew. Everyone knew you were on welfare. The thin-soled Buddy gym shoes could be rolled up in your hand like a glove. I'd rather wear socks than compete with my classmates in their Converse athletic shoes. As soon as they saw me wearing Buddies with that black circle on the side, my stock of coolness took a slide. It was the same with any piece of clothing the county provided. Those thick winter coats, goofy sweaters, and nameless blue jeans were all as square as a box, yet I wasn't humiliated enough to want to find something new.

I didn't know of any other way to live. I didn't know how to live free from the changing seasons, free of a foreman's whims, and free from reliance on the county. It overwhelmed me. Everywhere I walked, everywhere I went, my friends and all the adults laughed and talked and worked within the same bubble. The loss of a job or a family member or a long illness was enough to burst that bubble and ruin a whole family. Downtown, where the streets were short and the buildings close, the neighbors were like families and the neighborhoods our villages. When the bubble burst it strained the rest of the village with the wounded family's pain. That was my village. My home. And unless something helped me find a way to change, it would have become my future.

My graduation from college was enough to change everything for me, but almost of equal importance, it could change things on Gest Street. Growing up without having a single college graduate in the neighborhood left a hole that we didn't know was there until we left. Like a kid being raised by a family of one-eyed people who goes to school and learns all the other kids have two, we were raised by families that didn't go to college. In school, we discovered that many of the other kids had parents with degrees.

Having a college graduate like me on Gest Street meant something to us both. Like so many others, I'd been to 2020 Auburn Avenue as a juvenile and served time in the Workhouse as an adult. They either knew me or knew of me. I had stacked pop-bottle cases at Sonny's store. I had run errands for Miss Louise and hung out with Jim all day. And for dancing with Big Otis's girl, I nearly got beaten to death at a dance in the Lincoln Court. Yeah, I was from the West End. I used to live on Gest Street. And if someone like me could go to college, anyone could.

My degree meant that you didn't have to be white, or live in the suburbs and be a square. You didn't have to believe that white school counselor who said, "You don't qualify for college. Anyway, it's much too expensive. Why don't you consider going to vocational school?" It meant that you could live downtown, be black and cool, dance and fuck, and still go to college.

My having a degree was a two-edged sword—a source of pleasure and one of pain. Some folk treated me as if I'd become a traitor. By getting a degree, I'd joined the establishment and left them behind. I remember stopping at Jim's house the first time I passed through the neighborhood after graduation. I wore a black shirt with side splits worn outside my pants. In place of Florsheims, I wore a pair of Chukka boots. They were easier to walk in and complemented my dark gray slacks. Jim wasn't home, and his sister, Barb, opened the door and said to those in the room behind her, "Say hi to Junior. He's the one I told you about. He's got a college degree." A couple of guys stood up, looked at me as if I were some sort of alien, and sat back down. Three others kept their seats and sent noncommittal nods my way. Two girls feigned interest, walked over, smiled, said hey, and turned away. I nodded all around, adopted my stoic street face, and told Barb to tell Jim I'd catch him another time. Taking my time, I turned around and walked slowly away. I heard someone say derisively to Barb, "Is that the Junior you were talking about? Nigger's squared up. He don't look like any Junior that I know. That college shit has fucked him up."

I didn't look like the Junior he'd heard about was all that he could say. I knew how he felt. As a kid walking along Fifth Street in the middle of the shops downtown, the only impression I had of them was from outside. My parents never took me inside because they'd never been inside themselves. I had imagined what it looked like inside but rated the shop from its exterior. I learned to do the same with people. So I wasn't surprised or angered by the way the guy in Jim's apartment had rated me. After my graduation from college, he could no longer identify me as my former self. For him, it was as clear as the nose on your face: that college shit had fucked me up.

Unintended and mostly unavoidable, loss and separation are mean by-products of my degree—like coming back to Gest Street and feeling I'm a visitor, not a person returning to an old home. Guys like those at Jim's house saw me as an alien, and under their gaze I felt like one. Getting a degree was more painful than I'd imagined. Chasing after it, I looked only at the upside: a great job, better standard of living, expanding my cultural horizons, and making my place in the greater society.

Incremental changes both inside and out make a difference, building a wall earning after the degree. I still speak the same, but to Gest Street ears, I don't sound the same. The same old familiar references ring true, but the new ones shut them out and often bring mistrust. It's too obvious when I try to compensate for it. Conversation gets sticky, nobody's comfortable, and everyone wants to leave. Not every part of getting a college degree is comfortable. If you're going to go back to Gest Street afterward, you better have some guts. It takes guts to come home with a college degree where I come from. It takes guts.

ACKNOWLEDGMENTS

Thanks to my wife, Jeanette Terrell, for watching the back of my head for hours, and to Ayana Pressley Harris for having the courage to never stop believing in her Dad.

Thanks to my editor Melissa Delbridge, who helped bring clarity and focus where I needed it; to my good friend Vito Niesluchowski, who spurred me on by his own efforts; and to Ceil Cleveland who, by inviting me into her Writer's Group, helped sharpen my skills under criticism.

Finally, many thanks to Patrick Washburn, Ph.D., Director of the School of Journalism at Ohio University, for giving me the foundation and the skills that built my career. Neither this book nor any other writing achievement in my career could have been achieved without him.